CHAIN LINK ZEN

Hard Lessons Learned
in Dangerous Places

Rick Chatenever

Segue Press   Tucson, Arizona

This edition was prepared for publication by
Ghost River Images
5350 East Fourth Street
Tucson, Arizona 85711
www.ghostriverimages.com

To communicate with the author
contact him at
rickchatenever@gmail.com

Cover photos by
Karen Chatenever

Cover design by
Rick Chatenever

ISBN: 979-8-9876495-0-3

Library of Congress Control Number: 2023901038

Published in the United States of America

First Print Edition: February, 2023

Contents

To live outside the law you must be honest.

– Bob Dylan

Some names have been changed. Everything else is true.

For Karen, who waited

1

Alhambra

Once our eyes adjusted from the dark to the blaze of morning sunshine, men in dog runs were the first thing we saw. We had left Tucson two hours earlier, our feet shuffling as the chains of our ankle shackles clattered across the concrete floor. Our wrists were in handcuffs attached to chains around our waists.

"Gonna put a picture of this on Facebook," someone said of the heavy metal. "See how many Friend requests I get."

There were maybe a dozen of us packed into a white van with hard plastic benches along the sides and blacked-out windows behind heavy mesh screen. We shifted in our seats as the van exited the county jail yard and proceeded through Tucson. The pink light of dawn strobed through a slit in the window paint before the van clattered onto an Interstate on-ramp heading north. We spent the two hours it took to get to Phoenix bouncing on the benches, never figuring how to get comfortable in our chains.

Our destination was a facility called Alhambra, hub of the Arizona State Department of Corrections. In recent American history, Arizona-style justice has worn the face of a Maricopa County sheriff named Joe Arpaio. Five-foot-seven "Sheriff Joe" – as he was called by President Donald J. Trump when he pardoned Arpaio from a contempt of court conviction – made a name for himself for racially profiling Mexicans, dressing convicts in pink underwear, housing them in 120-degree tent cities and feeding them slop cooked in industrial troughs.

But in the state's corrections system, in 2018 Alhambra's reputation is even worse than Sheriff Joe's. It's a former mental institution turned clearing house where orange-clad convicts are processed from county jails to state prisons.

One of the guys I had ridden in with from Tucson was named Raymond, or Ray, or Rakish Ray or Racy Ray or Reprobate Ray or any number of alliterative nicknames he would pick up in the coming days. Aside from a few unfortunately missing teeth, Ray bore a striking resemblance to Jim Carrey, or "Cuckoo's Nest" era Jack Nicholson with his vulpine smile. In Hawaii, where I had lived for thirty years before coming to Tucson to get in trouble, they had a word for guys like Ray: *kolohe*, a rascal.

Ray was in for shoplifting, or whatever the legal term was for crimes against Walmart. His brain was encyclopedic when it came to larceny. Another of my van mates was Martin, with piercing eyes and strikingly handsome features behind his bushy black beard. Martin was in for stealing $10,000 in cash from a safe in the closet of a home where his mother was the housekeeper. It had taken him three days of trial and error to get the safe combination off the keypad. He stole the cash to pay for heroin.

Almost everyone I was destined to meet over the next six months would be a junkie. Their crimes were the business they were in, to pay for their habits.

We were helped out of the van, our legs like jello, our balance unsteady thanks to the shackles and the long drive, and herded into an outdoor chain link cage big enough to hold us all. Nearby were smaller cages the size of closets, one holding an inmate clutching the locked gate like a monkey in a zoo. From another a voice kept asking to use the nearby outhouse.

Freed of our restraints, tentatively rubbing wrists and ankles, we checked each other out through irises still adjusting to the late morning light under a bright October sky. Some of us vaguely recognized each other, but Pima County Jail houses thousands of prisoners in its different cell blocks. Like canines sniffing each other on first encounter, we checked each other out, looking for signs. With prison inmates the signs are literal – tattoos. The guys around me were covered with them, beginning with letters on their knuckles, then assortments of desert reptiles, skulls and arcane symbols circling their forearms like brace-lets, before disappearing under their short sleeves. The ink reappeared emerging from their collars, vines, tentacles and names of loved ones clutching at their necks, sometimes continuing onto their faces with reckless abandon.

I didn't have any tattoos. They had to seek other clues to establish my identity.

"Cool shades, dude. Transition lenses? "

I nodded.

"Hey, bro, how'd yer teeth get so white? "

"Veneers," authoritatively stated a little fella, a Chicano rap artist whose tattoos shared space on his face with a long scraggly beard.

"Nope. Just my teeth," I answered. "I brush regularly. And floss."

After a month in county jail I had learned to dispense information judiciously. Teeth aren't generally a strong suit when it comes to prison populations. Jails are hardly fertile territory for Crest commercials. When my daughter informed me on the Pima County Jail phone that my grandson had lost two front teeth shortly after I was first incarcerated, I told her he'd fit right in with the homeys in the joint.

Actual front teeth are at a premium among men with picket fence smiles. Shades of white, as opposed to dingy gray or yellow, are rarer still.

"Hey, man, how old are you? "

"Guess," I answered. My age had turned out to be an unexpected secret weapon ever since I first found myself in my current legal pre-dicament..

The guesses usually came in way low, sometimes by a couple of decades. Heads shook when I finally said, "Seventy-three."

"No fuckin' way, man!" The shock briefly provided cover for the obvious question:

Isn't that old enough to know better?

Months earlier, when it became clear that I actually was going to prison, my age felt like one more liability, casting me as a frail target for extortion schemes, or the yard fights and shower-stall rapes providing endless storylines for the "Lock Up" and "Locked Down" documentaries I had taken to masochistically watching on reality TV.

Turns out the silver hair had a more positive effect, inadvertently casting me as an appealing stand-in for the abusive addicted fathers missing in action in so many of their lives. Better yet, I reminded a lot of them of the grandpas they loved.

"OG," was prison parlance for men like me. It was a title of considerable respect. Prison is one place where older is assumed to be wiser, probably because not many of the offenders live that long. On the street the initials stood for "original gangster." I just assumed they stood for Old Guy, which was more to my liking anyway.

I got extra credit when I started doing burpees and pull-ups in the yard with guys young enough to be my grandsons. When they learned the charge that resulted in my one-year sentence – Aggravated Assault with a Deadly Weapon – it produced more cognitive dissonance. I didn't look the part. It would be like discovering that Mr. Rogers had been an extortionist or serial killer before he got into children's television.

In Arizona courtrooms, "assault" doesn't mean what it means in the dictionary. It's a statutory term … whatever that means. It doesn't have to be maliciously motivated, or even intentional. Careless or reckless qualify just fine. The victim can be a total stranger. As for the dangerous weapon? A 1997 Chrysler Town and Country minivan, painted a senior citizen shade of maroon. The victim, a pedestrian in a crosswalk, had suffered a seriously broken leg.

"Were you drinking? "

"Allegedly." There's another one of those legal terms for you.

Considering that I hadn't had so much as a speeding ticket in the 72 years preceding the incident, a lot of people found the sentence severe.

"You're getting fucked, brother," was the general consensus, non legally speaking.

Eventually guards arrived to unlock our cage and march us down a walkway. Behind the chain link fence on one side, two muzzled dogs, a German Shepherd and a Rottweiler, strained at the ends of their trainers' leashes as we filed past them.

We were directed to stop, turn our backs to them, and squat as they sniffed for drugs. From there it was on to a trailer manned by burly, bearded guards who directed us into three-sided enclosures like voting booths without a privacy curtain, and told to strip. Our jail-issued clothing, all orange except for the white socks and boxers, wound up in mounds at our feet. It was awkward trying to figure out what to do with our hands before being told to hold them out in front of us, palms up, then down. The instructions also called for "squatting and spreading."

The reason for the naked search, we were told, was to check for identifying tattoos, especially gang symbols and the occasional swastika. I couldn't help noticing that the guards were pretty heavily tatted themselves. Theirs was an interesting line of work, not for everyone: flipping testicles and otherwise checking out naked men all day.

It doesn't take long to stop noticing the ubiquitous rolls of razor wire topping the chain link fences in all directions. They're subliminal reminders that even Arizona's blue, blue skies are behind bars when you're in prison.

Inside, Alhambra has low ceilings and dingy walls along long echoey corridors that pass narrow windows and heavy metal doors to the cells. We were led into a big office for processing. It took all morning and included shaving off all our facial hair, before being fingerprinted and having mug shots taken for our Arizona Department of Corrections IDs.

Standing in a line of guys in orange wielding electric razors in front of a mirrored window, I watched my silver goatee that some had likened to Sean Connery's disappear in a shower of whiskers into the huge trash cans in front of us. I hadn't been beardless in decades. The color corrections on our mug shots would spark a chorus of complaints. Several black inmates wailed that it looked like they were wearing lipstick. In mine, above the newly exposed and suddenly vulnerable mouth and chin, my eyes looked like darkened ovals, like comic-book renderings of aliens from outer space.

The photo was laminated onto a yellow plastic ID card bearing my new identity: ADC#339331. The first three numbers meant there had been 339,000 prisoners locked up ahead of me through the years. Considering my age, it was another anomaly – a young card for an old guy.

We were issued orange jumpsuits, one size fits none. Mine was almost shapeless, its front opening extending from my neck almost to my knees. Then we were herded into another dog-run cage, this one at least out of the sun, where we received lunch. The tight, cellophane-wrapped bundle contained a slab of unidentifiable lunchmeat, four pieces of bent bread, a couple of cookies, a packet of condiments and another of sugary powder to flavor water. A knotted baggie squeezed into the bundle was ingeniously folded into two compartments. One contained a dollop they claimed was peanut butter but looked more like a deposit a poodle would make on a lawn; the other held a glob of colorless jelly. The smell alone tested my gag reflex as I tried to smear it on the bread that tore at the slightest touch of the plastic spoon with tiny teeth known as a "spork." The menu was fixed, with only the slightest variations in cookie flavors or what they called the meat. It was as immutable as the sun in the sky, and would become an all too familiar daily fact of life in the months to come. It was called "a sack," the staple of Arizona prison cuisine.

Our cage contained a multiracial assortment of Arizona lawbreakers. The Caucasians were called white boys or "woods," short for pecker-woods, whatever that meant. The blacks, I would learn, were "kinfolk." The Indians were "chiefs"; the Chicanos were Chicanos. And then there were the "paisas," taken from the Italian word, paisano. It meant foreigner, but in prison it generally referred to non-English-speaking Mexicans. The paisas would prove to be the bane of every yard I hit.

Racism is alive and well in the second decade of the 21st century in the Arizona prison system. When inmates talk about things "being political," racism is what they're talking about.

On the metal benches in the cage, guys vied for space to lie down on. It wasn't yet midday, but we were all already exhausted from long drives in from jails all over the state to the shock that was Alhambra. Among us was a tall, plum-skinned African man named Joseph, who bore an uncanny resemblance to a young Harry Belafonte. Joseph couldn't stop jabbering unless he was breaking into song, with a voice as silky as Al Green's.

"You've got to stop being so beautiful," he would croon whenever a female correctional officer in her brown-and-khaki uniform walked by.

Despite his charisma, his unflagging self-confidence and oblivious-ness to things like personal space, his overall effect fell somewhere on the autism spectrum. Wherever it originated from, it got old in a hurry. Annoying takes on new meaning when you're locked in a cage with it, especially with a posse of even sketchier hombres whose violent instincts are a matter of public record and often their most distinguishing traits.

We would spend the afternoon in Medical, where the waiting room was another cage. We took urine samples, read an eye chart, and talked to the psychologist before eventually getting to our assigned cell. Our group wound up in the biggest in Alhambra's E Wing with seven metal bunkbeds bolted to the concrete floor around the perimeter. Six more bunks – twelve beds – had been added, bolted down to the open floor area in the already crowded space. In one of them a guy named Harry was thrashing under the scratchy gray wood blanket that passes for bedding throughout Department of Corrections facilities. He would continue to writhe and moan all night, getting up to vomit or pace the narrow spaces between bunks. This is what Day 1 of heroin withdrawal looks like.

Ray, Martin and I wound up in a far corner of the cell. Latecomers who kept arriving in the following days often had to find room for their "beds" – thin, deformed plastic mattresses with extra stuffing at one end for a pillow – on whatever bunk happened to be open, or, more likely, on the floor between them. The facility ran out of blankets, but new prisoners kept coming.

Several days later when I told a sergeant that we had thirty inmates in a twenty-two bunk cell, she corrected me.

"It's a fourteen-man cell," she said. "That's what it was designed for."

Another C.O. would inform me that the whole complex was out of blankets because they had spent that money in the budget for Xboxes and game chairs.

Slit windows ran floor to ceiling on one wall. Through them you could glimpse the chain link exercise yard, a basketball/tennis court and the mess hall on the other side of the courtyard. Maybe a foot wide, the windows were intended to let in daylight, at least until the inmates on the bunks in front of them would turn their scratchy gray blankets into curtains, transforming their bunks into "jack shacks." The window glass was thick and shatterproof. Even if someone could somehow break or remove it, even if he could miraculously contort his body through the opening, there was no way his head was going to squeeze through.

And besides, once you got out to the yard, then what? The walls were red brick, two stories tall with rolled razor wire filling whatever don't-even-think-about-it openings you could spot. There were little guardhouses for sharpshooters on the rooftops, although I never saw anyone up there.

Our cell was the big one in the wing, like the executive suite. It had a large paneled picture window looking out on the central hallway. Some of the inmates, including the Harry Belafonte guy who quickly took on the nickname "Africa," were inclined to tap or pound on the tempered glass, as though it were a percussive musical instrument. This didn't go down so well with some of my new roommates including one named Roland. Roland had spent most of his life since adolescence behind bars on a law textbook's worth of charges, punctuated by long stretches in solitary confinement, AKA "the hole."

"I'm going to kill that motherfucker," was his music review every time Africa got near the window.

Being a newcomer to prison life, I was inclined to take him literally.

With little oval glasses on his round face, Roland occupied the bottom bunk closest to mine in our corner of the room farthest from the cell door. It was prime real estate, the whiteboy gated community in the racial subdivisions that sprang up in the bunks. The racial divisions served as a social safety valve, a circuit breaker to avert certain, uh, misunderstandings before they occurred.

Adorned in prison tattoos like graffiti across his chest and belly, Roland's droll demeanor suggested Rodney Dangerfield, only in orange. I got his humor, even as I recognized it as a thin shell over volcanic rage.

Roland had recently been released from SMU, a special management unit for prisoners "who present unique security and management concerns." In SMU inmates were locked down twenty-three hours a day, only bathed when a portable shower was brought to them, and only let out of their cells in handcuffs. Roland was in Alhambra like the rest of us, for reprocessing. But where we were headed into prison, he was headed out. He would regularly complain that he would rather be back in SMU than the pressure cooker of our cell. Whenever a guard was unwise enough to poke his head into the cell, Roland would plead, or demand, that they get him out of there before he seriously lost it and someone got hurt. Roland was the one regularly bestowing nicknames on Ray in the bunk above him.

Common sense dictated that anyone in his right mind should be seriously scared of Roland. For some reason, I wasn't. An inexplicable mutual respect developed, I'm not sure why; maybe because I helped him calculate the percentage of his sentence he had to serve before release.

There was one toilet to serve the thirty inmates in the cell. It was metal, part of a sketchy, multipurpose antique plumbing contraption that also had a built-in sink operated by a button rather than a faucet. It was the source of our drinking as well as hand-washing water. My daughter, who's a nurse, had reminded me to hydrate whenever we had a video visit or phone call back in Pima County Jail. She might have reconsidered if she had seen the toxicology report on the cloudy, luke-warm stream that came out in a weak, priapic arc when you pushed the button in the sink in our cell.

The sink/toilet was enclosed by low walls on two sides and a swinging door in front. The seatless, stainless steel commode was so low to the floor, a man sitting on it was hidden from view to the rest of the cell. A hand-lettered sign advised sitting down to urinate. And cleaning up after yourself. Some of my cellmates followed the instructions; some didn't. It seemed wise not to press the point.

In prison where any little thing can turn into a big thing, for no good reason in the blink of an eye, bathroom etiquette and diplomacy are essential for a smooth running community ...not to mention, your own survival.

Paying attention, the be-all catchphrase of the mindfulness move-ment from corporate boardrooms to new-age retreats, takes on greater urgency in close quarters surrounded by a bunch of scary reprobates with anger management issues.

The cell's overhead light fixtures that never turned off had been papered over with pages from the rape prevention fliers every inmate receives on entering Alhambra. This turned the illumination pale yellow, almost too dim for reading, which dashed my intentions to use my in-carceration time to finally read the Bible. A Bible is one thing you can find in any jail in America, but the gray-print fine type along with my aging eyesight meant it was a no-go for me in the dim light.

Roland was the lending librarian for the meager assortment of read-ing material. Seeking any break in the monotony, I finally wound up with "The Warlord," a coverless paperback about a crossbow-wielding paramilitary survivor in post-apocalypse California. The binding had long ago decomposed so the book was literally a pile of pages. Roland assured me they were all there. I would have to fish them out of the stack, one a time, putting the book back together as I went.

For several days we were locked down, unable to leave the cell at all. With sleeping mats blocking the aisles and nowhere to go anyway, we were mostly confined to our bunks. Oh sure, milk cartons could be torn into waxy playing cards, a bar of soap could yield a pair of wildly unbalanced dice, a pair of rolled up socks could be tossed at a makeshift dartboard on the wall, but gambling wasn't worth the effort when the stakes were creme-filled cookies from your sack lunch.

So what there was to do each day was mostly … nothing. This is a noble goal to attain for Zen Buddhists, but in a prison cell, not so much. Those fortunate enough to have extra blankets – dodgy, torn, scratchy gray remnants – might fold them into pillows under their heads, or put them over their faces to block out the light as they assume the fetal position. At any given time of day in any prison facility across America, a sizable number of inmates are sleeping, or doing an impersonation of slumber, their bodies motionless mounds on their bunks. In prison sleeping is a form of recreation.

Seemingly as a matter of policy there are no clocks in sight at Alhambra. This adds a sense of dislocation to the process of breaking spirits, the unwritten mission statement of prisons everywhere. Being lost in time adds to the sense of being lost, period, drummed into us 24/7. Daylight becomes a rare, valuable commodity when glimpsed through a window slit. Our sack breakfasts were brought to us at a still pitch-black ungodly hour of early morning, further skewing our already tenuous grasp of reality.

Our cell got an unexpected solution to the paradox of time with the arrival of an inmate named Keith. He was gray haired and wiry, his compact physique in good shape for his fifty-plus years. His elaborate, colorful tattoos, more artistic than most prisoners', were his body armor beginning with a dragon across his back amid other critters and warning signs, becoming more menacing as they climbed his neck. Keith was handsome, his mouth naturally forming a smile. Convict smiles and the deranged cackles some called laughter aren't the signs of cheer or hope they are on the outside. In jail exposed teeth, what teeth there are, usually signify cunning … or craziness.

Keith was well read, the first conspiracy theorist I would encounter behind bars. From the first time I heard him speak and saw him smile, I was just waiting for the diatribe about the Rothschilds and their kind, the shadowy horned Zionists secretly controlling the world. For some reason Keith decided not to go there with me. At that point early in my residency with the Arizona Department of Corrections, I was still keeping my promise to my wife Karen not to talk politics behind bars, but ignoring her advice to claim the origin of my family name was French, rather than admitting its Russian-Jewish origins.

I knew it was only a matter of time before someone broached the subject and led me into the minefield.

"Trump," said Ray one afternoon, wearing his best Jim Carry leer, "love him or hate him?"

Binary choices are hard to wiggle out of.

"I'm not a fan," I ventured.

Turns out, neither were a lot of guys I met during my incarceration. Granted, convicts are as gun crazy – actually considerably more – as everyone else in red-state Arizona. And while they're not well educated or able to do many things well, besides make really poor decisions, the ability to spot bullshit artists is built into their DNA.

Hearing my reply, Keith went quiet on the subject of Trump. Happily, the conversation quickly steered elsewhere.

Another thing Keith was was diabetic. He had an insulin pump around his waist with a tube running into his torso. The digital display included a clock, so in our cell we could always find out what time it was, if we had the nerve to ask Keith.

Being diabetic in a prison cell presented extra challenges for him. Although the medical staff had him on a special regimen of prescriptions and extra feedings to keep his insulin up, they didn't always get it right. One night we were awakened by Keith up on hands and knees on his top bunk, moaning and cursing, one step away from going into a coma before guys jumped up to keep from falling while others called the guards for help.

Such excitement was rare, a break in the enforced ennui that made days disappear in a mindless blur. Nurses would show up twice a day wheeling cabinets full of pills for inmates with prescriptions. I had more than most. Some of the nurses, male and female, were sharp and efficient; others unbelievably slow and obtuse.

One, a voluptuous black woman with wide blazing eyes, a lilting African accent and a blond streak frosted in her hair, was the stuff of dreams.

It's easy to fall in love in prison. What else do you have to do with your time? But at the other end of the estrogen spectrum was the female C.O. with the Spanish accent who was dumb enough to be extremely dangerous. She was the one accompanying the pill nurse one day, unnecessarily bossy as she ordered the guys in the pill line to stand with our backs against the wall, calling us "Dude" as she issued the command.

This didn't go down so well with the cellies, who tended to be a reasonable enough bunch when treated with a modicum of respect. One of the hot-headed youngsters on his bunk punched one open hand with the other, trying to enlist a posse to take her out.

"You go first, bro. We're right behind you."

"Thank you, dude," said Roland to her as he took his allotment of pills, muttering about killing the bitch as he made his return to his bunk.

Tensions and threats mounted throughout the cell before Africa broke out of the pill line to approach her.

"You're going to get rolled," he began, before she cut him off. She ordered him to the floor, barking into her shoulder radio for backup, which quickly arrived.

"He threatened me," she told the arriving officers.

"Did you hear him threaten her? " asked the kid on the bunk who had been punching his hand.

"Did anyone hear him do that? I didn't. Did anyone …?"

There was no response. Africa, who had been sitting on the floor, surrounded by guards, was led away …

And then he was back a short time later.

He hadn't been threatening her, he explained, lost as ever in his Asperger's fog. He had been trying to warn her. Seriously, dude.

The correctional officers would appear morning, noon and night for what was called "the count," just to be sure no one had escaped from the locked cell, or died, since their last visit.

We would be herded out into the corridor and up against the wall for roll call. They would call our names and we would respond with the last three digits of our prison ID number before filing back into the cell.

"Chatenever? " said one black, bearded guard, surprising me by pronouncing it perfectly. "Is that Russian? "

I said yes automatically before remembering my wife's warning.

For breakfast and lunch count we'd file back to our bunks with the wrapped packets of so-called food you wouldn't consider consuming under any other circumstances. I marveled at the kitchen crew's dexterity with cellophane, wrapping the turd of peanut butter so uniformly, tying such perfect knots. Cellophane has many uses in a prison cell. Rolled tightly, it provides a serviceable enough strand of cord. Alhambra's bill for cellophane alone was probably enough to provide a whole orphanage with Christmas presents.

For dinner we'd eat out. We'd be queued single file on sidewalks stretching around the basketball court, through a metal detector, past more one-man cages to the dining hall across the yard. Sometimes just being outdoors for the first time, breathing fresh air, drinking in the twilight sky, was our only reward for the day.

In the dining room the food came out of a slot in the wall. An inmate on the other side loaded the overcooked canned vegetables and comfort food entrees into the compartments of the molded red trays with no sharp edges, as thick as a swimming kick boards to prevent being used as weapons. The entrees, whether called stir-fry, stroganoff or jambalaya all tasted surprisingly like the same recipe, heavy on rice or potatoes or pasta, meant to be spread onto the ubiquitous two slices of bread, which were, at least, whole wheat. The meal concluded with some sort of pudding or pastry, frosted with sugar.

We would file quickly onto the next available seat, a legless round metal stool welded to an arm attached to a the podium of a round metal table, like four buds around a flower. A gray dead flower. Everything in prison is bolted to the floor, so it can't be picked up and thrown.

At the table there was no time for anything but eating. We shoveled our food, more like a pack of savages than a group of buddies meeting at Olive Garden. We were eager to clean our trays before being ordered to exit, one row at a time, with military precision. No morsel left behind. There's no place, or excuse, for a fussy eater in a prison chow hall.

The Arizona Department of Corrections was in the process of integrating during my stay with them. This was less out of a moral sense or desire to join the 21st century than to avoid losing federal funding. In the Alhambra dining hall you took the first empty seat no matter the race of the men already at the table.

Interracial eating is still a cardinal sin in many prisons throughout the state, and was in full effect the last time Keith had been locked up. If you didn't get beat up by your own race, the other race would see to it. Moving through the chow line with another white inmate, Keith stopped when they saw the next two open seats were at a table with two black prisoners. When they hesitated, then made a move for a fully open table, the dining hall froze.

I was suddenly aware of stern-faced guards of both genders moving in from all corners of the room. A race riot was exactly one second away before Keith and his friend had their aha moment. They sat down with the black guys, silently praying that they wouldn't have to face a white-boy tribunal when they returned to the cell.

On my third morning in Alhambra, I was in a group taken out of various cells for testing. It was the first time my fingers touched a keyboard in the more than a month since I had gone into custody in Pima County. I had almost forgotten digital communication even existed, having gotten used to the stubby, eraserless golf pencils and whatever scrap of paper you could find in a cell as the sole medium for recording ideas.

It's my guess that prisons keep their inhabitants in the dark ages of technology on purpose. True, the practice of imprisoning people predated the creation of the iPhone by thousands of years, but any way of depriving an inmate of his autonomy or dignity adds up to a plus in this system. Just making a collect call from prison is a clumsy exercise on clunky equipment requiring punching in elaborate code on an antique keypad, then going through voice recognition that often denies you're you. It's another reminder of all the things we take for granted "on the outs," like Steve Jobs' crowning glory, that magical link to cosmic consciousness most people have in their pockets, purses or on their nightstands, 24/7.

The testing involved a high school equivalency exam. Inmates had to hit the eighth-grade mark to qualify for a reduction in the length of our sentence and other benefits, like extra phone time. I got a perfect score. A lot of guys didn't pass, either one or another section, or the whole thing. One of prison's postures of rehabilitation is that an inmate – and there are a lot who are eligible – can get his GED while incarcerated. That's if he's so inclined. Not many are.

After finishing the test we headed outdoors. It was rec day, our first time out. Hundreds of inmates formed an impromptu parade, a listless counterclockwise march following the chain link perimeter of the dusty yard.

Many of the men were shirtless by the time I arrived, forming a cavalcade of tattoos in a never-ending procession of scary faces you didn't want to make eye contact with. Heavy metal pipes had been bent and welded into exercise equipment, their surfaces taped, their bases sunk in concrete. In between them – some of their shapes reminiscent of medieval torture racks – guys played volleyball or tossed a football around.

The blacks staked out one sector; the Chicanos and paisas laid claim to others. Reading cues and signs with heightened vigilance were essential survival skills, especially with so many well-inked, heavily muscled physiques around, preening in all directions. Being in prison is a form of tightrope walking. From the first moment I was locked up, I took note of where the nearest wall was, in case I had to back up against it in a hurry. There were no walls for protection outside, but the yard would prove my path to salvation once I joined the line at the pull-up bars and started knocking off sets of them, five at a time.

"Hey, look at OG!" I heard a voice call.

"Way to go, old school!"

"Whoa, grandpa!"

Suddenly being seventy-three stopped being a liability. Instead it became a badge that provided some momentary breathing room. Between pull-ups, push-ups and sit-ups, I felt my status changing. I was still an old man, but now an old man with heart. Strangers would call out, give me high signs when we passed. There was not only an endorphin rush, but a glimpse of security.

Rec days were also shower days, when the old jokes about not bending over to pick up the soap become words to live by. They crammed all of us from the cell into a white-tiled room with five shower stalls on one side and a tiled bench on the other. Then they locked the door. We had been instructed to throw our boxers and socks into a bin on the way in; we would get new ones on the way out. Our jumpsuits served as our bathrobes. We each had a prison towel, never to be mistaken for an actual bath towel, and a little plastic bottle holding a liquid purporting to be shampoo and body wash.

Our serpentine line filled whatever space there was in the white-tiled bath facility. Whoever was at the head of the line got the next shower. The water was – surprise, surprise! – actually hot.

There were different methods of disrobing, then getting dressed again, after. Roland admonished that anyone not maintaining eye contact at all times would be in serious trouble.

That meant Ray.

"You sure took your motherfucking time," Roland complained to him after our first group shower.

"You pranced around that place naked forever," he went on, "making everyone look at your penis."

"Did he have a penis? " I asked. "Must have been too small to see without my glasses."

By our last shower together we had it down. I used my towel, what there was of it, as a wrap.

"Very Adonis of you in the loin cloth, dude," said Ray afterward. "Especially what was hanging out at the bottom."

Someone nodded agreement.

"Didn't even need glasses, huh? Maybe you can get one too, when you grow up," I ventured.

In that confined space the racial boundaries may have been an invisible line, but they were always there, and easy to trip over. The simian-looking little fella who had commented on my veneers when I arrived turned out to be a talented rapper, inflecting the black hip-hop rhythms with his own Chicano worldview, but confining his recitations to the brown-skin end of the cell.

Chicano gangsta culture was a weird hybrid. "Nigga," one word absolutely forbidden in every social circle I moved in, was a form of greeting among many Chicanos along, with the black kinfolk. It was just one more acknowledgment of a friend, or fellow human, like, "Homey ... dude ... dawg ..."

A young black guy who had been in Pima County with me arrived at Alhambra a few days later. I almost didn't recognize him, since he had been shorn of his signature Afro with a comb sticking out of it. He had an irrepressibly sunny disposition and an inescapably loud voice, two stripes against him as far as Roland was concerned. His accent sounded Southern, and his nonstop chatter sounded gay, even though his topics of conversation rarely strayed from the prison staples: bitches, baby mamas and pussy. His woman waiting for him on the outside outweighed him by a hundred pounds, he cheerfully boasted.

Even from his bunk across the cell, his voice sounded like it was coming from the monkey house in a zoo, putting him right at the top of Roland's to-kill list.

As I got used to calling Native-Americans "chiefs," one named Philip wound up sleeping above me. In the foot-dragging Department of Corrections efforts toward integration, Native-Americans and Asians were the OK boxes to check when white inmates were asked for their bunkbed-sharing preferences. It's kind of the opposite of Hawaii, where aloha is color blind, and after a few generations of local marriages, everyone is everything anyway.

Like me, Philip was in on DUI-related charges. A welder, car customizer and motorcycle mechanic from a mining ghost town turned artists' colony called Jerome, Philip had an easy smile resembling Wayne Newton, and a tattoo on his forearm saying, "Cops Lie."

"Lawyers lie ... witnesses lie ... judges lie, too ...," he would explain if anyone asked, never losing his Wayne Newton smile.

He had kind eyes and a creative mind. Sometime during a past incarceration, he had thought up a board game like Scrabble. He sent his idea to the Milton Bradley company and got a letter of interest in reply. Put in wood land – the white sector of our cell – Philip was mostly quiet, lying motionless on his bunk for hours, whether he was asleep or not.

Another cellie with eyes as kind as a Golden Retriever's was a gray-haired Chicano close to my age named Jose. He had ridden in from Pima

County chained next to me in the van. Jose was the one always sweeping the large cell or cleaning the toilet without being asked. One day he mustered the courage to come over to our side of the room, stopping at my bunk to tell, in broken English, the story that had landed him in prison. Like me, it was his first time. He wasn't a career criminal but a good man who had made a bad mistake. His entailed overriding his better judgment and making a one-time delivery of drugs to a friend behind bars. The whole thing was caught on the jail security camera.

He told me about his son in college, waiting for him to get out. The light had not been extinguished from his eyes. His words were philosophical, not bitter. He was a rarity.

Prisoners don't have much, but almost all of them have stories. Once you get past the sordid details of their crimes, they speak of wives and partners they've lost, families they've broken with their selfishness. For the lucky ones, there's still love and support awaiting them "on the outs."

Roland often spoke of a remote piece of land owned by his family in the desert cactus and scrub brush south of Tucson. His plan was to fill a backpack with Spam, get his guns and head out off the grid.

Feeling especially loquacious one night, he talked about his childhood. He was still in grade school when a friend invited him over to play at his house one afternoon. The friend showed his guest a family treasure, a cookie tin filled by his father with foreign coins. On top was a hundred dollar bill.

When his friend wasn't looking, Roland stole it.

Then he went shopping. He went to JC Penny at the mall and bought all new clothes for school. He threw away the receipts, thinking there would then be no evidence of the crime. He went to the food court and treated himself to anything he wanted. Then he took a Yellow Cab home.

"When my parents found out, they weren't mad," he said, wistfully. "Maybe because they never had anything to give us themselves."

His teenage years were spent in and out of juvenile detention. One time he and a friend burned down a house to cover up the mischief they had been up to. I think he said it was accidental, but I'm not sure.

Roland had a sense of irony it takes most people a master's degree in literature to acquire. He spoke of the night he shoplifted a warm jacket, then a bicycle from Walmart. He took them across the street where he swiped hot dogs, nachos and a bottle of Crown Royal from a Circle K. He woke up the next morning in a ditch behind a hedge, hungover, but warm.

The consensus among my new pals was that it was a wonder that any Walmart or Circle K was still open, what with all the shoplifting they enabled. This was Ray's area of expertise. Although he had resolved not to reveal any trade secrets when he was imprisoned, one night he couldn't help himself. Switching tags on Walmart items was for amateurs, he began. Ditto for rolling a loaded supermarket cart out the fire exit. That was chump change for artists on his level. Printing up fake bar codes on his computer at home, or procuring a device to remove the magnetic gizmo that sets off the alarm at the door ... that was more like it.

Ray's fashion sense ran toward dressing in layers, one on top of the other, all under the clothes he had walked into the store wearing. I couldn't quite grok the fine points of the great Swiffer switcheroo, but it had something to do with procuring the expensive pads but paying for the cheap ones, then advertising them for sale online. And here the Walmart bosses still thought self-checkout was a mark of progress, he laughed.

He was the king of copper wire heists, from job sites to warehouses. He and Keith would compare fantasies for the perfect crime. One involved using bolt cutters to make a hole large enough to drive a car through in the fence around the railroad yard, then driving off in a new Mercedes fresh off the train car carrier. Apparently the vehicles, bound for local dealerships, were not yet registered and were transported with the keys in the ignition and a bit of gas in the tank.

And then there was the great ATM getaway. You'd need a pickup truck and a battery-powered sawzall. The plan called for strong-arming the cash machine from a store – Circle K once again being the target of choice – then throwing it in the back of the pickup, which had a designated driver. You'd be in back with the saw. Since ATMs are outfitted with GPS trackers, you had to cut fast in the moving vehicle, remove the contents of the safe, then toss the ATM by the side of the road before scurrying away as pronto as possible.

What could go wrong? Criminal minds were wondrous things, I would come to learn, wired differently from noncriminal minds ... their smarts located in all the wrong places.

The next night, standing out in the corridor for the late evening count, I was one of the guys notified that we'd be leaving in the morning. We would be awoken at 4 a.m., groggily packing our few hygiene items into a mesh bag and hefting our bed mat in the other arm. We'd be herded out, back to the processing office where our lives at Alhambra had begun. Once again we'd be stripped naked, our testicles checked for contraband, before we were given new clothes, orange of course. Then we'd be cuffed and shackled before being packed into another vehicle – a bus this time, with mesh in the windows – to be transported for hours across the state to another godforsaken dot on the Arizona prison system map.

It had been a month and a half since the bailiff had first snapped handcuffs on my wrists and led me out of a Tucson courtroom. It felt like a lifetime – several lifetimes, actually.

But I knew that the story had barely begun.

2

Maui

In a movie this would be the scene that begins with the words *One Year Earlier* ...

From our deck on the slopes of a volcano named Haleakala on the Hawaiian island of Maui, I can see for miles. Other islands – Lanai, Molokai, Kahoolawe – dot the horizons. The scene stretches out like a panoramic postcard you can buy at the airport.

From our elevation, we have what Realtors' brochures call "bicoastal views." You can see a fringe of white beach sand on both the north and south coasts. Off the north shore, with its curved horizon meeting the blue of the sky, are the monster waves that draw demigod surfers from all over the world to ride down their fifty-foot faces. On the south coast, opulent resorts rise from the sand. Their palm-framed sunsets and warm turquoise waters teaming with Day-Glo fish, wise-looking giant turtles and frolicking dolphins continually get Maui named the top island in the world in travel magazine polls.

For almost thirty years Maui has been my home, and my life. As a journalist, college instructor, documentary filmmaker, and entertainment and features editor of the island's daily newspaper, my words have helped paint the island's portrait. I swim with dolphins and write about it. When Elton John does a concert at the Maui Arts & Cultural Center, I review it. In thousands of newspaper stories and a half-dozen documentary film scripts, I have explored the history of slack-key guitar; the sensual spirituality of hula; the ways the first inhabitants of these islands communicated for a millennium before the missionaries arrived to convince them they needed a written language.

And before that, a thousand years before the Europeans realized the earth wasn't flat, I write about how the first voyagers in large wooden canoes navigated by the stars across thousands of miles of open ocean from Polynesia to the chain of islands they would name Hawaii. About how the first whalers to arrive would give the natives syphilis; about how the descendants of the early missionaries along with speculators in the sugar business would steal the islands from their rightful queen in 1893, under threat of shelling the natives from naval vessels offshore.

Everyone comes to the islands from somewhere else – some just arrived centuries, or eons, before others. My own path to get here was a humble version of manifest destiny, always heading west. I was born in Brooklyn but had moved with my parents in the early 1950s to Norman, Oklahoma, when my father accepted a position as a professor at the university. I was six when my mother died in Oklahoma, giving birth to my twin brother and sister. As soon as I got old enough, I started heading west on my own, first to California for college, arriving in time to catch the '60s at their epicenter; then, eventually, to Maui.

I belong to a small fraternity of lucky writers tasked with probing the soul of local culture and turning it into words. I'm part of Maui's stir-fry of ethnicities, found nowhere else on the planet, descended not only from those first Polynesian voyagers but also from strong laborers lured from around the world to work its plantations. More recently the arrivals have been entertainment icons, software moguls and other cash buyers from California. My assignments include glossy articles in in-room magazines in the most expensive resorts, and interviews with gorgeous movie stars at the Maui Film Festival, outdoors in the balmy night air, sometimes in front of audiences of thousands.

I am so not worthy, but telling stories is my job. Like most of the island's other resident writers, I also teach English at Maui College. Idle rich on Maui is defined as only having one job. It was moonlighting when I started teaching at what was still a community college. The students were mostly local kids from a whole United Nations of ethnic backgrounds, some of whom didn't speak English as a first language. But even after I retired from my "real job" at the newspaper, I continued to teach. My students encouraged me to. It meant a lot to them, they said.

It even changed some of their lives. That worked for me.

My journalistic career had made me what I teach my students is called a "primary source," observing four decades of American culture. It also made me an aging poster boy for Joseph Campbell's adage to follow your bliss. Living on Maui, it's easy to think you've won the reincarnation lottery. Now I can no longer tell which part is work, which part play; what is spiritual and what is recreation; where nature ends and God begins.

I swim more than a mile a day, religiously, drinking in great gulps of sky and sunshine as my internal pharmacy pumps out the endorphins. The joy of the ritual is a precise balancing act between the muscles of my body and the state of my mind.

We live in a rural part of the island called Kula. Residential neighborhoods border cattle ranches and persimmon farms. Acreages growing lavender, coffee, exotic tropical flowers and the sweetest onions in the world are still owned by the descendants of the Chinese, Japanese and Portuguese families that planted the first seeds.

Kula perches twenty-five-hundred feet up Haleakala. The mountain was the spiritual home of the demigod Maui himself, but now its ten-thousand-foot summit is topped with futuristic domes housing the world's most powerful solar telescope and lots of satellite tracking equipment. Haleakala's moonlike crater was the piko, the navel of the earth in ancient Hawaiian lore. According to acoustic research measuring noise pollution around the planet, Haleakala's crater is the quietest place on earth. I wrote the script for a documentary film about that phenomenon.

Even from our deck at a lower elevation, the power of the mountain is palpable. From the deck I look over what my wife Karen and I call the orchard. The crowns of orange, avocado, lemon, lime, grapefruit, coffee and mango trees, most of which I planted myself, have fruit on their branches. The late afternoon sun tinges them gold.

I know that in the human realm nothing is perfect. But on my deck, as the sky begins to morph from soft blue to wisps of pink, turquoise and lavender, for a moment or two it's possible to believe perfection exists.

On this particular waning day of late summer, I am on the deck engaged in my nightly ritual. True, it's always five o'clock somewhere, but it's my practice to wait for the hour hand to strike in Hawaiian Standard Time before I begin. I'm a creature of habit that way, predictable to the point of dullness, a boring, methodical Capricorn.

The rite begins with tequila, either from the brown bottle straight to the shot glass, or else over ice with juice from a grapefruit or orange just picked off a tree in the orchard. Then it's on to the beer – Mexican or Japanese or Australian or Kiwi are my taste – by the case from Costco or whatever 12-pack is sale at Longs Drugs. I never have more than two … well, maybe three sometimes. If there's any marijuana around, I'll have a couple of puffs.

The ritual is a nightly occurrence, making the gauzy darkness descending into purple twilight that much more gorgeous, that much more perfect. I never get drunk – I know my limits. When I drink I recalibrate my central nervous system accordingly, especially if I have to drive somewhere. After my personal tequila sunset, I think nothing of jumping in the Tacoma pickup – an island classic at 200,000 miles and counting – and barreling the 20 miles down the mountain "to town," to catch a movie or concert that I'll review in the morning. It's my job, after all.

I never get drunk. I'm not an alcoholic. It's the buzz I'm after, as finely tuned as a family recipe or Jack Daniel's well-guarded secret formula.

The fruit trees in the orchard are reassuring. Sometimes, looking down on them from the deck railing, I feel I know each one intimately, every branch, every leaf. My domain is, as always, orderly. Karen's grand design as gardener-in-chief, and my convict labor with shovels, shears, loppers, chainsaws and my trusty Toro seamlessly blend with what God has wrought, the sublime endless wonder of nature itself.

My mood is wistful, knowing this night will be the last time in several months that I will savor the view from the deck. We're going to be flying to the Mainland tomorrow morning for our annual fall sojourn to help our daughter and her husband with our three grandkids in Tucson.

A sense of trepidation hangs unexpected in the still air, marring the enchanted evening. An unfamiliar sensation tilts my usual implicit trust in the order of it all, and my steady faith in being able to handle whatever comes my way.

I don't know if I can do this, I think, picturing getting on the plane in the morning. It's a strange, unwelcome feeling. I wonder where it comes from.

3

Tucson

One drawback to being a Hawaii resident is that it's the most remote island chain on the planet. It's hard to reach, or even to get around. Its islands were once linked by canoes. Now it's 727s. For those not island-born whose relatives live elsewhere in America – or as it's known in the islands, *on the Mainland* – maintaining family ties comes at a price, paid in airline tickets.

In our case, despite my wife's roots in California, and my cross-country upbringing from New York to Oklahoma and California, our destination was Tucson, where our daughter Lisa had moved and started a family. Leaving our tropical tranquility to become the designated drivers, feeders and lion tamers of three little people who called us Mimi and Grampa had become an annual balancing act of love, service and a vague sense of anxiety, wondering if we were still up to the challenge.

As opposed to Oprah and the other billionaires driving the millionaires out of Maui, our lifestyle there was frugal. Local-style. And Karen had found a way of keeping down the costs of our extended stays in Tucson, too. We traded houses. Between house-swap websites and Craigslist, there was no shortage of folks wishing to put their homes along with their vehicles up as collateral for a basically free Hawaiian vacation. Over a decade, trading places, stepping into the lives of strangers, had proven spectacularly successful for all parties involved. Instead of a generic hotel room or cookie-cutter condo, we would step into cozy, relatively new, furnished homes – in one case a mini-mansion – with ketchup and beers already in the fridge. Across the Pacific our traders could rest easy knowing they were getting the better end of the deal.

True, putting virtual strangers who are neither friends nor family in such intimate proximity to all your stuff, along with locked file cabinets full of financial records, is an act of supreme faith in humankind. Or maybe sheer foolishness. But what's the worst thing that could happen? I joked once with a Maui friend who also traded houses when his family took vacations. I realized almost as soon as the words came out of my mouth, the answer wasn't a joke at all.

I would soon find out how unfunny it was.

We had been in Tucson for about a month before the accident occurred. For all the Hallmarky little pleasures of resuming our roles as grandparents, our time hadn't been without its stress points. For the third year in a row we helped Lisa's family move, this time to a modest little fixer-upper they were able to buy in a charming, family-friendly neighborhood right out of the '50s. Doing my share of heavy lifting, loading then unloading two big container pods in the driveway, was an uncomfortable reminder of what being seventy-two feels like.

The morning of the fateful day had been spent in Tucson Medical Center, the hospital where Lisa was an ortho nurse. Taking advantage of medical resources Tucson has and Maui doesn't, plus our Medicare Supplemental insurance, X-rays revealed the sorry state of my left knee. Surgery more than fifty years earlier to repair an athletic injury in college had evolved into its current bone-on-bone condition.

The pain was not extreme … yet. But, considering my AARP demographic profile, there was probably a new knee somewhere in my future. For the time being arthritis-strength Tylenol would do the job.

So I took one.

Later in the afternoon, the kids and I did a little science experiment growing crystals in a glass of water. As Karen prepared dinner in the kitchen of this year's house trade, I engaged in my nightly ritual, Tucson-style. That meant minus the deck, minus the sense that all was right with the world. Tucson-style meant sneaking a couple of swigs straight from the the Hornitos bottle in the cabinet, then leisurely sipping dos cervezas with dinner.

After Karen headed for bed, I struck out for I didn't know where. I didn't know why, either. I would have the opportunity to ask myself that question about ten-thousand times in the coming days. Our first month in Tucson had been a tough slog, what with the move and the other challenges well known to parents everywhere. Worries about the future, not for yourself but for your kids, and now your grandkids. Wanting everything to be okay for them, wanting to fix anything that might go wrong, despite knowing that you can't. And then blaming yourself for not being able to fix it, even though you know better.

It wasn't what anyone would call a healthy state of mind. Or a good time to get behind the wheel to go for a ride. Of the two vehicles at our disposal, I decided against the snazzy Buick SUV and went instead for the grannymobile, a 1997 Chrysler minivan. Leaving it in the parking lot of whatever country-and-western honky-tonk I might wind up in drowning my sorrows, the van would be one less thing to worry about.

As evidenced by my decades without so much as a speeding ticket, I always thought of myself as a responsible driver ... and an even more responsible drunk driver. No, not drunk. Buzzed. It was that little extra hit of juice I sought, and had cultivated with Epicurean detail.

Being aware that I might be slightly impaired led me to seek out roads less traveled that night, although my knowledge of Tucson city streets was still limited.

Months later I would watch a TV documentary about how the young cities of the American Southwest developed simultaneously with the rise of the automobile. This in contrast to the pedestrian-and-public-trans-portation metropolises of the East that were more than a century older. Which partially explains, I guess, why Tucson city planners and traffic engineers decided to put a barely marked, poorly lit crosswalk across a five-lane avenue where the traffic is flying thirty miles an hour through neighborhoods of low-rise apartment complexes. And why the number of accidents involving cars hitting pedestrians on Tucson streets keep going up each year.

Of course I didn't know any of this at the time. I didn't know a crosswalk was there, in a place no one would expect to find one. In the minivan's cloudy, twenty-year-old headlights barely above the front bumper, I didn't see the signs. When I saw a car ahead of me slowing in the left lane, I assumed it was making a left turn into an apartment parking lot.

The car had come to a complete stop as I approached in the right lane, preparing to pass. I didn't slow, but as I pulled abreast of it, a voice called out frantically from the right side of my car.

"Watch out, asshole! What the hell are you doing?"

My eyes turned in the direction of the voice, catching a blurred glimpse of two terrified faces dangerously close to my van's side window whizzing past them. It took a microsecond to turn my eyes back to the road, just in time to see the body hit the windshield.

The glass broke into a spiderweb of fissures, sprinkling particles onto the dashboard like flakes in a snow globe. Through the shower of glass in an endless second, I watched the body of a man bounce like a rag doll, off the front of the car, through the crosswalk, coming to a stop in the left turn lane. He was for a moment upright, in a seated position, before slowly sagging down to the roadway.

It wouldn't be until the next day that I saw the dent in the van's roof above the windshield. Had it been caused by his head, or the force of his hand flying up? I'll never know.

My brain was useless as I hit the brakes and steered over to the curb. Where had that man come from? What was he doing in the middle of Pima Avenue? Where had that voice come from?

What just happened?

I was absolutely confused, the shock yet to set in. It felt like that excruciating moment in a nightmare when something truly awful happens, before your consciousness jumps in to save you, telling you to wake up.

Except it wasn't a dream.

I didn't know what just happened. But in the space of that split second, one thing was perfectly clear: My life, as I knew it, had just ended.

Getting out of the car on shaky legs I was confronted with two people, a man and woman in their twenties or thirties.

"You asshole!" yelled the man. "You didn't even slow down! What's wrong with you?"

He was taller than I was, wearing plastic-rimmed glasses, something smug and patronizing about him even in his furious anger. His eyes, framed in plastic, burned into my eyes. His smug hipster demeanor was struggling for words.

"You're …you're …you're old, dude! You are fucking … old!"

Still in the dark about what I had just done, I stood there dumbly, feeling his words hit my face.

"You shouldn't be on the road, you shit. You fucking almost hit us. You don't belong on the road. You're not going to be driving again for a long time. We'll see to that."

This, instead of rushing to help his friend, stricken in the street.

The scene had drawn a crowd of onlookers by now. Some of them attended to the victim.

The cops started arriving minutes later. The lights on the roofs of their Chevy SUVs strobed the darkness with flashes of red and blue.

The man had stopped haranguing me by then and was comparing notes with the woman who had been driving the car I was trying to pass.

"… Didn't slow down," I heard him repeating. "Didn't even touch the brakes, the fucker."

The cops went to them first. I eavesdropped as they gave their statements, hoping for the slightest clue to help me piece together what just happened. The other driver had apparently stopped when she saw the pedestrians crossing from the left side of the broad avenue. Their friend, a black man about their age, was a few steps behind. I hadn't seen the two of them as I focused on the stopped car, which obscured the third pedestrian from my view. Startled when they yelled out at me in alarm, I was unaware of the third man until he walked into my path.

The cops told me to pull the van into a nearby parking lot. I got out, and stood alone in the darkness feeling waves of shock and shame washing over me in equal measures. The ambulance arrived minutes later. From the time the paramedics took attending to the victim before driving him away I dared to hope his injuries weren't life threatening.

In the shadows, my head feeling disconnected from my body, ramifications and repercussions started exploding like a private fireworks show inside my mind.

What if he died? Would I ever drive again? Was I insured, driving someone else's car? Could we be sued … lose the house … lose everything …? Would our house swappers sue me, too? Would they rush home, throw us out on the street … ?

I had become, in that instant, something unforgivable. Is there any alternative for someone – especially an honest, responsible someone – found guilty of drunk driving and hitting a pedestrian ... besides suicide?

When the cops finally got around to me they were nice enough, considering. They inquired whether I was okay, asked about my health in general, and whether I was on any medication.

I had forgotten about the arthritis-strength Tylenol. I shook my head.

Then they got to the words anyone in America can recite by heart, having heard them so many thousand times on cop shows on TV.

Anything you say can and will be used against you in a court of law ...

It was the *and will* part that got to me. As a journalist for decades who moonlighted teaching English, I had built my life trusting words. The concept that my words could be used against me felt as unsettling as anything else that had happened in the last hour.

I was hardly the typical suspect. For openers there was my age, the fact that I didn't live in Tucson, my Hawaii driver's license. I had no previous record – it took forever to locate me in any database they could find on the computer screen in their squad car.

Through it all they were respectful, deferential to my age, even helpful. But no matter what I said or didn't say, it didn't take long to ascertain there was alcohol involved.

From that point on, it was an out-of-body experience, hearing the voices of the cops and my own as though they were underwater or in an echo chamber. All those sobriety tests that are so hilarious when you're watching them on the reality-TV cop shows aren't funny at all when it's your feet you're trying to put heel to toe, arms out like a scarecrow, as you walk a parking line painted on the asphalt. Or do your imitation of a flamingo when they tell you to stand on one leg.

I figured there would be no percentage in telling them how challenging those commands would be under any circumstances, what with my seventy-two-year-old equilibrium, my toes that naturally point out like a duck, or my knee problem and all.

I learned much later that following the officer's finger with my eyes was the most damning test of all, even though I thought I did it perfectly.

Under the impression at the time that the accident had sobered me right up, it was a shock several months later when the cops finally released their heavily redacted body- cam footage and I had to relive the evening. Imagine the worst moment of your life – actually, the worst two hours – in super slow motion, preserved forever for anyone to see, unspooling one humiliating second after another, all night long.

Only a million times worse than that.

Did I want to call an attorney? the cops asked.

I did, but didn't have a clue how. Their offer to show me the yellow pages of a phonebook only complicated matters. Did they have my permission to draw my blood?

Uh, did I have a choice? Really? My Hawaii driver's license was another complication. By law Arizona authorities couldn't confiscate a license from another state… but mine was destined to accidentally get lost in the confusion.

I was going to be arrested, they told me, almost apologetically. I was going to jail. Then one of the cops offered me his cellphone. I knew that Karen was home in a deep sleep. She didn't keep her phone by the bed; it was down the hall. As I left her a message, I tried as best I could to choose words that couldn't, as they said, be used against me.

"Something horrible happened," I began, with at least enough sense not to admit on the officer's phone that I had even been behind the wheel.

"I'm going to be arrested … and taken to jail. I don't know what happens after that."

By the time the cops turned me to face the vehicle, putting my hands behind my back to lock on the cuffs, my mind had gone blank. By the time they guided me into the hard plastic backseat, protecting my head from the door frame, it wasn't even my mind any longer. I didn't know who it belonged to.

Next stop, the abyss. Other than complete surrender I couldn't think of a single thing to do.

4

The pit

In the backseat, my wrists cuffed behind my back, the ride was a flashback to a '60s light show. Tucson's city streets were swirls of colored lights to my eyes not familiar enough to recognize landmarks. The police radio crackled with meaningless chatter, adding to the sense of being adrift, set free of morality, no longer bound by the social contract.

The ride took forever, yet was over in an instant as the police car approached a high chain link fence topped with rolled razor wire. Welcome to Pima County Jail.

The arresting officers removed the handcuffs before buzzing me into the jail's booking room. Molded metal benches bolted to the floor held men and women arrested earlier in the evening. Their faces showed various signs of being high, drunk or beat up; they wriggled through one uncomfortable posture after another on the benches as they shivered in the air-conditioning turned up high. Their inebriation was going stale, but it was too early for the withdrawals to begin.

One wall of the room held a row of glass windows, each with a number above it.

Behind the windows sat booking officers, processing the paperwork for that evening's new crop of losers. Whether it was their disgust at the sorry specimens of humanity facing them through the windows, or just boredom and job burnout, they weren't happy to see us. Later in my imprisonment I would meet an inmate who got a year added to his sentence for getting to one of the workers behind the windows and punching him out.

"Was it worth it?" I asked him.

"You'd better believe it," he said.

Trying to find an open space on the bench between ominous tattoos, facial lacerations, missing teeth and furtive eyes like rodents in a cage, my sympathies briefly went to the folks behind the windows. What were they dealing with here? Crack whores? Carjackers? Extortionists? Knife fighters? Bar brawlers? Shoplifters? Wife beaters? Daughter rapers? Strong-arm men? Killers?

The only thing I was sure of was that at least one of the new arrivals was a drunk driver.

At the first window a woman asked if I was having any suicidal thoughts.

In fact, I was having nothing but. But despite being new to this world and mistaking her question for actual concern for my well-being, a little voice inside told me not to answer honestly. I was still operating on the real-world assumption that people behind glass windows – bank tellers, say – were there to help you. Courteously, to provide service to the customer, who was always right. But that little voice warned, not here. Not now. Not anymore.

Tell anyone in county jail that you're feeling suicidal, the guy next to me on the bench later advised, and you'll find yourself in a "turtle suit." It's like a baseball catcher's vest, or a mattress that fastens around your chest, with a hole cut out for your head. Other than that bulky encumbrance you're naked as they throw you in an empty cell where the lights are never turned off above the cold concrete floor that you'll eventually mark with your own excrement.

You may recall the 2015 news story about Sandra Bland, a young African-American woman arrested for arguing with a cop about a minor traffic violation in Waller County, Texas. Sandra was on her way to accept a position teaching at the local college, but instead they threw her in a cell where a few days later she killed herself.

Sadly, the question about suicide from the woman behind the window wasn't prompted by her compassion for me at all, but rather from following protocol to protect Pima County from future litigation. Behind the windows I could overhear banter between the clerks processing our papers. Their voices were cynical, world-weary, practiced at the gallows humor I was pretty good at myself after decades in newspaper newsrooms. Their stabs at humor provided flimsy distractions from the pathetic career choice they had made with their sorry lives.

"Hey, look at this," one told another as he did a background check on his computer screen.

"This guy is born in New York, then California, then thirty years in Hawaii ... then comes to Tucson to get arrested! How fucked up is that?"

Pretty fucked up, I had to agree, as I listened to the morons sharing guffaws.

It would soon become clear that being lucky enough to be a mellow, longtime resident of Hawaii – land of aloha, frequently mistaken for paradise – wasn't going to count in my favor in this bloodthirsty, vindictive red state. Just the opposite, actually.

I have no idea how long it took before the processing was completed, and a group of us was moved through doors that clanked shut behind us to another holding area known as the pit.

It's a large open room, brightly lit, freezing cold. It's on two levels; a catwalk around the perimeter looks over what's below. The catwalk's where the guards, who tend to be big boys, bulging in their brown and khaki sheriffs' uniforms, greet the inmates. They jingle when they walk with all the keys, weapons and equipment hanging from their heavy belts.

You enter the space along a wall that has rooms and offices opening onto it. In one of them I was weighed, then told to undress. Taking note of my body type – lean from swimming my two-thousand yards a day, with little excess body fat – the guard took pity. People being held in jail are only allowed one layer of clothing on their upper body. He let me keep my heavy flannel overshirt. That made me luckier than most of the other arrestees including the women, who had to hand over their bras and wound up in flimsy, county-issued white T-shirts. They quickly pulled their arms inside the short sleeves and tried to cross them over their chests for warmth. It didn't help in the pit's relentless air-conditioning.

I had to give up my belt but got to keep my jeans and leather slip-on shoes. This again set me apart from many of the other arrestees who wound up in baggy, orange jail-issued pants and plastic shower shoes.

Getting a mug shot makes you laugh when you watch Kramer do

it on "Seinfeld." When you have to do it yourself, not so much. The opposite of a selfie – a happy act of vanity and narcissism – a mug shot is a moment of truth, ringing with mortification, ramifications and consequences, caught in the click of the shutter, there for evermore.

Being fingerprinted seals the deal. After seventy-two years of living legally and never giving it a second thought, you suddenly have acquired a record. Regardless of whatever verdict awaits you, you are now officially a criminal.

The pit was down a low flight of stairs; at the other end, a long ramp made it wheelchair accessible. The women were segregated into a quarter of the space, next to the ramp. The male prisoners were ordered to have no contact, or even look at them.

The pit's walls were ringed with molded metal benches; two more rows of them ran through the middle of the room. As the night went on they filled with one scary character after another, their tattoos and facial expressions like Do Not Disturb signs. Their faces progressed through increasing stages of pissed off as they tried to bend their bodies to fit the unforgiving benches and go to sleep.

Sleep wasn't an option for me. Half of my senses were numb, the other half in adrenaline-fueled overdrive, the needle well into the red zone of my built-in safety gauge. Between fear and guilt, trying to lie down or even close my eyes was fruitless. The guys sharing my bench were not inclined to share their personal space. Many of their faces had fresh abrasions from whatever had happened earlier that evening, either before the cops arrived ... or after.

A row of pay phones was available to us. But the calls had to be collect and the code for accessing the system was indecipherable for first-timers like myself. Besides, the hour was late, Karen would be in deep sleep, and whatever message I could leave would be more alarming than helpful.

The pit is one place where there is a clock. But its second hand seems to move in super slow motion, making the nightmare that much worse. By now my mind had become my worst enemy – the judge, jury and prosecuting attorney, all talking at once. The verdict was a foregone conclusion.

It wasn't just a matter of breaking the law but worse, of breaking my own code of conduct. In a split second I had shattered a priceless vase, violating everything I had spent a lifetime building. I wasn't a doctor, but had my own creed to do no harm. I had flunked the karma test ... after assuming I must have had great reserves of it accumulated in my savings account. I had no defense attorney – I didn't deserve one. Whatever charge I faced, I was guilty. After forty years of a trying-my-best marriage, I had joined the ranks of fuck-up husbands. There was no way of facing my daughter, no way of explaining to the kids what Grandpa had done. Over and over my mind played the tape. Over and over, but the hands on the clock barely moved.

The jury verdict was in. All that was left to do was to round up the firing squad.

The agonizing unfolding of the longest night was broken up with each new arrival.

One Pima County Jail inmate in orange was up on the runway with the guards. He was a trusty, the "sandwich guy" dispensing as many as we wanted. I didn't want any. There was water, available from a sketchy fountain at the bottom of the ramp. Considering the necessity of staving off dehydration it was best not to think too much about the quality of what flowed from the spigot. We had to raise our hands to ask permission to go up the ramp to the restroom. Otherwise we stayed put.

The guys in the sheriff shirts – I would later learn to call them C.O.s for Correctional Officers – surveyed the scene from above. There were a lot of them, including several females whose jokes and vocabularies tried to match their male counterparts, F-word for F-word.

The officers were clustered at the end of the room where the arrestees arrived.

Obviously well fed, the C.O.s' shirts tight around their bulging upper bodies, they were a jolly bunch, playing grab ass as they traded homophobic insults with each other, but ever on the lookout for trouble from down below. Sometimes it arrived through the front door. One arrestee rolled in in a wheelchair, bellowing about having been man-handled, hurling insults at every cop in sight, squealing whenever one got close to him.

Troublemakers, or just guys with attitude, were periodically escorted out of the pit to one of the interrogation rooms along the catwalk. They'd arrive back maybe a half-hour later, with the same sneers on their faces, along with some fresh raw spots. Sometimes the C.O.'s couldn't wait that long. One arrestee, his hand in his pants as he made a collect call to his girlfriend, was set upon by three or four guards, who had rushed down the stairs, one of their knees pinning him with his face pressed to the concrete floor, the rest on the ready if he moved.

The minute hand crawled to 6 a.m.

The morning after finally arrived, and with it my day in court. My first day, at least.

One public defender, looking chipper in his suit, little beard and glasses, was there to defend everyone who had been arrested the night before. We would appear before a judge on a video screen in the make-shift courtroom off the catwalk. Our attorney instructed us all not to say a word beyond identifying ourselves when our case was called. On the screen the judge went down his list mechanically, our names like items on a laundry list.

Despite the verdict I had already pronounced for myself, the public defender was optimistic about my case. I would be released that morning, he was sure. All of the interviews and processing I had gone through since being booked had resulted in a recommendation that I be released to something called Pretrial Services.

The police report would be sent to a grand jury that would decide in a week or two whether I would be charged with anything at all. The public defender didn't think so.

Not realizing that giving false hope was part of his job description, I didn't know how he could be so positive.

In my mind, a body slammed into a windshield, which shattered into endless cracks in front of my eyes. The scene was destined to screen, slo-mo, in an instant replay loop, daily. Sometimes more than once a day, right up to today.

" ... Sloppy police work ... your age ... your spotless record ...," the attorney said to justify his rosy assessment. "It was an accident, for Chrissake."

At least he had read the paperwork and was familiar with my case. Unless they wanted to make an example of me – and he didn't know why they would – a slap on the wrist would probably be the extent of it. The case could be dismissed outright. Worst case scenario: probation …

After all, we had to get home. We had our return tickets to Maui for the end of the year, a month and a half from now. I was slated to start teaching in January.

The paperwork for my Pretrial Services release had a long list of conditions: No drinking. No driving. Checking in with the office the following Monday.

The accident occurred on November 15, 2018, a Thursday night. It was a historic date in my family history. Exactly sixty-six years earlier, my mother had given birth to my twin brother and sister. She had been able to hold the newborns briefly, but died a short time later of eclampsia following the delivery. I had been six at the time. Six, six … six. My brain tends to find symbols, even when they don't really exist. Failing that, it makes metaphors.

The public defender was relentlessly cheery. There was nothing to worry about, he reassured me. But just in case, he gave me the name of a private DUI attorney he said was the best in Tucson. Susan Caruso. I was probably too well off to qualify for a public defender, he deduced – and I definitely didn't want to let the court know what my assets were.

Nothing to worry about, he repeated one more time with a smile, before saying something I would come to learn were the two words you never want to hear coming from the mouth of a defense attorney.

"Good luck!"

5

Thanksgiving

When you're released from jail, all your belongings are returned to you. The rest of the clothes you were wearing, your belt, your watch, your wallet, your shoelaces. All of the items in your wallet have been gone through. Your cash has been confiscated. In its place, if you're lucky, is a debit card. You're instructed to use it just once and pull the whole amount out, as close as you can in $20 ATM increments. Use it a second time and there's a hefty fee.

All of this was new to me. Despite my advanced years, in this realm I was the babe in the woods, the newbie, the virgin. The leering guy sitting next to me with fresh scrapes on his cheeks as we waited to be released was already talking about hitting the strip clubs that night. I, on the other hand, was one step above catatonic. When it was my turn at the property window, I went through my belongings with unsteady hands, putting some items in my pockets and replacing the cards in my wallet. Hmm, where was my driver's license? I went through all the IDs and credit cards, and then went through them again. Nope, not there, even though the arresting officer had made such a big deal about not being allowed, under law, to confiscate it.

I told the woman behind the counter and she gave me a lost-and-found phone number. No problem, she said cheerily. It happens all the time.

I wouldn't be able to call until next Monday – it was Friday morning now – but she was reassuring. Or impatient. Missing items can always be replaced. She was as anxious as I was for me to get out of the building.

A blast of morning sunshine was waiting outside the heavy jail door. It hit me in the face, my eyes weak and tired from all they had seen in the lifetime of last night. I took a deep breath and realized for the first time what freedom feels like when you can no longer take it for granted.

Later that afternoon we returned to the accident scene. The minivan was still in the parking lot where I had left it. In the daylight the spider web of cracks in the windshield sparkled like crystal. The hood was as crumpled as an accordion.

We called a Triple-A tow truck to take it to a discount auto glass shop we found online. New windshield in place, the van was drivable by the next day. The owner of the glass shop also gave us a lead on a body shop, the owner's name – Alejandro – and a phone number scratched on a piece of paper.

Alejandro's shop was on Tucson's south side, an area easily mistaken for Tijuana or Mexicali. Its tire shops, taquerias, dollar stores and mini mercados filled one strip mall after another, all painted in shades of day-glo, broken up with murals and graffiti.

Alejandro's garage had no sign over its chain link gate. A big tree shaded the yard full of vehicles in various states of repair. Garage bays and tin sheds ringed the perimeter.

A big fluffy stuffed dog sat on a table next to the entrance, taking the place of a live pit bull. With a short-cropped white beard and a kind, handsome smile, Alejandro looked like a stone engraving of an Aztec king come to life.

He had a thick accent more comfortable in Spanish, and a reassuring twinkle in his eye. Surveying the damage to the van's front end he brushed aside the shame I felt showing it to him.

"It's only a car," he said. "It can be repaired. More important that you're okay." I didn't know how to tell him, a complete stranger, that I wasn't.

He had that startling X-ray vision of a saint. It felt like he could look right into my soul, and forgive whatever he found there. I wasn't ready to join him. I had a lot more down to go before starting back up.

It took a few days to track down a replacement hood and other parts at assorted junkyards. Then came matching the paint color from a fistful of paint chips, all of which looked like the same shade of maroon to me. We made several trips to the shop while the work was going on. One time we brought our oldest granddaughter, and Alejandro brought his granddaughter, too. They were both named Lilie.

We were looking for cheap, a quick-and-dirty job, but Alejandro proved to be a perfectionist, and an artist. Legally we were in dangerous, uncharted waters, paying cash, avoiding insurance claims, not even conferring with the car's owners. Hey, the van was twenty years old, and we had more pressing matters on our minds.

This was all unfolding in the days leading up to Thanksgiving. The chance encounter with Alejandro was a brush with redemption, an unanticipated blessing in this week devoted to thanks. It felt like free therapy, a little flicker of light in the descending darkness.

But it couldn't hold off for long the knowledge that I was a man who had lost his identity and was now living in the Twilight Zone.

6

The Twilight Zone

The Monday after the accident I contacted Pretrial Services and went to see the lawyer the public defender had recommended. I also continued on the mission to find the missing driver's license. Nothing on my new to-do list was easy. I felt like a zombie, an impostor inside my body. My voice sounded like it was in an echo chamber, coming out of someone else's mouth.

Karen didn't know any better than I did how to respond to the stranger who had taken my place. To my surprise, she didn't yet share the guilty verdict I had placed on myself … but the role of trying to give moral support to someone who had never asked for it before wasn't comfortable, either. As for forgiveness, that was a ways away for either one of us, although it came easier to her than to me.

Beyond all the new tasks at hand were the even harder ones I was trying to put off: Calling the people whose house we were staying in; calling their insurance company, and my own.

Pretrial Services is located in the sterile '70s architecture of the Pima County Courthouse complex in downtown Tucson. You enter through a security checkpoint and metal detector in what would become a routine in the months to come.

On the first visit, and occasionally in subsequent ones, I would be interviewed. It didn't take long for my case worker to shake her head.

"You don't belong here," she said. "You're not like any of my other clients."

But the main reason for going to pretrial services was to breathe. The breathalyzer that had helped seal my fate on the night of the accident was there waiting now, twice a week. It had to come up all zeroes, or else.

The missing license wasn't helping lift the sense that my ego had become a beachball with a slow leak. Being twenty-five-hundred miles away from my comfort zone, I was acutely aware of the empty place the license had left in my wallet, and my self-assurance. Without a license you have a much harder time proving you are who you are … especially if you've got your own doubts. Using a credit card becomes iffy. You need an ID to get medical treatment. And don't even think of going anywhere near an airport.

Worse than that, it was a Hawaii license, more valuable than the rarest aloha shirt. It was legal proof of my paradise connection. Over three decades of assimilating the culture, my heart had learned what aloha meant. I thought I had paid my eternal debt in all those words I had written. Now the bond was broken. I was Adam, banished from Eden by his own poor judgment.

I called the woman in the police lost-and-found. She couldn't find it either, but said she'd refer the search back to others in the department.

The next day I got a call from someone identifying himself as Detective Murphy. He was so courteous and helpful on the phone, I almost forgot the public defender's warning that for people facing possible indictments, the police are not your friends.

Anything you say can and will be held against you …

Detective Murphy sounded so solicitous, I kept telling him things. Like the reason we were in Tucson was to help our daughter and grandkids. Day after day the search kept coming up empty, and my ego kept shrinking. Methodically, he kept following new leads, leading me to believe he actually cared, but he was down to his last one.

And then he found it.

The license had fallen off the cop's clipboard into a crack in the squad car between the seats.

As elated as I could be, all things considered, I thanked him. "Wow, I guess that's what makes you a detective," I said.

"I suppose," he answered, the humor lost on him. He added that he was sorry about what had happened, and about my grandkids and family and all.

The sympathy part apparently didn't come up when he had to give testimony to the grand jury a week later.

The lawyers' office was in what was once a modest brick home in Tucson's historic downtown district, echoing with 200-year-old Spanish history. It was a homey, unpretentious office with "10 Best Attorney" plaques and a photo of a softball team instead of chrome and glass fixtures. A woman named Blanche, older than either of the partners, with a shaky voice but a sure grasp of legal details, was the entire staff.

The lawyer, Susan Caruso, was short and trim with dark hair, glasses and a directness where I longed for something more warm and fuzzy. In the coming months she would become increasingly attractive to me, maybe because my dependence on her was so total.

She listened impassively, without judgment as I stumbled through recounting the accident. There were still lots of holes in my recollection. It would take weeks to add more details, piece them together, amidst the PTSD.

Still in a state of shock, bottomless guilt and shame coloring my words, I realized Susan had heard it all before. Lots of times. DUI attorneys' place in Dante's Inferno must be just above drunk drivers themselves.

If Susan wasn't making judgments, she wasn't offering much in the way of reassurance either. Instead she produced a sheet of green paper, laminated because she used it so frequently, showing the penalties in the Arizona legal code for most of the cases she handled. My victim and his injuries, whatever they would turn out to be, took it well beyond a standard DUI. She didn't know at that point if I would be charged by the grand jury or not. But on the green sheet the felony sentencing ranges for possible charges I faced ran between three and fifteen years. On each count. For a seventy-two-year-old defendant that added up to a death sentence.

When I told her the public defender's cheery prediction, she shook her head. "That was pretty irresponsible of him," she said.

My first visit had been all it took for Susan to reach the same conclusion most people familiar with my predicament did. Wrong place, wrong time, could have happened to anyone. But sentimentality wasn't part of her job description.

A couple of weeks later the grand jury would forward its indictment to her office. "This is horrible," Susan said as she went over it with me. It seemed unusually punitive, vindictive and mean spirited, even to her eyes that had seen it all.

She had her work cut out for her.

But in the meantime, she said, "Go see Frank."

7

Weekend with Frank

With his shaggy gray hair, faded jeans and light blue T-shirt, Franklin Delaporte was a rarity: someone bigger and older than I was, still going strong. He was prone to mumble or slur his words like the guy on the next barstool, even though he had been sober for decades. His voice was liable to trail off mid sentence, his eyes visualizing whatever scene from his past he was reliving ... except, instead of a patient in this particular rehab program, he was the leader.

In my first meeting with him we wound up comparing notes about how we had spent the '60s – our adventures on beaches in California and Hawaii, psychedelic cosmoses we had flown to, spiritual paths we had wandered on and off of. Had he not gotten passionate about clinical psychology and finally fulfilled his considerable hidden talents and intellect, Frank would probably have remained a world-class drunk, addict and screw-up.

He lived in a little cowtown two hours south of Tucson where, among his other business interests, he sold prefab metal buildings to his neighbors. He was a hard one to put a label on, falling somewhere on a scale with new-age visionaries and charlatans at one end, and Arizona rednecks at the other. During the week he would commute to Tucson where he ran a family services and alcohol treatment program in a shabby suite of offices behind a strip mall. He had a guitar in his office that he'd rather be playing than playing doctor. He was always stoked when he'd get a musician busted for DUI so they could jam together.

Despite realizing that Frank was probably more interested in telling stories about himself than listening to my problems, I still liked him instantly. I recognized a holy man lurking under the good ol' boy disguise. Listening to me describe my accident he said it sounded freakish enough to have happened even if I hadn't been drinking. But that didn't get me off the hook. He didn't want to know any more details; he didn't want to be called as a witness if it went to trial.

Filling in the bubbles on his scanner paper questionnaire about alcohol use reinforced my certainty that I wasn't an alcoholic. I had no incidents of violence in my past. I never experienced road rage. I knew when to stop. I didn't suffer from bouts of anger, insecurity or depression. My self-esteem was off the charts, bordering on insufferable.

Looking over my computer-scanned test results, which translated the sublime reveries on my Maui deck into precise liquid measurements, Frank reached the opposite conclusion.

"Yep," he said, "you've got a serious drinking problem." There wasn't a hint of judgment in his voice.

"Shouldn't have gotten caught in Arizona," he added. "It's got the worst DUI laws in the country."

He signed me up for his next weekend workshop.

"Bring a cushion," he told me. "Those chairs get uncomfortable by late afternoon."

Taking the class meant missing a violin recital by my oldest granddaughter.

Welcome to your new life, I thought.

There were maybe twenty of us in the workshop that mostly consisted of watching videos. Frank would cue one up, nod off while it was playing, then wake up with a start at the end and begin free associating stories from his past. He had a million of them. He was an authority on addiction. And on how to get relationships wrong.

At the beginning of the class we had to introduce ourselves, AA-style, and talk about what had gotten us here. I had been instructed by my attorney not to talk about my case at all. My classmates recounted their situations. One was a border patrol agent who was going to have to get a breathalyzer in his patrol car. Another was a security guard in a cannabis greenhouse. One middle-aged woman knew she had some jail time coming – it was her third DUI. A younger woman in yoga pants couldn't get past the shame she was feeling.

When my turn came to speak I said, "I'm Rick, and it sounds like I'm in the most trouble of anyone in here."

I could relate to the woman talking about shame. It was my shame speaking, too. It had replaced my confidence, it had pushed aside the person who used to have my name.

Frank wasn't buying it.

"You're still the person you were," he said matter-of-factly. "You just made a mistake. That's what humans do."

He had been in this line of work a long time, long enough to know a lot more than I did about forgiveness.

Most of the others in the group weren't happy to be there. It was part of their sentence, not a choice. Several of the men wavered between boredom and impatience, skeptical of anything Frank threw our way. On the other hand, it was hard not to notice the tattoo on the back of the young woman with the shame problem, just above the whale's tail of her thong disappearing into the waist of her yoga pants. She kept getting cuter as the weekend went on, no matter how horrible she claimed to be feeling about herself. It wasn't long before she was flirting with Frank. She couldn't help it, that's how she rolled.

Being stuck on hard chairs sharing the errors of our ways as a gorgeous fall weekend happened right outside the windows was punishment enough for everyone else. For me it was an epiphany. I felt like I was attending my own personal drunk driving film festival.

I absorbed everything, starting with the clinical studies of alcohol's effects on perception. There was one case study after another, one doctor and psychiatrist after another, like the blind men with the elephant, each describing a different part. There was a particularly gruesome New Zealand public service TV spot showing the bloody consequences of wrecks on the highway. A vivid reenactment of a vehicle hitting a pedestrian caused me to recoil involuntarily. The video screen in the room was interchangeable with the memory that was still waking me in a cold sweat at three a.m. The body hitting the windshield, the windshield shattering, playing over and over in the cinema of my mind.

My favorite video was called "Pleasure Unwoven," by a charismatic doctor named Kevin McCauley who had done prison time himself for his own problems with addiction. (Stop me if you've seen it. All my revelations that weekend were old hat to anyone who has ever attended a single AA meeting. But it was virgin territory to me.)

The video was shot in the awe-inspiring national parks of Utah. Under the big skies, the sheer cliffs, the jagged ridges and the shadowy valleys each represented a different region of the brain. The film makes the case that alcoholism is a disease, not a choice. It illustrates the bio-chemical reactions, the tricks the brain plays on itself, convincing your rational mind that it craves poison.

Bingo! A lightbulb started flashing on and off in my mind like a warning alarm in a submarine movie.

It had never actually been the alcohol for me. Well, maybe a little. Well, maybe more than a little. But what it really was was the image.

When I had studied literature in college so long ago with fantasies of becoming a novelist, the fact that most of America's Nobel Prize-winning authors were alcoholics had not been lost on me.

Drinking and driving, often at the same time, was something I was sure Ernest Hemingway would do. The buzz was not only worth the risk, but, more importantly, was proof of one's manhood. Real men could handle it, as I went on to so coolly demonstrate for decades.

It had been the night vision, the slowing seventy-two-year-old re-action time, the narrowing of peripheral vision that had finally caught up with me. It left an innocent man I didn't even know crumpled and bleeding in a Tucson crosswalk.

Technically I still didn't think I was an alcoholic.

But an arrogant jerk who took stupid risks with dangerous conse-quences? Yeah, for sure.

8

Purgatory

I hadn't had a full night's sleep since the accident. There was no way to silence the recriminations that began when my head hit the pillow each night. It was that irritating jingle you can't turn off or chase from your head. Even worse were the three a.m. heebie jeebies, surprise attacks on a defenseless victim.

My efforts to prioritize the requirements of my new life – calls to lawyers, case workers, cops, insurance adjusters – were complicated by the lingering requirements of my old life. No one on Maui knew what had happened to me on November 15 in Tucson. I was still the same old me as far as they knew – a trusted, sometimes loved columnist for the island's daily newspaper. My Maui Connections appeared every Tuesday morning in the paper, and on Facebook when I would post it later that afternoon.

What was the column about? you ask. I wondered too. I still had trouble answering the question, even after doing it for six years. It was easier when I had been the entertainment editor and could write about movies all the time. Now it was the Connections part that I focused on – the segues, the little acknowledgments of the connective tissue tying us all together, making us part of the same thing. Being an island in the ocean, Maui was a mini version of our planet in space. If I could perform little magic shows with words I was happy. I tried to make the column about Zen each week, but never use the word. That's what I thought I was doing. The column's handful of regular readers on the other hand, just liked seeing themselves in the name-dropping bold-faced type.

Maui Connections was 808 words long each week. Exactly. 808 is the area code for Hawaii; the word counter on my MacBook Pro made the precision possible. The word count was my secret code for an island state of mind. It was a certain form of discipline, and a way of turning each column into a piece of sculpture. It required making each word – and the spaces left by each word cut in the final edit – matter.

My handful of regular readers weren't aware that it added up to 808 each week. Just as well.

Thanks to a very supportive editor, I kept the column going long distance during our extended visits to Tucson. This questionable form of local journalism was made possible by social media, and just plain media, and the virtual world in which Maui and Tucson aren't that far apart. It also helped to have sources on the ground, who loved hobnobbing and keeping those bold-faced names coming.

A smart phone and email were also all I needed to do freelance stories for magazines from a long way away. The night of the accident I had two such assignments with deadlines approaching, for a glossy, in-room resort magazine. One was about two-time Pulitzer Prize winner and former United States poet laureate W.S. Merwin, who happened to live on Maui in a magnificent palm forest he had planted and cultivated. The other was about the Maui Film Festival, which I had been an integral part of since its inception twenty years earlier.

It was my job – tough, but someone's gotta ... – to interview the festival's celebrity honorees each year. They ranged from icons like Pierce Brosnan and Laura Dern, through up-and-comers like Adam Driver to heart-stopping ingenues like Bree Larson and Karen Gillan. In recent years I was the guy conducting their star tributes, doing the interviews outdoors in the balmy night air before audiences of thousands. They were my close encounters of the celebrity kind, two-shots with superheroes and some of the most gorgeous women on the planet. All of that now shattered like the minivan windshield and the femur of my victim, in the blink of an eye.

One silver lining was that the accident happened in a place where I was invisible. On Maui it would have been front page news. But here it remained my secret that the aging but still well-regarded revealer of Maui Connections had been usurped by that most vile of social violators, a drunk driver. It had been challenging enough trying to decipher W.S. Merwin's poetry when my mind was still in synch with the universe. His lyrical precision, mythic echoes and reverberating nuances had eluded me when my mind was still functioning properly. Now he had become utterly inaccessible, a revered bust on a pedestal with a "Keep Out – This Isn't For You" sign at its base aimed at people like the new me, and my fellow Pima County Jail inmates. I was so ashamed. The poles of my existence couldn't be further apart as I bounced between them, rudderless.

It helped a little to still be Grandpa. Taking the kids to and from school, feeding them, teaching them, provided a sense of being useful, at least. We were still early in a new school year. The shared morning ride to three different destinations – an elementary school, a kindergarten and a preschool – sometimes provided philosophical discussion bordering on cosmic. Of our three grandchildren, the boy was the youngest.

One Monday morning he was particularly excited. His teacher had let him bring something home for the weekend, and he was returning it. It was a giant wasp, its gossamer wings and threadlike legs perfectly preserved in synthetic amber.

"It's an amazing creature," he began, with four-year-old earnestness.

"It's not a creature," corrected his middle sister, two years older, already a contrarian although she was still in kindergarten.

A spirited debate ensued about the definition of creature. Like disagreements among people much older, it didn't hinge on semantics or logic, but on who had the stronger will. Wisely realizing he didn't have a chance (and never would in negotiations with the opposite sex), the boy began again.

"It's an amazing little fella …"

My daily rendition of Dead Man Walking was also broken up each afternoon with a swim. One thing Tucson and Maui have in common are public pools where you can swim outdoors all year long. They both have palm trees with glossy emerald-colored fronds as big as I am, gently brushing the sky in the breeze.

For years I had been swimming a mile and a quarter each day, the methodical routine rarely changing. I swam the medley – butterfly, backstroke, breast stroke and freestyle – changing stroke each time I flip turned at the lane's end. I never stopped for the forty or so minutes it took. It was my version of what Michael Phelps did every four years at the Olympics.

"Only he doesn't do it right," I would tell whoever was listening.

"He does it too fast" – too fast to take notice, too fast to savor the Zen of the matter.

A pair of futuristic shaped, blue resin fins made the challenges of the butterfly stroke not only doable, but an endorphin-pumping pleasure. To strangers on Maui or in Tucson who never spoke but still recognized each other like members of a dolphin pod from our shared time in the pool, I was "the guy who does the butterfly."

Long before the accident that changed my life, swimming was my grail, my philosophy, my drug of choice. And it's almost free, I would point out. You've got your own pharmacy right inside your body, filling the prescription for joy juice. It was my medication and meditation, my daily happy dance with the sky.

Now I was looking at a sentence, maybe a life sentence, without it.

Living on Maui provides constant reminders that you're part of nature. Tourists might mistake it for Disneyland as they look out through their snorkel masks at all those bright zebra-striped fish they think are "Finding Nemo" cast members putting on a show for them. But locals know better. Every piece of Maui's landscape and ocean is dynamic proof that God is alive. Or, if you prefer, gods are alive.

Tucson, in contrast, is more conventionally measured in trips to the mall. It's a flat grid of straight streets, a big university, a large Air Force base, a vibrant Hispanic population, all surrounded by jagged-toothed mini mountain ranges on its various horizons. Its low-to-the-ground, flat-roofed architecture and its cuisine are reminders that its earliest inhabitants were desert dwellers, and its earliest conquerers came from Spain, not northern Europe.

It's easy to get around if you can ignore the almost daily traffic accidents, including the long record of them at the crosswalk that got me. There's a certain magic in its cobalt blue skies, especially at twilight when the sun paints the foothills gold and lavender, as the city below them begins to twinkle with lights turning on like an electric train scene.

With my driving privileges revoked and my confidence shaken, I was relegated to the passenger seat of the assorted car trades, auto rentals and the fifteen-year-old minivan, very much like my assault weapon, that we eventually bought. Which meant that aside from my swims, I basically went where my wife went. I stifled my complaints about the supermarkets, health food stores, the huge hardware stores (actually, those were my idea), and the one particular thrift store that had become her obsession.

As on Maui, Costco was the Mecca of our consumer universe. No mere store, it was more a cultural center and meeting place. Where some Maui tourists actually buy tacky T-shirts saying, "I survived the road to Hana," to commemorate the spectacular but white-knuckle winding road to the remote tropical hamlet, actual residents of Hana prefer T-shirts saying, "I survived the road to Costco."

The Costco we favored in Tucson had another function: It was easy to make lunch out of the samples they handed out each day. It was Costco's version of an early-bird special, the store's founders' realization that whatever they gave away for free would be repaid many times over by impulse buys by customers with their mouths full.

I was in Costco at the pizza counter a few weeks after the accident when the phone in my pocket began to buzz. It was an email from the secretary in my lawyer's office. "You've been indicted," said the words in the subject line. Dispassionately, matter-of- factly, just like that.

The ramifications got more ominous when I followed up with a phone call with my attorney Susan that evening. Although it meant her fee would go up considerably, she wasn't happy with the development.

"This is terrible," she began, momentarily losing her professional detachment. I had been charged with one felony count of aggravated assault with a deadly weapon; one count of misdemeanor DUI; and something called endangerment, another felony, for putting the nearby pedestrians in harm's way.

There was something especially draconian in the way it was written, she thought. Reading the grand jury transcript, between the part where they snidely wondered about how to pronounce my name, the tone sounded to my ears just a bit envious about my home in Hawaii.

If my case went to trial, my career, my decades of service to my community, the value system I lived by, (or had, up to that unfortunate moment), the photo of me standing in a group around the Dalai Lama when he visited Maui would not be part of the instructions to the jury. Neither would the excessive length of the sentence – dictated in Arizona by something called mandatory minimums – be admissible before they had to reach their verdict. Their instructions would be that a poor black pedestrian in a clearly marked crosswalk had been hit by a driver – a seemingly affluent driver from Hawaii – with alcohol in his system. End of story.

She kept telling me it was my choice whether or not to retain her services. It sounded like she might be trying to talk me out of it. Was it out of concern for me, or did she just hate to lose and know she was going to?

She put my odds of winning at thirty percent. Which meant a seventy percent chance of all those years adding up to that unwritten death sentence. Under no circumstance did we want to go to trial, she went on, extending the slender but unlikely hope that if things went exactly right – she likened it to threading a needle – maybe I could avoid any jail time at all.

"If you do go with us, we'll fight like hell," she said.

Her words barely registered in my brain, numb since first getting the news. It didn't feel like either of us was convinced.

9

Heart break

Twice a week I would "go breathe" at Pretrial Services, and every few months I would go to court, only to have my case continued another sixty days awaiting this piece of evidence or that bit of legal procedure. It felt like I was doing my own episode of "Better Call Saul." Tucson's courthouse with guards and a metal detector at the entrance, echoey corridors leading to ominous elevators, fading judges' portraits with wax museum expressions on their faces, and smarmy lawyers joking in the hallways, was interchangeable with the TV series' courthouse in Albuquerque. A sardonic Southwestern sense of doom hung over both cities. My wife and our daughter, sometimes wearing her hospital scrubs to get sympathy for her dad, would accompany me for my day – more like fifteen minutes – in court.

The brief appearances offered a chance to get a bead on the judge assigned to my case. Her name was Janet Purdy, and she had recently been appointed to the bench after a long stint as a prosecutor. She was a large woman, seemingly comfortable in her skin, her face unexpectedly kind. Watching her go through her docket, I noted that she had little patience for lame excuses or inept defense attorneys, but seemed empathetic to genuine remorse or sincere attempts at atonement.

I couldn't say the same about my prosecutor. She had a reputation as a one-woman mission to rid Tucson streets of drunk drivers. The single time she bothered to show up for any of my appearances, she reminded me of women I sometimes met at chamber of commerce mixers, wearing just a little too much makeup, their confidence brittle, their business cards providing the uneasy basis for whatever bravado and confidence they could feign.

Considering what a omnipotent role she would play in determining my fate, not to mention paralyzing my life for the foreseeable future, it didn't seem to weigh very heavily on her. Her office happened to be in chaos for the months my case dragged on, a rash of resignations adding to her workload. Had my case not been such a slam dunk, low-hanging fruit to bolster her conviction percentage – pedestrian in crosswalk hit by drunk driver *from Hawaii* – she might have been more inclined to bargain.

No such luck.

We'd file into the wooden pew-like benches of the gallery to wait for my name to be called. The seats around us would fill with families and girlfriends, most clad in their Walmart best, here to show support, no matter that the time for it was long past. More than once the bailiff had to order them to remove the family dog sitting in someone's lap from the courtroom. In many cases it would be the last time they would see the accused, maybe for years.

Convicts already in custody would be paraded into the courtroom for sentencing before the judge would get around to me. With sheriffs at both ends of the line, they would shuffle in their shackles, chained together at the waist, their mouths missing teeth, their faces looking sheepish or confused or defiant or ashamed under their shaved- sidewall prison haircuts. They were all dressed in what would become my least favorite color, their particular shade of orange faded by the length of time they had already spent in county jail. They were a disconcerting sight, beings from some underworld, adding to my nightmare that I could find myself chained in their line one day.

It couldn't happen … could it?

Turns out, when it comes to justice, Arizona is a place that believes in power to the prosecutor. There's something called mandatory sentencing that largely removes a judge's prerogative when it comes to determining a case's outcome. If I could just talk to the judge for five minutes, I thought, if she could see the person I was instead of my list of awful sounding charges … But things didn't work that way.

My family and friends, the handful that knew about the accident, responded with tears and horror to my predicament. The person they loved and admired bore no resemblance to the one who was being charged in my case. It was cognitive dissonance, as though the guy they knew had been replaced by his evil twin no one even knew existed. The very term "assault" was an assault on the person they knew by my name, who was nothing if not a man of peace.

My crash course in the perils of drunk driving, first from Frank and later from Mothers Against Drunk Driving victims' panel I was required to attend, put me in a somewhat different mindset from theirs. Consuming even the slightest amount of alcohol can result in impairment, I learned. You're guilty as soon as you get behind the wheel, before you even turn on the ignition.

It made me wonder each time we'd pass a bar or restaurant surrounded by a big parking lot. What's wrong with this picture? The biggest problem with drunk driving, the one I had gotten away with all my life, was thinking it didn't apply to me. But once caught, accepting guilt came naturally. It always had, long before I ever set foot in Tucson.

Self-destructive impulses were turning into mantras, beginning and ending each day.

Instead of starting the morning with an affirmation and smile as recommended by my favorite Buddhist monk, Thich Nhat Hanh, "I wish I were dead," were the first words that popped into my head, still on the pillow. The were also the last words as my eyes closed that night; they'd show up for an encore in the three a.m. follies.

Curiously, I didn't find the message alarming.

I wasn't even sure it qualified as "suicidal thoughts" in those warnings in TV ads about some drugs' unintended side effects. Why couldn't it just mean I had gotten an F on this particular incarnation, and was anxious to get onto the next one to see if I could do better?

When I was younger I fancied myself capable of the grand Hemingway gesture, right up to the last one – kerboom! – when called for. But now I wasn't so sure. I read a particularly vivid picture of souls burning in hell in a novel called "Lincoln in the Bardo" by George Saunders that undercut my certainty that hell didn't exist. I was still pretty convinced, but what if I was wrong …?

And besides, thanks to my swimming addiction, there were just too many endorphins in my system to let me get certifiably depressed. Throw in the Buddhist part of my outlook that didn't consider taking one's life a "sin" – Buddhism doesn't seem to know what that word means – but rather a cosmic miscalculation that you can't take back on second thought the morning after.

If there were just some way my life, which had become worthless and indefensible in my estimation, could end in a way I wasn't responsible for, that would be fine with me.

Who would have thought my heart would take the concept and run with it?

Exactly one month after the accident, I woke one morning sensing something other than my usual death wish was going on. It was a feeling of mild but persistent discomfort, like a bad case of heartburn, less serious than annoying, fixable with a handful of Tums.

I suffered through it stoically, periodically checking my watch, counting the hours until the pool opened and I could swim it off. I was old school when it came to pain or discomfort; I didn't buy into the concept that keeping things bottled up caused psychological harm. Just the way I wore alcohol as a badge of machismo, so denial was a quintessential part of being a man as far as I was concerned.

But something about what I was feeling this morning caused me to take a different action. Despite misgivings that it was probably a big mistake, I told my wife.

Surprisingly, she didn't react the way she often does, anticipating the worst possible outcome whenever she sees me with a chainsaw in my hands or going about any number of other semi-dangerous chores. Instead she did something altogether reasonable: she called our daughter, the nurse, who happened to be on duty at the hospital that day. Wisely, my wife knew I would listen to her.

"What's going on, Dad?" Lisa asked at the other end of the phone, her concern buffered by professional calmness.

I told her my symptoms, and my heartburn diagnosis. I told her that I didn't want to spend hours in a hospital answering questions and filling out forms over something that was probably nothing. I'd rather be swimming. I was trying not to sound too whiny.

As Lisa listened, she took the elevator down to the emergency room. It was pretty empty, she reported.

"Here's what you're going to do," she began. "You're going to have Mom drive you to the hospital. You're going to go to the emergency room. You're going to go up to the receptionist, and you're going to say the magic words …"

"Which are?"

"Chest pain."

"You won't be filling out any forms," she went on. "They'll roll you right in, give you an EKG to be sure everything's okay. Then you'll be free to go swim the rest of the day away. Knock yourself out."

Karen drove. It didn't occur to us that an ambulance might be a good idea. The mid-December morning air was achingly blue and clear. When we arrived, the emergency room was calm, quiet and mostly empty.

The receptionist was attractive enough to make me forget why we had come. I put on my lame imitation of suave – my fallback position whenever I get flustered – feeling like I should apologize for wasting her time with my hypochondria. When she asked what the problem was, I shook my head.

"I'm sure it's nothing," I began, "but I'm having this, uh, pain in my chest …" Before I could add, "very slight," they were ushering Karen and me inside.

We sat down at a desk where a nurse had barely gotten my vitals and started going through her questionnaire before a bearded EKG technician showed up to lead me to his nearby cubicle. He deftly applied the sensors amidst the forest of hair on my chest and got the reading before I had even gotten comfortable on the table. I returned to the nurse and her questionnaire, but hadn't gotten very far before the EKG guy was back, with a wheelchair and a worried look on his face.

The urgency of the matter was lost on me as I got into the wheelchair. I was still in faux suave mode as he broke into a trot, rolling me to a triage room where a team was waiting. They started undressing me before they even got me on the gurney, alternating questions and encouragement to me while starting an IV and wiring up more sensors as they exchanged tech talk with each other.

One started shaving my groin, another peered intently at the image of my beating heart on a monitor by my bed. I was still coming up with clever answers to their questions; I didn't know what the rush was all about.

It wasn't until my gurney was moving, a nurse running by my side as the hospital corridor walls flew by in a blur, that I noticed the defibrillator paddles right next to me on the gurney.

In the operating room another team was waiting, led by a dapper cardiologist with an Eastern European accent. He explained what was happening as his team scurried about, prepping me. Despite the increasingly hazy – thanks to the IV – state of my mind, he explained the situation with a precise yet wry bedside manner that downplayed the fact that it was an, uh, emergency.

On the monitor, the artery feeding a chamber of my heart jumped around like a piece of blocked hose on the floor, with no blood coming out.

I was having a heart attack.

Not until much later would I learn my good fortune that Dr. Constantin Boiangiu happened to be the guy on call that afternoon. He was, according to my very unscientific survey, one of the best heart doctors in Tucson.

Through the anesthetized cloud of the next hours, the doctor succeeded in opening the blocked vessel by feeding a stent – a little mesh tube – in through an artery by my groin and up to the heart to unobstruct the vessel and keep it open. Now when the artery pulsed on the monitor, a little jet of liquid shot out.

Over the ensuing days Google would help me understand what a heart attack was, exactly – the way plaque develops over time on the inner walls of our arteries, constricting the opening so that a blood clot can stop the flow entirely, like a dam.

Visiting me in my hospital room the next day, the cardiologist told me the heart attack I had experienced was "not insignificant." Bringing me in when we did was fortuitous.

So were all my years of swimming. He prescribed a long list of meds, but the incident hadn't left any damage to the heart itself.

I was released from the hospital twenty-four hours after being admitted. The doctor said it would be fine to start swimming again – just take it easy. I took that to mean no flip turns. That lasted about a week.

When I had been on the operating table with the anesthesia doing its work, I kept trying to tell the doctor I was "under a lot of stress." He didn't find that information all that relevant at the height of the emergency. When a chaplain showed up in my room everal hours later, I chose not to tell him about it.

But, true to form and regardless of the medical explanation, I had my own diagnosis.

My heart had carried out the sentence handed down by my brain. It was committing suicide for me, while taking me off the hook for eternal damnation. It was a noble gesture. From that point on, my heart itself became noble in my estimation. I promised myself I would treat it better, beginning with silencing any more idle mental chitchat about wishing I were dead.

10

Scene of the crime

We came home from the hospital to our borrowed townhouse where I spent the afternoon wondering WTF had just happened. With no scar on my chest, no pain or discomfort other than a certain wooziness from the residual hospital drugs, the reality that I had suffered a heart attack hadn't sunk in. It existed more in my head than my body, more like a dream I had to convince myself was real than anything my body was feeling.

I didn't remove my white paper hospital ID bracelet when we got home, just as a reminder. I still had it on when I got a visit later that night.

In my first meetings with my attorney, she recommended hiring a private investigator to check out the scene of the crime. We scheduled the investigation at the same time of month and the same time of night, to get the moonlight just right. Who knew then that I would go one step further, personally marking the date on the calendar, exactly one month later, with my little medical emergency?

There were two PIs at the door. Aubrey was the blond with wire-rimmed glasses and holes in her jeans; Laura was the one in yoga pants.

They reminded me of once seeing a TV interview with Willie Nelson. Willie's another Maui guy who lives on the island permanently enough to have raised several kids there, and to play unannounced concerts in a local saloon called Charley's in the funky surf town of Paia. The interviewer was Englishman Piers Morgan. With his London accent, he asked how many times Willie had been "properly" in love.

"You mean today?" Willie answered.

I don't know why, but the line stuck with me.

The women investigators were concerned and solicitous about the heart attack. Of course they were also being paid fifteen-hundred dollars to feel that way.

"You're pretty amazing," said Aubrey, the chief investigator. "You and your wife came all this way to help out with your grandkids. My parents live five minutes from me.

"They never show up to help with the kids."

We climbed into the minivan, a.k.a. the assault weapon, Aubrey behind the wheel, me in the shotgun seat, Laura in back to shoot the pics and video. We had fixed the windshield and replaced the hood, but had left the headlights – twenty years old, cloudy and dim, located barely above the bumper – just as they were that night.

We chatted idly as Aubrey drove. Laura had been a cop before crossing over to the defense side for this phase of her career. It only took a few minutes to get to the accident site; I hadn't realized how close to home it was.

I had to point out the crosswalk, which wasn't readily apparent in the darkness. A couple of small signs on the sidewalk marked the crossing, painted white over four lanes of traffic, five counting the left-turn lane in the middle. Streetlights on poles arched over the roadway but no flashing light or warning signal marked the crosswalk. It was actually on a slight rise, camouflaging it even more from the casual glance.

If you were looking for the crosswalk you couldn't miss it. If you weren't looking for it, it was one step from invisible.

"Jesus," said Laura in the backseat. "This is fucked up. It wasn't your fault."

The traffic wasn't heavy, coming intermittently in little waves from stoplights in both directions. By the time the cars reached the crosswalk they were going thirty miles an hour, at least. No one showed a sign of slowing.

"Are you kidding?" asked Aubrey behind the wheel.

We made several passes through the crosswalk, shooting photos, then videos. Then we parked on a side street and got out for a reenactment.

Laura was the pedestrian, Aubrey shot the video. Trying to cross the street meant taking your life in your hands, we all realized simultaneously. Laura stood on the sidewalk waiting to cross, but the stream of traffic didn't slow.

"Are you kidding me?"

Even in the dim light of hindsight, it was obvious that a pedestrian could see a car coming long before the driver would see him.

Despite the romance of the open road associated with historic Route 66, and the glorious photos appearing for decades in a beautiful magazine called Arizona Highways, I had never found the state's roadways to be friendly places for drivers from elsewhere. The first time I drove across the state in 1966, patches of Interstate 40 were still being constructed, leapfrogging with Route 66 through the Western movie landscapes. I was with a high school buddy from Tulsa; we were heading for college on the West Coast. Our plan had been to drive straight through, nonstop, but we now found ourselves bleary eyed on a two-lane stretch of highway in a pitch-black night, a slow lumbering semi in front of us, a state trooper riding our back bumper.

He had been tailing us for miles, so my pal who was driving this stretch was being especially careful to wait for the yellow no-passing stripe to end before he made his move. Turning on the blinker, we passed the truck safely, only to see the cop car still on our tail, now with its red light flashing.

The trooper pulled us over for passing in a no-passing zone. When we pointed out, as politely as we could, that the no-passing zone had ended, the cop informed us that it had started up again while we were passing the truck, before we got back to our lane.

The magazine circulation probably wouldn't be so high if they called it Arizona Speed Traps.

We paid the ticket in a justice of the peace office under a color photo of John F. Kennedy on the wall. The office was attached to a red-neon-lit bar and cantina in the middle of nowhere on one of those storied Arizona highways.

The stakes were higher this time around.

A bearded, pony-tailed man walking his pit bull emerged from the apartments across the street. We watched as they perilously navigated the crossing through the cars whizzing by. When the man reached our side of the street we stopped him.

"Is it always this hard to cross?" one of the women asked him.

"Always," he said. "It's dangerous as hell. Everyone around here knows that."

The women and I shook our heads. Impairment hadn't been the only thing going on that night. Shit-bad luck also played a role. A pretty big role, in fact.

The mix of sympathy and outrage from the women investigators was genuine. But somehow I knew it wasn't going to help.

11

Stuck

Months went by. By law I couldn't leave Pima County without getting written permission from Pretrial Services, the judge, the prosecutor and the victim, and I couldn't ask without reminding everyone that I wanted to go home *to Hawaii*. Not a good idea, said my lawyer. It will mean more work for them and make them like you even less than they already do. So I was under de facto house arrest despite the fact that we didn't have a house. Karen and I were American nomads in a new millennium, a half-century after our hippie days, homeless despite being owners of a very homey domicile in Maui, right down the road from Oprah's place.

Our house traders turned out to have empathy and forgiveness of biblical proportions. They were a happy, optimistic pair of adventurers, up for anything, high school sweethearts now a few years younger than we were. It didn't hurt that they were able to extend their Maui stay for an extra month through the holidays as we tried to get our bearings.

Tucson hosts a gigantic gem, mineral and fossil show every January and February. It draws thousands of gem enthusiasts from around the world, making last-minute condo or Airb&b rentals impossible for anyone else. Desperate enough to briefly ignore the obvious question – What were you thinking? – we put our "Our Maui for Your Tucson" house trade ad back on Craigslist. It didn't take long to realize what a truly insane move that was, but before we could pull the listing, we got a call.

Which is how we wound up for the month of February in one of the mini-mansions dotting the foothills along Tucson's northern city limit.

The houses are gigantic, architecturally opulent in a casual Southwestern way, with towering front entryways and entire walls made of glass. From our living room you could watch each morning's pink-striped sunrise gently bring Tucson to life. The vistas of flat-roofed homes on hillsides dotted with cacti went on for miles. Despite feeling like every room was twice as big as it needed to be, and being awed by the four-bay garage holding a Dodge muscle car and BMW convertible among its fleet, the place was quite comfy. Cozy, not pretentious. Our grandson turned the leather furniture in the living room into trampolines; his sisters tooled around the expansive patio on assorted bikes and scooters the owners had for their grandkids. A pair of hummingbird feeders outside the plate glass drew squadrons of the chartreuse aerialists, zooming and hovering on wings blurring into invisible. An unexpected February snow storm was a white miracle for the kids, who couldn't wait to get out into it, making balls of the stuff to throw at each other.

It was all serene and beautiful, or would have been if the grandfather clock in the entryway wasn't ticking off my hours and days of borrowed time. My life, long measured in Zen thought-for-the-day desk calendars, had mysteriously morphed into the Book of Job.

After the home owners returned from their month of whale watching, sampling Hawaiian regional cuisine and reading the Buddhist books on our bookshelves, we knew better than to tempt fate with another house trade. Instead we rented a one-bedroom apartment, also in the foothills. And after months of showing up in enough traded and rented vehicles to make crossing guards at the kids' schools think we were car thieves or repo men, we finally bought a car of our own. It was, ironically enough, a Dodge minivan, a few years newer with a lot less miles on it than the one I had driven straight to hell on that fateful night. Karen drove; my driving privileges were still suspended.

Spring arrives in Tucson heralded by the paloverde trees erupting in yellow waves covering the foothills and sprawling down into town. The paloverde are weed trees, their trunks like sticks that turn green along with the leaves. The paloverdes are rugged and tough, as with so much about the desert, their beauty is subtle, requiring stopping to take notice, which brings a sense of stillness and peace at no extra charge.

The apartment complex was unassuming but large. Its mud-colored buildings were built into hillsides so they were two stories on one side, three on the other. They were like latter-day Anasazi pueblos with parking lots full of Toyota sedans and SUVs. It went on for blocks. They nestled right up to the mountains, with glimpses of gorgeous sunsets from our little deck. There was a swimming pool surrounded by orange lounge chairs where the kids and I became regulars. There was also a manmade creek meandering through the property. It was surrounded by unkempt desert landscaping full of scrub brush, dozens of succulents that erupted into colorful blooms in the spring, and a biology class's worth of lizards, toads and insects darting across the pebbly paths that followed the stream. Javelina kept their distance. Rattlesnake sightings were rarer still. The stream emptied into a tiny pond with a family of resident ducks, who sometimes sometimes buzzed swimmers in the pool like a squadron of carrier jets, or if the pool was empty, made their landings there instead of the pond.

On the paths it was possible to entirely forget that this was an apartment complex. The kids and I would head out every time they visited for what they named "nature walks." They would lead, becoming more and more sure-footed each time. I would follow, my seventy-two-year-old equilibrium and my Maui-style beach flip-flops – they're called *rubbah slippahs* in the islands – put to the test. The kids were oblivious to the scenes from "Tom Sawyer" or "Penrod" they were reenacting. Following them, traipsing down to the water, crossing the creek on a fallen log, or hopping over from one side to the other when it narrowed, it was easy to feel like we were all the same age.

I was still writing my weekly newspaper column for The Maui News, still maintaining my other life from afar. I was grateful every day that my plight remained secret and hadn't become an instant bulletin on the "coconut wireless," the island's true communication network that predated social media, and all other media, since petroglyphs. I was well-known and high profile enough on the tiny island to have earned the tabloid-cover curse: the secret satisfaction most people can't help feeling as they watch high flyers spiral downward out of the sky, their wings melted from traveling too close to the sun.

But thanks to my "sources on the scene," my column still reliably appeared every Tuesday morning at the bottom of Page 3, full of name dropping and reports on this party, that concert or art exhibit opening. I had spent decades staking out the paradise beat. Even if I wasn't on Maui in person, my column was still the place to check to see if we were having fun yet.

The arrival of spring brought another annual assignment from the paper: the Maui Film Festival. The festival would be celebrating its twentieth anniversary that year. I had, as they say on NPR, "been present from the creation," covering it for the paper. Its founder and director was another longtime Maui guy and sixties survivor, but unlike me, hadn't jettisoned his Jewish roots in Brooklyn.

He was brilliant and pugnacious, his mouth moving faster than most people's brains. He had directed the festival from the beginning with his wife, a small staff and an army of volunteers. Considering the sandy chic reputation Maui Film Festival had gotten in the industry, it was still a pretty mom, pop and the kids family-run operation. I was like the brother-in-law.

There wasn't much to the festival when it began besides its venue – a gorgeous amphitheater big enough to hold more than three-thousand people, created on jaw-dropping real estate that was a golf course driving range the other 360 days of the year.

It was called the Celestial Cinema. It featured a huge screen, crystalline Dolby sound and cinematic postcard vistas of Maui in all directions at twilight. It couldn't compete with Cannes or Sundance when it came to the movies it screened, but it still attracted iconic film artists like Clint Eastwood, Geena Davis and Tim Burton for me to interview in the early years.

More recently it had skewed its tributes younger, often to film stars like Jessica Chastain, Lupita Nyong'o, or Adam Driver, at the very moment they were making the leap from anonymity to the Oscar A-list. And my own star had also risen, mostly because unlike snooty interviewers from Variety, I came for free and didn't even need an airline ticket. For the last four years it had been me doing the celebrity tributes in the Celestial Cinema in front of huge audiences in their beach chairs in the balmy night air.

I made a point of thanking the festival director for my good fortune whenever given the chance. "You're putting on this whole festival thing just for me, right? Don't think I don't appreciate it, Bro."

"You're fucking welcome," he'd answer.

Brother or not, when he started making phone calls in March to give me a head's-up about the upcoming schedule, I couldn't bring myself to tell him what had happened. Besides the waves of shame that were still daily occurrences, I didn't want to burden him with having to keep the secret that the island would certainly love to discover.

I was in the same boat with the editor of the newspaper. Young enough to be my son, he was Japanese, a Maui native, a Buddhist by birth unlike those of us who came to the beliefs later, by choice, adding mindfulness to the acquisitions in our fortunate white lives. My editor was my ally, covering my back in newsroom politics, convincing me to keep doing the column long after I had been ready to pull the plug on it.

I couldn't tell him, either.

The first part of covering the festival was writing a story each time they announced a new star or film artist to be honored that year. I could do this part from Tucson thanks to Google, the Internet Movie Database and my friendship with the festival's co-director in charge of celebrity wrangling. He was a millennial who had grown up on the edge of the L.A. entertainment industry, where he was on a first-name basis with figures most of only knew from star-gazing magazines, with names like Brie and Zooey and Zac. He and I had become buds over years of working together. He talked in a fast, fascinating mumble that I had learned to decipher, mixing industry business news, marketing strategies and Hollywood gossip in a way that made me feel these storied creatures were my friends, too.

In fact they would be, for the thirteen minutes I interviewed them on the Celestial Cinema stage. Cameras in front of the stage put our faces up on the big screen behind us, perfectly lit two-shots of me and Viola Davis or Frida Pinto.

"You don't need erotic fantasies," a friend once told me. "You've got memories of the real thing."

"Yeah, but they're all PG-rated," I answered, "like 'Singin' in the Rain.'"

Literally. A light mist was falling the night I did the tribute to Karen Gillan, soon be known to the world as bare midriffed Ruby Roundhouse in "Jumanji." She had a Scottish accent, she was funny, she was delightful.

Now what had Willie Nelson said again, about falling in love?

The guy in rubbah slippahs with the silver goatee and bald head so deeply tanned from swimming every day wouldn't be available to do the tributes this year. The guy who knew better than to think he was one of the beautiful people he shared the stage with, but was still grateful to have been invited, had been the casualty of a traffic accident in Tucson, Arizona. He didn't exist anymore.

But I was still available long distance to do the lead-up announcement stories in May and June. Many of the year's honorees were too young to even be on the radar for people my age. But one was almost as old as I was. His name was Louie Schwarzberg. He wasn't an actor but a cinematographer who had pioneered time-lapse photography. Back in his hippie days, along with an engineer who built guitars for the Grateful Dead, Louie had jury rigged a battery to his bulky old 35-mm camera so it could go outside to reveal flowers unfolding, make lilies in the field bloom in unison, observe clouds scampering across the sky like a flock of sheep, or behold an entire day in the life of a city of twelve million people unfolding in a few seconds.

From the first few seconds of talking to him on the phone, I recognized a brother of the soul, a fellow beholder of the connections that make us all part of the same one thing. Louie's career had taken him around the world turning his bliss into his art; these days he was the kind of guy who gives TEDx Talks. In his latest one he showed a documentary film he was making on the theme of gratitude.

His spellbinding visuals were accompanied by the the Austrian-accented voice of a ninety-three-year-old Benedictine monk, Brother David Steindl-Rast.

"Look at the sky," Brother David says, his accent like syrup around his words. "The formation of the clouds in the sky will never be the same as it is right now ... Open your eyes, and be grateful you have eyes to open ..."

His words would echo in my mind months later, when a little patch was all my eyes could see of the sky, there above walls twenty feet high with wire mesh at the top turning an entire courtyard into a cage.

As the mid-June dates for the festival approached, both festival directors called me separately entreating me to fly back to Maui to conduct the tribute interviews. They upped the offer telling me that Olivia Wilde was a last-minute addition to this year's star lineup. They had first-class tickets for me on the festival's airline sponsor, and if there were someone staying in our place in Kula, they had a luxury suite in one of their sponsoring resorts – tropically elegant accommodations with marble lobbies and perfectly groomed palm trees outside the open-air walls. This was the stuff once-in-a-lifetime Hawaiian vacations are made of.

"C'mon, Rick, it's only five days …"

I couldn't tell them that instead of getting lost in the almond eyes of Olivia Wilde in night air as soft as silk under a full Maui moon, I had a previous engagement in the Pima County Courthouse, where the décor and the company weren't nearly so nice.

12

Swim season

The hot months brought swim season to the neighborhood pool, a short walk down a dusty alley from our daughter's back door. Under towering palms next to a big park where middle-aged men who spoke Spanish played soccer every Wednesday afternoon, the pool felt like a throwback to the '50s, when innocence was more innocent, being cool was less cynical and growing up wasn't as dangerous.

The pool was home of the Wahoos, the neighborhood swim team. A big painting of a Wahoo leaping out of the water graced the wall of the locker rooms. In Hawaii the fish is called "ono," which translates as "delicious to eat." Some former Wahoos were now parents of current team members. I had been our grandkids' first swim teacher, but swim team was the next level – stroke training, flip turns, lots of laps, meets against other teams all over east Tucson.

In my blue, red and white Wahoo T-shirt I joined the parents in the cheering section. The meets happened at twilight, wholesome beyond belief. Colorful camp chairs filled the grassy spots around neighborhood pools like ours, where the youngest swimmers had all they could do just trying to get to the other end. Last place finishers got cheered as much as winners. Whenever our granddaughter Vivie heard people chanting her name in the middle of a race, she would stop and wave.

Taking the kids to swim practice provided brief respites, but they didn't last. My life in limbo was some sort of spiritual whack-a-mole. Every time I thought I had finally gotten beyond the sinking sensation, something would pop up somewhere else to bring me down again, lower each time.. The next blows came in the form of a letter from a personal injury attorney, and a phone call from a man identifying himself as an insurance adjuster.

The victim of my accident had almost disappeared from memory. After my first court appearance where I learned I hadn't killed him, I kept thoughts of him at bay. The only thing worse than imagining his injuries was the sharp pain I felt for causing them.

But now it was all back, the windshield cracking all over again in PTSD slow-motion with each new details in the lawyer's letter. The impact had caused a serious compound fracture in her client's leg, she wrote. He had been in the hospital for days, then in rehab for weeks. The accident had put him in a wheelchair, then a walker. He was still in physical therapy. It had caused great pain, suffering and financial distress.

"He's lucky to be alive," said the letter. "He will have pain for the rest of his life, and may require additional surgery thanks to the reckless actions of the driver."

The writer of the letter wasn't one of those snazzy dressing ambulance chasers with advertisements on TV and the sides of Tucson city buses. Instead, she had been doing it for almost twenty years, and was rock solid, my insurance adjuster told me. I never met him, face to face. I knew him only as a voice on the phone whom I assumed thought as badly of me as I thought of myself. But he had become my ally. I didn't have any other choice.

Complicating matters, I had been driving someone else's car. The attorney had already contacted their insurer and had filed a claim to the max of their policy limits. Then she contacted mine, and was in the process of maxing that one out, too. Together the claims came to a cool $400,000. But that wasn't all. In her due diligence she had discovered our house on Maui, where fixer-uppers go for a million bucks. She was demanding a list of my assets. So, besides the eternal damnation I received in the split second of the accident, there was also the very real possibility of losing everything we owned.

Welcome to rock bottom. It's a hell of a place to visit, and there's no way you want to live there. Trust me.

Luckily, the impulse to destroy rather than defend myself, playing both cruel judge and willing victim, had its limits.

"What if I don't tell her my assets?" I asked the insurance adjuster. "What if I refuse the demand?"

By law, he couldn't advise me, he said. But the way he said it convinced me it was worth a shot.

In cases like this, he went on, the victims, and especially their lawyers, were more anxious to take the money and run than get tied up in court for years trying to get more. The lawyer was going to walk away with a quarter of the proceeds, a hundred grand, for her troubles.

Our house traders were understandably upset when they got her demand for their assets, too. It fell to me on the phone to try to defuse their fear and anger and talk them off the ledge. I put on bravado like a Halloween costume, hoping they wouldn't notice how poorly it fit.

"Ignore the demand," I told them, hoping I was right.

Turned out, I was right. After two weeks of insomnia that had me making nightly appearances before a skeletal judge in the Tijuana courtroom of my imagination, I got a call from the insurance adjuster.

The victim was going to sign off, he told me. The adjuster would be hand delivering the settlement check that afternoon. The other insurance company had reached the same settlement. I and the owners would be off the hook for any future liability.

The call came around 10 a.m. as I sat by the pool watching the kids' swim practice. The June Arizona sun shone like a thousand-watt bulb burning a hole in the blue fabric of the sky. The big palms stood silent sentinel, their giant fronds like umbrellas over the synchronized splashes as the kids swam their laps. A few weeks later Lilie would win a first-place ribbon in her age-group heat at the city championships.

"Indemnity" was the legal word for our settlement outcome. It felt like the sunniest word in the English language that morning. Our assets were safe. But my sentence still waited.

At my next court appearance there was a black man with a walker sitting in the gallery a few seats away from us. My victim had always had the prerogative to attend any of my hearings; I had been dreading the day it would happen. I hadn't gotten a good look at him that night, but the guy on the next bench was the right age – thirties or forties – and seemed to have the same build, if he hadn't been bent over his walker.

Courtroom confrontations between perpetrators and their victims
– or their victims' survivors – were standard Mothers Against Drunk
Drivers practice. We, the accused, had to stand for judgment before
them, the judge and their deity of choice.

Karen by my side and I kept stealing glances at the man with the
walker as we waited for my case to be called. What would he say? To
me? To the judge? But instead, the judge called a different case number,
and the black man got up to approach the bench accompanied by his
attorney. He wasn't my victim at all, but instead a defendant. For all I
know, he may have been a drunk driver himself.

I had been living in suspended animation for more than half a year
now. My guilt was a foregone conclusion; any plea we reached could
easily turn into a death sentence for a now seventy-three-year-old defendant. Especially one who had just had a heart attack. I was one step
away from being a convicted felon, guilty of assault with a dangerous
weapon that had almost left someone dead. Yet some part of me remained
as naïve as Dorothy in Oz, still believing in happy endings. Bad things
didn't happen to good people. After a long life conscientiously trying
to do the right thing, I assumed I had built up a hefty savings account
at the karma bank.

Turns out I didn't know karma at all.

And then finally one morning in July the plea came. It arrived at
9:30 the night before my next scheduled court appearance. When Kar-
en and I arrived at the courthouse that morning and saw my attorney
Susan sitting in the corridor outside the courtroom, I could tell by the
look on her face that the news wasn't good.

13

Nothing to fear but …

The prosecutor's offer had me pleading guilty to two felony counts. Besides the ag assault, there was something called Endangerment, basically for imperiling the two other pedestrians even though they hadn't actually been injured. The DUI was a misdemeanor, ten days in county jail, nine to be suspended.

The felonies were both eligible for probation, especially for an upstanding senior citizen with a spotless driving record. But the prosecutor had taken that option off the table. Her offer called for one year of incarceration in state prison, rather than county jail, followed by four years of probation. My driving privilege was revoked; whenever it was reinstated I would have to have a breathalyzer in my vehicle.

The plea offer was nonnegotiable, the prosecutor told my attorney Susan. If we turned it down and went to trial, I could be facing five years behind bars on each count. Jury instructions would be open and shut: poor black pedestrian struck in crosswalk by drunk driver. White drunk driver. Affluent white drunk driver. Affluent, impaired senior citizen white drunk driver … from Hawaii, one of those liberal blue states.

It was an "artful" plea, cynically conceded Susan. The prosecutor, undoubtedly getting pressure from the other side, had weighed my positive mitigating factors against the victim's understandable desire for me to feel his pain. When I tried to explain all this to friends and relatives almost as distraught and terrified as I was, I had to remind them that I wasn't the victim in the case. It was a hard for them wrap their heads around the concept.

As the date approached to accept the plea, my psyche was well into the red zone on the terror meter. One of Karen's friends got busy Googling jails and prisons in the state of Arizona. It didn't help. Neither did all those TV series on the reality cable channels. On some windswept yard in Colorado or California, they'd go behind bars to focus on one or another inmate. Often they'd pick the most vulnerable and pathetic, with thick eyeglasses and weak chins, all their belongings in a cardboard banker's box under their metal bunk. Their loved ones' faces occupied a crude montage of faded photos on a tiny piece of wall. They were the ones forced to hide someone else's hooch – crude liquor clandestinely distilled from fermenting fruit, jelly packs, water and bread – in their cell whenever there was an inspection. They lived in a constant state of being bullied, extorted and/or raped by the sinisterly tattooed skinhead running the politics in their cellblock.

I superimposed my face over theirs in my mental movie and kept running a cruel tape loop of possible outcomes, over and over. My emotions bounced erratically between terrified and numb.

But then something truly unexpected happened.

Visualizing horrible outcomes was pointless, said a little voice in my head. The voice should have had a Tibetan accent; I expected it to address me as "Grasshopper."

Especially when you don't have a clue what you're visualizing. You don't have the details, the peripheral vision, the faces of the players. You're making it all up. It's the Zen koan about the great artist who paints a realistic picture of a tiger … than gets terrified of the painting.

What was I doing? There would be plenty of time for actual fear when I got where I was going.

Along with my age, or because of it, there were also my meds to worry about. My cardiologist said I'd have another heart attack if I didn't keep taking all my prescriptions, especially the expensive anti-clotting one preventing my heart from rejecting the stent he had put in.

But the Department of Corrections was notorious for taking these matters in its own hands. It went for cheap and generic whenever it could. It was currently facing a million-dollar lawsuit from the ACLU for poor prisoner healthcare.

Susan's law partner, Clint Kowalski, had also become involved in my case. He had a journalist in his family and had a high opinion of the profession, even ones who accidentally drove cars into pedestrians. He gave me the name of still another attorney, Marnie Mercer, who specialized in prisoner rights. The DOC was afraid of her, Clint said. When she sued, she won.

I gave her a call.

When I told her I wasn't actually a prisoner yet, she asked if I was in danger.

"Well, no," I answered, thinking, not yet. Or not that I know of.

"I just want to know what to expect."

I made an appointment and Karen and I went to see her. She wore jeans in her office and had a large mural of Ruth Bader Ginsberg on one wall and a picture of her father standing next to the Dalai Lama on a shelf. She had reassuring presence; her role could be played by a younger Meryl Streep.

But the picture she painted was hardly reassuring.

Prisons are run by the prisoners, she told me. Prison society is divided along racial lines. I would have to declare my race – the choices beyond Aryan Nation or Mexican mafia were pretty slim. As soon as I got there, the "head" of my race would want to see "my papers." That meant the court documents on my case. They needed to be sure I wasn't a child molester or snitch, the two unforgivable offenses behind bars. If you were guilty on those counts, you would live 24/7 awaiting sentencing and punishment by your fellow inmates, carrying out the unwritten code of the yard.

The more we talked, the worse I felt. There was no protection, you couldn't go to the authorities without being labeled a snitch.

How did the Aryan Nation feel about Jews?

Probably a good subject to avoid. Jail wasn't a good place for political discussions about Donald Trump, either.

"Just keep your head down," she advised. "You'll be all right."

What about getting raped?

"You're not that pretty," she said, almost apologetically as though she hated to break the news to me. Besides, homosexuality was high on the list of things convicts didn't tolerate, she added.

She did agree, for a hefty fee, to write a letter to the Department of Corrections, demanding that they provide the medications I needed. It seemed worth the price to have something with her name on it in my file.

The secret of my survival, I realized, was simple:

Just pay attention.

It's just that there was a lot more on the line now, then simply reading those words on a Zen calendar.

I had one more meeting with Susan and Clint before my next court date, when I would be taken into custody. It was part briefing about what to expect, part pep talk, part suicide prevention hotline. I had just assumed I would be incarcerated in Tucson, but they told me I could wind up anywhere, even out of the state. Prisons were rated on the basis of security – the least dangerous offenders usually went to what was called a "two-yard"; more dangerous criminals wound up in three- or four-yards. They were all over the state. Some were privately run, for profit. The decision about who went where was in the hands of the Department of Corrections, otherwise known as the DOC.

One Arizona prison yard was under contract to the state of Hawaii. All the Hawaiian prisoners were flown there. I wanted to go there, I told the lawyers, "to be with my people."

Clint kept trying to reassure me.

"You'll have your own TV," he said. "You'll get a little job, maybe in The library.

You can write a book. Something on prison reform – it's a very timely subject."

I didn't know how to tell him I wasn't up for the job.

Then Susan said something that stopped me cold. "You're going to do something good."

I looked at her in total disbelief. WTF?

Locking eyes with me, she went on, "Many of those guys have never had a positive male role model in their lives. No authority figure who didn't beat them or bully them. No father, no teacher, no one who ever believed in them. They don't know what that's like. You're going to show them."

I looked at her blankly.

"I didn't sign up for that," I finally told her. "I'm not interested." She looked at me as if to say that didn't matter.

"They need you in there, Rick."

With craggy mesas distantly visible in all directions, statues of Wyatt Earp and Doc Holliday stand at the Tucson railroad station commemorating their killing of the man who murdered Wyatt's brother on the train tracks nearby. Arizona has a proud tradition, a distinctive version of justice that makes for good movie scripts.

Under the blazing sun, the saguaro cactus standing like men with their arms raised in surrender, the state pays pious lip service to loving Jesus. But in its heart it subscribes to the Old Testament wrath of Jehovah. Vindictive sadism trumps turning the other cheek every time. And punishment that's not cruel and unusual isn't really punishment at all.

Once you sign a plea bargain, the deal is done. No trial, no appeal ... for which you get a reduced sentence in return. Once you sign, the judge is essentially powerless to undo it. It's not until the night before, or even the morning that you go to court to sign your plea that the judge actually reviews your case. It wasn't until then that she saw my letter of remorse, plus a sheaf of letters from family members and high profile friends on Maui. Every one of them cast me in a light almost saintly. They made me feel I was reading my own obituary, en route to heaven. I could tell the file had gotten to the judge. I could see it in her eyes, hear it in her carefully chosen words of empathy.

When you sign the plea you stand before the judge as she goes down a checklist of questions. You swear that you have not been bribed, coerced or otherwise forced to accept the verdict. Non-negotiable offers don't count as coercion. $400,000 civil settlements don't matter. High-handed prosecutorial zeal is immaterial.

Everyone in the courtroom knows that what you're swearing to is a lie. Or at least not quite true. It's a negotiated bargain. But none of that matters as you're taken into custody and led out of the courtroom in handcuffs.

14

Deja vu

The bailiff took me out through the door in the back of the court-room, past the judge's wood paneled chambers, down a long corridor to an elevator. When we got out, we were in different world. Instead of wood there was drab paint and metal office furniture. Instead of stately courtrooms and judges' chambers, there were mesh-walled jail cells.

I was still in handcuffs. The bailiff handed me off at the elevator door to one of the guards.

"No problems with this one," the bailiff told him. "He's chill."

The guard put me in a cell with one other inmate, an old man, although probably younger than I was, sleeping off a bender. We didn't speak. We sat on opposite sides of the space, waiting.

Waiting is something you a lot of in jail. It's one of the few things you're free to do in there. If you're resourceful you can make a hobby of it.

The night I had been arrested was my first experience of incarceration; I could barely function. Between shock, terror and whatever intoxicants were still floating around my brain, it was a trip to hell. This time was different. For one thing, it was daytime. My brain hadn't had any alcohol in it since the night of the accident, almost a year ago now. The realm was just as toxic, but I knew what was in store this time.

The cuffs and shackles didn't come as a surprise for the short ride to jail. The wrist and ankle chains would be required any time I had to be transported from now on. The only thing missing was a molded mask with metal nails over the mouth to make the resemblance to Hannibal Lecter complete. This time when I got to the jail's booking area, instead of fretting, the journalist in me kicked in, observing the other inmates who had been brought in that morning.

There was an almost attractive young woman, I don't know what her charges were, wondering who was going to pick her kids up from school. She didn't seem too worried about it. There were two guys who had come in from Yuma and Cochise Counties on the southern border. One had been in jail in Mexico, where getting beat up was part of the daily routine. After that, Arizona was a step up. And compared to the other Arizona county jails he and his pal had sampled – it was a long list – they rated Pima County's as an all-expense-paid vacation to the Ritz.

For me, even the encore visit to the pit wasn't too bad this time. I had worn running shoes to court; they let me keep them for the day, minus the laces. On Susan's advice, I had worn a plain white T-shirt to court under my dress shirt. They let me keep the T-shirt, too. You start figuring things out fast, like how to meditate while seated on a molded metal bench without anyone around you noticing.

And you wait. I dispassionately watched the guards on the catwalk, without fear or alarm this time. I even got up from my bench occasionally to take a sandwich from the orange-clad inmate, the sandwich guy, as the afternoon went on. When it came to the oozy circular slabs of supposed protein, part pink, part gray, labeled "lunchmeat" in Arizona correctional facilities, it was clear I would have to adjust my standards of what's fit for human consumption if I hoped to survive the next several months of my life.

And you wait. The pit is windowless; time would be a complete unknown if it weren't for that damn clock on the wall ticking the day away. It was early evening before they got to my group for processing. We handed in the clothes we had been wearing and got orange ones in return. Our shoes were replaced with orange plastic shower slides.

All sizes were approximate. Somewhere along the line we got a few hygiene items and a scratchy gray woolen blanket. And we got our tablets.

Some months earlier Pima County had allocated funds to give jail inmates tablets. Such programs are what pass for rehabilitation in the minds of prison authorities, and make for great local features on the Five O'Clock News. "Innovative Program Helps Arizona Convicts."

The tablets could barely get online, there was no Google, social media, word processing, dictionary or, heaven forbid, porn. But on your tablet you could do email, play solitaire, purchase music, movies or radio reception. And be distracted from boredom or more sinister impulses for hours at a time.

That's if the tablet works.

They give you a flimsy plastic bag to hold what from this point on constitute all your worldly belongings. Then you move on to your new home.

Pima County Jail is a big facility housing almost two-thousand inmates. There are several different sectors of the sprawling complex, ranging from the high-rise Towers holding dangerous offenders, to the Mission, where some inmates leave the complex each day to go to work.

I wound up in the area called 1-A in the Towers. You enter a large open space ringed with several floors of cells where men, most of them shirtless, stand framed in the heavy glass windows of their cell doors. Some have their hands on the glass in futile defiance. Their stare out blankly, menacingly – gorillas in a zoo, their cages torture chambers. It was Dante's Infermo, Tucson style.

I was put in a two-man cell that already had two men in it. One was middle-aged, an Indian with a graying pony tail. He was in for burglary and struck me as a thoughtful type as he sat at a desk writing something. A letter perhaps? A poem?

The other was white, in his twenties, looking like he weighed about ninety pounds.

Shirtless, his ribs were easy to count under the parchment skin of his chest. His arms were muscleless. He was in for attempted carjacking. The vehicle's owner was an off-duty cop, who happened to be standing nearby, probably with one foot on the bumper, when the incident occurred. He had no trouble subduing the perpetrator single-handedly.

The kid was a junkie. Almost everyone incarcerated was a junkie. He had been high when they brought him in, a few days ago. He had gone through withdrawals cold turkey, a process of nausea, tremors, vomiting, listlessness, sweats, insomnia and agony in waves that go on for days. He was better now.

The cell was cramped, more a pen than a room. There was one vertical slit of a window, too narrow for a human body to pass through, its thick, unbreakable glass was opaque so you couldn't see out of it. The two guys had the bunks. They told me to lay my bed mat on the floor, its foot touching the base of the metal toilet. Navigating what open floor space there was required the balance and grace of a tightrope walker. I wondered how that was going to work, but my new roomies told me not to worry.

"You're not going to be here that long," they said.

They were right. Cell 1-A was a temporary stop before I got to my final destination. In a while the guards opened the door so I could join another group of inmates heading elsewhere. The skinny inmate gave me a twelve-ounce plastic cup. He had an extra.

"You'll need this," he said. There's nothing that's not valuable when you're in jail.

Our group, plastic bags in hand, were herded into a sally port, a fortified room with security doors at either end like a pressurized chamber in a space station. You had to be buzzed in, then buzzed out. Among us was an older guy in a wheelchair. He was bald, wore glasses, looked frail and maybe deranged. Instead of a plastic bag, he had his possessions in a cardboard banker's box, indicating he had been in for a while. He had bandages on his head and over one lacerated ear, sloppily applied to wounds that were obviously fresh.

"Jeez, what happened to you?" someone asked him as we waited in the confined space.

"Somebody hit me in the head with a phone when I was trying to make a call," he answered. He had no idea why.

He and I were headed to the same place – cellblock 2-R. It was in what was called "the new jail," the most recently constructed wing of the complex. It incorporated all the latest thinking in incarceration; there were pictures of it online to show how progressive the jail was. Two-Romeo was for non-dangerous offenders, blocks of eight-man cells, each one of them with its own TV on the wall.

I had yet to discover "non-dangerous offenders" was a relative concept.

I wound up pushing wheelchair man so we made our entrance together, through another sally port into a large airy dayroom whose far wall was all glass, opening onto a tiny, high-walled recreation yard. There were four cells on each side of the dayroom, two upstairs, two down, with heavy glass walls instead of bars looking onto the common area. I could feel dozens of eyes watching us as we entered, like jungle creatures shrouded by night, alert for new prey.

A single correctional officer oversaw the almost seventy inmates in the cells from a central control podium. They guy in the wheelchair was obviously a "lower-lower," an inmate either old enough or infirm enough to require a lower bunk on the lower level. I didn't get the same treatment.

The hostile glares from the surrounding cells indicated that we weren't welcome in any of them. It would take a while for me to learn that unfriendliness was the standard greeting for all newcomers. It was nothing personal; it wouldn't get personal till they got to know you.

As the guard at the console was processing us, one of the inmates from an upstairs cell signaled to be let out. The C.O. buzzed his door open and the man emerged on the upstairs landing. He was black, his head shaved, his muscles chiseled, his face movie-star handsome.

"The guy in the chair is okay," said the black man. It was obvious that his vouching for the newcomer was all it took to guarantee him safe passage.

I on the other hand got sent upstairs, buzzed into Cell 5, full of young, forbidding faces. I was the ninth man in the eight-man cell; a molded plastic "boat" held the extra bed mat on the floor. The bed space vacant for me was an upper bunk. But before I could climb up, one of the guys – Mexican, Indian, or some blend of the two, with long black hair pulled back in a pony tail – briefed me.

The cell had bunks along the three walls that weren't glass, with a bathroom area at the far end. There were two toilets, but the one on the right was for urination only since someone had, in a fit of rage, jammed a radio into the plumbing. Anyone sitting on the toilet should pump the handle with "courtesy flushes" to cover any sound of flatulence, I was instructed. In close quarters like these where no one likes anyone much to begin with, flatulence was a serious offense. It could get you a hot one. I didn't know what a hot one was yet, but it didn't sound good.

There was a vent in the middle of the heavy cell door that you needed to back up to, in the event you felt a fart coming on.

My guide's name was Thomas. No one else in the cell was extending any friendliness to either one of us. Thomas told me that the leader in there – the bossman, the alpha male, I didn't have the terminology down – was a guy they called Mano. Mano was sitting with his back to us, watching TV. When I went over to shake hands, he didn't acknowledge that I was there.

I finally climbed up on my bunk, but the welcome party wasn't over. Another inmate, in his early twenties like most of them were, sat backwards in one of the cell's molded plastic chairs looking up at me. He had one of those canine mouths that naturally forms a smile ... not to be mistaken for an actual smile.

"What are you?"

When I looked at him blankly, he impatiently added, "What race?"

"White," I answered.

"White power? Aryan Nation?"

"Just white."

He was Chicano, but had light skin and Caucasian features, prompting the slang nickname Guerro, Whitey. His real name was Jose.

"Where'd you get the cup?" he went on, barely waiting for an answer.

"A guy gave it to me in 1-A ..."

"Where'd you get the T-shirt?"

"Wore it to court ..."

He was shaking his head with each answer, tallying the strikes against me.

My age was at the top of the list. I realized that you could put three of my new roommates' ages together and it still wouldn't add up to mine.

"Look, old man," chimed in someone else, "we're young in here. We don't do ten to ten."

He referred to standard prison curfew – all quiet from 10 p.m. to 10 the next morning. It was strictly enforced, but this was jail, not prison, and that glass wall made the cell soundproof.

"We like the TV turned up loud, till they shut off the signal. Get it?"

I nodded. My bunk was right next to the TV, the speaker blasting my way. It was clear that my new living arrangement was neither safe nor secure. My new acquaintances, living in closer proximity to me than anyone in my family ever had, were dangerous as hell. But after a really long day, beginning in the courtroom that morning, I was too exhausted to care.

As I tried to settle in on my bedroll, struggling to fashion a lumpy pillow from an extra sheet that had been left on the bunk, I turned my face to the wall. The TV was turned up to 100, and the guys in the cell were yelling over it, all at once.

"Swear to God, dawg, it was fuckin' crazy …!"

They'd scream, they'd curse, they'd cackle then giggle like a bunch of girls.

"Homey, you better believe that shit's happening …!"

Over the din, including sexy music videos on MTV, the title of a song popped into my mind. It was by another Maui guy, one of the galaxy of silver-haired musical superstars who realized that for all its paradise beauty, what Maui really was was a sane, paparazzi-free place to live, especially for those who could easily afford it. This one had moved to Hana a long time ago, raised a bunch of kids there and spent the ensuing decades just blending in. He was known around the world as Kris Kristofferson, but he liked it better when the Hawaiian kids called him, "Uncle."

Of the thousands of celebrities I had interviewed over the years, Kris was the one I thought of as a friend. There had been some good times with him, and his wife, Lisa.

And although his iconic career had been lived in the shadow of Bob Dylan's quicksilver genius, in recent years it was Kris' lyrics that I found myself coming back to more and more, as momentary glimpses of ultimate truth in my own life.

The name of the song this time was "Help Me Make It Through the Night."

15

Home

Sleep came fitfully that first night, when it came at all, broken when my eyes sprang open with a jolt. Jail is a natural fit for insomnia. The three a.m. heebie jeebies are known to everyone, but when you're incarcerated they're the status quo. Many inmates compensate by sleeping the next day away, motionless mounds on bunks in cocoons made of scratchy gray blankets.

Just when the deepest phases of slumber should be kicking in, breakfast arrives. It comes on rolling carts in the dark stillness, somewhere between four and five a.m. The cellblock lights are flipped on and one inmate from each cell is buzzed out, returning minutes later with gray plastic molded trays stacked high in his arms. The tray compartments, sticky with syrup, might hold scrambled eggs, chorizo, cornflakes, potatoes, canned fruit or pancakes. Most days there are three slices of Wonder Bread, two packets of grape jelly, one envelope of fake sugar. Cartons of milk on top of it all make the trip up the stairs to the second floor a circus balancing act.

The men in the cell stir in their covers, barely awake. The ones on the upper bunks have to negotiate the ladders without kicking anyone in the head, a constant danger in the confined space. There are two plastic tables in the tight floor space, but not enough molded plastic chairs for everyone, so at least one person winds up eating on his bunk. In the dim light, the daily morning routine is carried out in silence, less like friends meeting for breakfast at Denny's than a pack of wolves in a cave, hunched over their food, sounds of chewing and grunts instead of speech.

After breakfast everyone crawls back into his bunk, some not waking up again until midmorning.

I spent the first week like a free diver trying to adjust to pressure changes without blowing out a blood vessel in my brain. The new normal was a state of heightened vigilance, always looking for the nearest wall to back up against at the first sign of danger. The guys in the cell weren't making it any easier, alternately ignoring me or flashing looks of disgust.

My cell, I would learn, was the worst in the cellblock, the one reserved for young Chicanos with attitude. Besides Thomas, my interrogator Jose, and the leader of the pack, Mano, there was a big, funny-looking guy named Arnie and a thin, pretty faced kid named Georgie Fitzgerald.

Georgie claimed to be Chicano although that conclusion wasn't readily apparent from his dyed blond hair and delicate features. Claiming that ethnicity felt like it might have been a flimsy stab at protection when he first arrived in the cell, although the other guys weren't buying it. They were suspicious of anything that came out of Georgie's mouth, especially talk of all his Chicano cousins and relatives, and his boasts of sexual conquests. Actually they weren't boasts. Georgie reported that beautiful women were continually coming up to tell him how much they had enjoyed sex with him, but he could never remember having done it. He had been stoned out of his mind. Drugs were his one true love.

Jose especially was always gunning for Georgie, taunting him with homophobic slurs, threatening him physically whenever he got bored and didn't have anything better to do.

The other white guy in the cell was named Bryce. He was older than the others, his face still handsome despite the false front tooth he could flick in and out with his tongue. His body hadn't totally gone to ruin despite the ravages of years of drug abuse; a reckless assortment of tattoos were like graffiti on his arms and chest.

In furtive moments he tried to hide from the rest of the cell, Bryce glommed onto me almost from the beginning. Probably it was because I was a fellow "wood," or white guy. The first time we were let out of the cell for rec in the dayroom, he told me the story of his life.

Unlike most guys in county jail, he had grown up rich and privileged on Tucson's east side. He was ambitious in high school and college where he majored in business, specifically the hospitality industry. He was a natural salesman and quickly became a mid-level manager at an upscale Phoenix resort. By then he had a beautiful wife, a big new home and a couple of kids he took to dance lessons and coached in Little League. It was the American dream, right up until he made the fateful decision that trashed it all.

It wasn't about drugs, at least not at the beginning, but about a perky co-worker. He made matters worse by using a vacant room at the resort for the seduction. It was the place, not the act, that sealed his termination. Had he not done it there, his higher-ups might have looked the other way, but now they couldn't.

The long-planned corporate-sponsored trip to Hawaii for his family was the first thing to go. The job, the wife and kids followed shortly afterwords, especially after Bryce's father-in-law intercepted a phone call with his girlfriend.

The drugs came later. Uppers, downers, he was up for whatever. Using them quickly led to dealing them; his addiction wasn't merely to narcotics, so much as to the effect they had on certain women who thought drug dealers were the sexiest men on the planet. Being a dealer made him lots of money at times, but it also got him beat up a fair amount. Seriously, by guys with hammers. He was in jail now, awaiting a sentence of at least five years after being set up by a narc who busted him with all kinds of illegal substances in hefty amounts on his person.

Bryce was crying by the time he finished. I wondered if he noticed all the other cons circulating around us in the day room as he relayed one sordid detail after another. I didn't know why he was telling me, but it seemed to help.

"I've learned this time," he concluded, wiping the tears from his cheeks.

"This was the last time. I'll never do it again. I'm in AA, NA, I'm going to meetings all the time. I've learned. I've finally figured it out."

I nodded, but doubted it.

All the glass windows added to the impression of being in a fish-bowl. Literally. Privacy is nonexistent in such a world; everyone knows everything that's going on. In my first few days I was stopped twice out in the rec area by white guys from other cells.

"They treating you okay in there?" asked the first. "Anything happens to you, you come to me."

I didn't want to ask him what "anything" covered.

"They still have you on that top bunk?" asked another, shaking his head. "They're fuckin' with you, bro. They do anything to you, you come to me ..."

It wasn't clear to me what coming to him would accomplish. Mano was a semi-professional boxer, with thirty bouts under his belt. In the prison world where fighting was the measure of all things, our cell was the one the others worried about, and Mano was its boss.

As for my top bunk, I had absolutely no desire to leave it. I learned that on day one. From it, and almost nowhere else in the cellblock, there was a clear view out the big windows, over the high rec yard walls, to the world outside. There were trees, Interstate 10 running south to Nogales, a VA hospital and occasional other big buildings jutting out of the low-rise cityscape. The Rincon Mountains that turned violet at sunset marked the horizon. I called it a room with a view. Surrounded by danger and craziness, my bunk was a port in the storm.

After a few weeks of getting deeper and deeper into jailhouse mentality, I started thinking all those vehicles on I-10 heading north from Nogales were carrying drugs or illegals crammed in their trunks.

Even people who have never been within a thousand miles of Tucson have a sense of the place, painted on movie and TV screens by decades-old classic Westerns, and gritty glimpses of the new West's seedy side. In them, gangs kill each other on the Mexican side of the border for the drugs that they then transport through tunnels under walls to wealthy American households and penniless street addicts alike. Past and present, Southern Arizona's leathery desert landscapes have given refuge to bad hombres with itchy trigger fingers, their faces rough with stubble, their corneas permanently etched, their brains fried by the blowtorch sunshine.

A single C.O. oversaw the cellblock; there were at least a half dozen of them alternating as the shifts changed. One of the morning guys was named Montero. He was a big boy in his early twenties, with thick curly black hair and almost cherubic innocence in a handsome face that would have been more at home in a alter boy vestments or priest's robes than a sheriff's uniform.

My second day in, Montero called me over to the control console, which dominated the day room like the bridge of the Starship Enterprise.

"Why are you here," he asked, "if you don't mind my asking ...?"

Contact between C.O.s and inmates was dangerous under any circumstances, carried out at great peril. Fraternizing was a no-no, and being perceived by the other prisoners as a snitch was a constant risk. Even worse, anything you said could still be used against you. Especially here, especially now, since most guys in country jail are awaiting formal sentencing. One of the scariest aspects of being imprisoned is the first time you realize you can't count on the guards for protection. But, as with everything else in there, limits were always being tested, boundaries always being pushed, exceptions always being made.

"Ag assault," I answered tentatively. "I hit a pedestrian in a crosswalk ... it was an accident ..."

Montero's face filled with concern. "Was he ...?"

"Broken leg," I answered, trying not to volunteer anything the court didn't know already.

Montero looked relieved. He would be the world's worst poker player. Then he repeated the verdict I had already gotten used to, although hearing it again just made things worse.

"You don't belong here."

A more pertinent concern at this point was whether there would be one injured victim of my mistake, or two?

No matter what I did, I knew I was on shaky ground. Everyone is. The trial period never ends, you never pass the initiation. A cellblock is a Machiavellian domain. Gossip and backbiting are rampant, there's always a war council meeting in one cell or another, deciding someone's fate for the slightest offense, real or imagined. The code is unwritten and arbitrary depending on who's passing the judgment, but the punishment is infallible. A "hot one," or hard slug in the shoulder, is the starting point for administering justice. The form of punishment works its way up from there.

I hadn't been there for long before Jose cornered me on my bunk.

"We want you out of here," he said. "You don't belong here. You're too old, you get in our way.

"You cramp our style. Go to the C.O., you'll have to fill out an inmate request form. Tell him you need to be a lower lower."

He wasn't menacing. I figured I was ahead of the game since I hadn't gotten hit. I planned to ask the C.O. as soon as I could, but we got locked down in our cell for the rest of the day. It wasn't until the next morning that there was an opportunity, but by then something had mysteriously changed.

"I'm going to talk to the C.O. now," I told Jose.

"No," he answered, "we changed our mind. We don't want you to go, we like having you here.

"You're old, but you've got heart. You're okay."

What had changed? What had the discussion been, when did it even take place? I would never know. But by way of a treaty, Mano showed up at my bunk bringing me a pair of earplugs he had fashioned from scraps of cotton enclosed in fingertips cut from blue rubber gloves. Thomas, who had been an ally from the beginning, started sharing items of food from his cardboard banker's box. Georgie and Bryce could openly talk to me now.

"They're all behind you now," Bryce confided when we were alone. "Each one of them, they've got you covered. They said anyone who comes at you has to go through them. All of them, Arnie, Mano, Jose, they're all saying they've got your back …"

"But why?"

He couldn't say. But by some calculation unknowable to a newcomer who would never fully belong in this world, I had changed. No longer was I the old man pain in the neck. I had become "Pops."

You could never be sure you were safe, and you could never be safe for long. Being in or out of favor could turn on a dime. You may never have been diagnosed or exhibited any symptoms of being bipolar before, but in jail it's a contagious disease.

You ride the roller coaster of every emotion you know in the course of every single day.

Thomas, my first friend, was a poster boy for a life spent locked up. From his long black androgynous hair down to the swirling discolored bruises in his calves from shooting up heroin, he was what Kris Kristofferson had once labeled "a walking contradiction, partly truth and partly fiction."

All of the males in his family had been or still were incarcerated. His mother, as with all Mexican matriarchs, was the long-suffering saint who never lost faith in any of them. Although still in his twenties, Thomas had spent most of his adulthood in state prisons. Since arriving in Pima County Jail, his temper had already earned him a months-long stay in the solitary confinement of "the hole."

"It changes you, it makes you even crazier" he said of the hole. He didn't elaborate.

Thomas had grown up in a strict Mormon household, and in school had shown all sorts of promise. But one wrong turn early on led to another, then another, until he was so lost in the wild woods it was impossible to find the path back out.

It was a pattern I would see over and over again, a demographic I would come to label "the guys who never had a chance."

But despite being an inevitable recidivism statistic, Thomas was smart, an avid reader, a philosophical thinker. And when the time was right, he was funny.

He would taunt the night C.O. Crystal – a lisping guy with glasses who looked exactly like Pat on "Saturday Night Live" – by standing on the landing outside our cell, bare chested, accusing Crystal of "getting all googly-eyed" whenever he saw a good-looking man.

Thomas had a large, esoteric assortment of books borrowed from the cellblock library downstairs that he was eager to share with me. In one of them I learned psychologist Hans Eysenck's theories on personality formation. It began with Type 1, characterized by a lifelong pattern of hopelessness; and Type 2, marked by constant blame and anger. This was invaluable data considering my new circumstances.

And here I had spent seventy-three years living at the Type 4 end of the scale, where you're all squared away.

In another of Thomas' books I read about the positive effects of DHEA hormone on longevity. When it came to picking a novel, I decided against the Baldacci and the escapist epics favored by prisoners who liked to read. Instead I chose "The Laughing Sutra" by Marc Salzman, a light, comic Buddhist odyssey set in modern times, from China to the Bay Area. I had read a lot of Buddhist books in the months before being taken into custody, searching for helpful coping mechanisms. I discovered some very useful tips in their ancient wisdom. Like being reminded that lust and greed were the major impediments to enlightenment. Or that overcoming the fear of death was the pathway to immortality.

They also gave me the sneaking suspicion that enlightenment itself might be a little bit boring.

The book Thomas was reading at the time was an academic tome by some professor examining the creative process in early 20th century artists and thinkers including Picasso, Einstein, Freud, Martha Graham and T.S. Eliot. He kept stopping to ask me definitions of words that he couldn't find in his pocket dictionary: Epistolary. Vignette. Epoch. Androgynous. Juxtaposition. Oxymoron.

Funny what happens when you take a guy who doesn't have a chance and get him out of the hole to a place where his brain can get some light.

16

Another Day in Paradise

The TV was on the wall next to my bunk. The remote had been cracked in half, probably in some long forgotten anger management lapse, and was now patched together with bandaids. You had to hold it just right to get it to work. Control of the remote was supposed to be democratic; everyone in the cell theoretically had a turn. I didn't push the point, figuring that putting on PBS, much less CNN or MSNBC was asking for trouble with the cell's prevailing demographic. My room-mates preferred mixed martial arts, Jay Leno's Garage and any other show about hot rods, British mechanics and classic car auctions. Or music videos with sultry Latina vocalists or slinky booty dancers in fishnets rubbing up against John Travolta. They were also fond of true-cop and inside-prison reality series, but their favorite of all was something called "Ridiculousness" on MTV.

The long-running series featured videos of young Americans of the male persuasion riding skateboards and almost anything else with wheels into walls. Or falling off swings, jumping off roofs or finding other ingenious ways of pulverizing their crotches and doing themselves serious harm. The show's host wore a flat-brimmed skateboarder cap and made snarky comments about their misfortune as he sat on a couch next to a buxom blonde woman with long legs up to her miniskirt, and a laugh reminiscent of a chirping dolphin or a machine gun. "Ridiculousness" was on at all hours of the day, which was fine with my cellies who couldn't get enough of it.

Most of the time they operated the remote at ADHD speed, never staying on a single channel for more than a second. The effect was dizzying. I always wished we could linger a while on the MTV videos, Ava Max singing, "Oh, she's sweet but a little bit psycho," Taylor Swift intoning, "You need to calm down …"

Thomas called dibs on the remote Friday nights when the History Channel aired "Ancient Aliens." I was with him on that one. I wasn't exactly a true believer in the "theory" that aliens from outer space were the progenitors of the human race on earth. But its explanation of how massive pyramids, giant stone heads and monumental temple complexes were created thousands of years ago by primitive cultures that hadn't even discovered the wheel was a more fun origin story than real scientists or ancient bible writers had come up with. Plus it was a trip to visit all those very cinematic, wonder-of-the-world sites around the planet, especially when they got to Hawaii, which some ancient alien theorists believe was the portal for the first space travelers.

Those were the magic worlds on the show: … *some ancient alien theorists believe* …, a convenient way of differentiating it from anything that was actually true, in a manner that undiscriminating viewers wouldn't notice.

Some of the Hawaiian footage had been filmed on Maui's volcano, Haleakala. Our home was on Haleakala's slopes, twenty-five-hundred feet up. Watching the show felt like a home movie. Despite the fuzzy science, pop anthropology and sketchy sci-fi theology, it touched me in the place I lived. It was personal.

Little did I know then that that was just a teaser. The TV screen, virtually the only technology allowed to Arizona prisoners, would become the transporter for my own spiritual journey during my almost year in captivity.

My tablet didn't work, but Thomas loaned me his when he wasn't using it. He thought it might be helpful when he caught me meditating on my bunk one morning when everyone else was still asleep. One of the few things the tablet was good for was music. Most Arizona inmates' tastes run toward violent, explicitly misogynistic rap, but I found other things more to my liking. Not just Japanese shakuhachi music for cellblock meditation, but livelier stuff, too. Like smoldering Rhiannon Giddens with her banjo on the New Basement Tapes covering Dylan's

"Spanish Mary":

> *Beggar man, beggar man,*
> *Tell me no lie,*
> *Is it a mystery to live*
> *Or is it a mystery to die?*

I was not the only newcomer to the cell. One bunk in particular, the upper next to mine, seemed reserved for guys just passing through who never fell into the cell's good graces, had problems with authority, and didn't last very long before they got rolled out.

The first one, there when I arrived, was named Anthony Rodriguez. Tall and thin with falcon eyes and a hooked nose, he looked like a cross between an Aztec warrior and Bruce Springsteen. When he opened his mouth to speak, the resemblance ended.

Like a lonely auctioneer he would sit on his bunk trying to join the never-ending food trades at meal times that constitute jailhouse commerce.

"Pancake for an egg, pancake for an egg ...," he would try. No one would take him up on it. The other cellies didn't like Anthony, and the feeling was mutual. But he spotted me as different – sympathetic at least, if not a complete pushover. Anthony tried to make me his friend. When the others played Spades with cutthroat determination, he enticed me into games of Uno with the cell's battered deck. He was like a puppy, thrilled with my attention. Pretty soon he was telling jokes, all of which were on the same subject: Christa McAuliffe, the science teacher turned astronaut, killed in the 1986 Challenger disaster.

"What color were Christa McAuliffe's eyes?" he asked me. I didn't know.

"Blue," he answered. "One blew this way, one blew that way ...

"What was the last word she said?"

I didn't want to know.

"'Goodbye' to her ass ..."

They seemed to be the only jokes he knew, as inappropriate as they were unfunny. It was as though some piece of his brain had gotten stuck at that moment in 1986, then it broke and had been flapping around inside his skull ever since.

"I was in eighth grade when the Challenger blew up," he went on, not that I had asked. "We watched it on TV in school. My science teacher started crying."

That moment was probably the sum total, and the end, of his formal education.

The rec yard outside the dayroom's floor-to-ceiling windows was surrounded by twenty-foot walls topped by escape-proof mesh on the sides and across the top. It was about the size of half a basketball court, with a backboard and hoop on one wall. Its side walls fanned out in a crescent. You could do laps inside the walls under a patch of blue sky caged above your head, dodging the basketball shots by other inmates as they bounced off the rim and backboard. A hundred times around might have added up to a mile, it was that tiny.

The black man who had stepped out on the landing the night I arrived was named Troy, and he was basically the god of the yard. Most days a group would work out together, doing pushups and burpees by the hundreds. Mano, with Thomas next to him trying to keep up, deferred to Troy. With his Greek god physique and effortless confidence, Troy was our Denzel Washington.

Troy was the first one to call me "OG"

I watched the workout routine a couple of times before asking if I could join. Troy nodded, with skeptical approval.

"Take it easy, old man. Don't hurt yourself."

I took my place in the lineup, and managed to keep up. Thomas noticed. Then, when I took my shirt off, so did the rest of them.

"Fuck, man, OG's ripped …"

"How old did you say you were?" Troy wanted to know.

I had made myself known on the cellblock. For better or worse.

It was still a delicate balance. Part of me clung to Susan's words, "They need you in there, Rick …" Part of me stayed on permanent alert, always ready to duck and cover. Working out every day upped my status, but more importantly got the endorphins pumping.

"You're seventy-three and you still know how to fight?" asked a kid from another cell. It made sense not to correct him.

"You've got to own it," Thomas advised. "When you were younger, you probably had more swagger. Get it back …"

But not too much. The one thing convicts everywhere hate more than anything else is anyone who thinks he is better than they are. Fortunately for me, I didn't. My own self judgment was still harsher than the formal sentencing awaiting me. I was in orange just like everyone else. I had fucked up as badly as they had. The orange was protective coloration, but also constantly humbling. The universal truth of inmates is that every single one of them made a really big mistake to get there. Every single one of us.

But there were differences, too. By now Bryce was referring to me as the guy on the yard with the halo and angel wings. Inmates from other cells, like Troy, were sharing their stories with me. One of them was from New York, DAVEY tattooed across his knuckles. Swarthy and hairy, he could have just stepped out of a Scorsese casting call.

He was in for extortion and racketeering in a criminal career that had filled most of his thirty-plus years with charges including murder. He had beat that one back in New York. He had started his life in crime before he was ten, getting paid a hundred bucks just to stand on a street-corner and be a lookout for a drug deal. He told me about other kids on his street, including the African immigrants who had been forced into conscription as child soldiers in their homeland. One had been ordered to kill his mother, Davey told me, by beheading. Kids like Davey didn't have childhoods. On the other hand, he was extremely bright, and had even earned a college scholarship back in his teens before squandering the opportunity.

He approached me out on the yard one afternoon.

"Do you have a minute?" he said, "I know you're older, all due respect, and might be able to give me some advice. I'm thirty-four now …"

He kept talking, filling in one sordid detail after another, furtively looking around to be sure he wasn't being overheard. For the last decade, he had his wife convinced that he had a legitimate business flipping houses as he kept engaging in his real profession, strong-arm shakedowns.

"… I've got a six-year-old daughter now. I want to see her grow up. I want to spend time with her, be her dad, take her fishing. Is it too late? Do you think I can turn my life around and go straight, once I finish my sentence?"

I thought about it.

"Yeah," I said slowly. "No question. You're smart enough to get a business degree, even go to law school. For you that's not going to be the hard part. But for anyone like you, used to the fast lane, I imagine going straight's gonna be the problem. No big payoffs when you're on the up and up. Lots of boredom, paying taxes, punching a clock instead. It's stifling …"

I left out the part about lives of quiet desperation. That was too much information, I figured.

"You can," I concluded. "Up to you whether you will."

Almost everyone I knew and everything I took for granted before didn't exist in this world. A high school diploma was a given; at least one college degree was the norm where I came from. What we knew of misfortune was pretty First World: Dysfunctional families. Alcoholism, drugs and shopping addictions. Neuroses and clinical depression. Trying to be good parents. And now the ravages of our bodies growing old, maybe with a cancer diagnosis to really sober you up.

It was rookie stuff compared to the guys in the cell, a third my age.

Arnie had seen his mother raped and burned alive when he was nine. Georgie began his shoplifting career at the same age, nabbing a fifth of vodka from Safeway, then scrambling out the fire exit and delivering it to his mother at home. These guys' missing and rotting teeth weren't solely the results of fights. They also came from heavy drug abuse from an early age, and the fact that there was no one in their homes who had the money, or cared, for dental hygiene when they were growing up.

The tattoos filling vacant spaces on their bodies were like war-paint warning signs to their peers. But also symbols of surrender to themselves, the realization that they would always be criminals.

And here I was, a prisoner in their world, sentenced to try to sort things out. Finding myself surrounded by life's dregs – robbers, thieves, thugs, abusers, addicts, bullies, punks – getting in touch with my inner Jesus was the only way forward. Not being able to pass myself off as one of them, it would prove my only option if I hoped to survive.

"Another day in Paradise," was a common answer from one inmate to another when asked how he was that morning. You hear that phrase a lot on Maui. It didn't mean the same thing here.

17

Taking notes

One thing prisoners live for in the relentless monotony of a long jail sentence is what's known as store, or Keefe. They pronounce it *Kee-fee*.

It's the weekly delivery of commissary goods from the Keefe Group, the Tucson-based purveyor for the statewide Arizona Department of Corrections. The commissary isn't a real place, like a market with aisles for food, toiletries, clothing and even electronics. It's not an actual room you can visit in the jail. Instead, it's an order sheet you fill out with your stubby golf pencil. In jail there's no such thing as cash; convicts have accounts where their "people on the outside" can deposit money on their books.

Once you have money on your books, you access the Keefe price list on your tablet – or on a friend's tablet that works – and you fill in the red-ink order bubbles on a scanner sheet. The following week your order arrives, delivered by a Keefe employee in a loaded laundry cart. The workers are usually short-tempered women with Mexican accents who grumble as they unpack all the orders on a dayroom table, then watch impatiently as you check the items on your list and sign for them. Attitude notwithstanding, they are jail's version of Santa Claus, or the Wells Fargo stagecoach pulling into a dusty town in old Arizona.

You can buy summer sausage, oatmeal, tuna in a pouch, big bags of chips, coffee, candy bars, cheese whiz in single-serving plastic packets. It's all processed food, the one health requirement being enough sodium to bust a blood pressure meter. The staple of the Keefe diet is packs of ramen noodles that inmates buy by the dozen, affectionately known as *soups*. Soups and shots of coffee are jail's version of currency. The value of any good or service can be measured in soups. A soup and a cheese add up to a dollar.

Your people outside can also place orders for you online. They can choose from prepackaged assortments of meats, crackers, candy and other treats; or maybe a breakfast-themed collection. It's like Harry & David for the criminal element. The assortments are called "secure packs" when they are delivered in big clear plastic bags.

The week I arrived, Karen aided by Lisa navigating the computer, ordered me the most expensive secure pack on the list, not realizing it could make me a target for theft or extortion. The secure packs aren't delivered on regular store days, so they get lots of attention. You're buzzed out of your cell and can feel the eyes of everyone in the cellblock as you walk down the stairs and pick up yours, almost as big as a Santa bag stuffed with packaged foods. The arrival of my secure pack may have had something to do with my cellmates' sudden decision that I was alright after all.

"Don't give it all away," advised Thomas. "People like you, it's in your nature to share … don't!

These assholes will take total advantage of you if you're not careful."

You can buy toothpaste, shampoo, boxer shorts, socks, bandaids, earphones, batteries or a hundred other items including a pocket-size transistor radio known as a "peanut" because of its shape. It was a peanut that was impeding the plumbing in our right toilet. My list of essentials also included a pack of notebook paper and as many ballpoint pens as I could order (three, at nine cents each, was the limit). The pens consisted of a ballpoint tip connected to a narrow flexible ink tube. The plastic part that says Bic that we normally think of as a pen is not included, out of caution that it can be turned into a weapon.

The words you're reading here were originally written with one.

It took a while to get used to using a flexible writing implement whose ink could puddle out if you didn't have the right touch. I also had to remember how to do actual handwriting. My computer had been my instrument for decades.

"How can you teach writing, Grampa?" Lilie once asked me, looking at my indecipherable marks on a note. But now that I was forced to, my ink-blot scratchings were yielding curlicues like those created with quill pens by pirates or signers of the Declaration of Independence. I did illustrations, too. Floor plans of the cell and cellblock; renderings of the view from my bunk or inmates playing basketball that might pass for New Yorker cartoons or a four-year-old's drawings.

The guys in the cell knew I was a journalist. When they asked what I was doing, I replied, "taking notes."

Trips to the clinic provided another break in the routine. Whether it had been the letter from the prisoners' rights attorney demanding that I receive the right medication, or the more obvious fact that they were dealing with a seventy-three-year-old recent heart attack survivor, the medical staff gave me their full attention.

That was good news, and bad news.

They subjected me to a battery of blood tests and an EKG shortly after I arrived, showing that my blood pressure wasn't taking well to my new living arrangements. I got seen by a couple of physicians, both women, who started tweaking with my meds, only to find that what was good for my heart wasn't necessarily good for my kidneys.

It would have been more unsettling if the tests weren't being administered by this gorgeous nurse. She wore her name tag inside out so no one could read it. I heard Diana, I heard Candice. But she was legendary throughout the entire complex as the one with the hair. His brown hair cascaded down her back past her waist, calling attention to the rest of her perfect body. She wasn't just jail beautiful, but beautiful, period. She was also smart. You could tell from her eyes, and the way she dealt with her "clients," never losing her cool despite some inner knowledge of the unspeakably lewd thoughts she triggered in every one of their deprived brains. The conversations by snaggletoothed, tatted inmates in the clinic waiting room watching her through a big window as they waited their turn was beyond the misogynistic pale, even by jail standards. Surely she knew, but ignored it. The psyches of women who work in prisons remained a never-ending mystery to me.

For the first couple of weeks I got called out of the cell every night, patted down by the C.O., then put into the sally port to await another guard who would walk me to the clinic for a blood pressure check. The soups, the new staple of my diet, each had a couple of days' worth of sodium in its little flavor packet. This was undoubtedly a contributing factor to the dangerous readings from the BP cuff … but so were Diana's (or Candice's) fingers on my arm when she put the cuff on. When, after several days, the readings started falling into the safe range, I was crestfallen.

"Nooo," I said softly, realizing that our nightly visits were going to end. Looking into her wise brown eyes it was clear the feelings weren't reciprocal.

The other nurses weren't as beautiful. They had more years and more ample backsides, but they sparked the same animal lusts whenever they appeared. Prisoners' libidos are as subtle and nuanced as beagles humping table legs. Nurses arrived in the cellblock twice a day, morning and night wheeling cabinets of prescriptions for the inmates on their lists. Their arrival, especially at night, was taken by the guys in Cell 5 as a mating call from a she-creature in heat, despite getting no signals to that effect from the women themselves. Led by Mano, the guys would rip their shirts off, then stand by the windows preening and striking poses. The delusion – shared by most of the men I met during my extended residency in the Arizona prison system – that they were God's gift to women was an error in judgment almost as huge as the mistakes that had gotten them arrested in the first place.

As a rule, inmates' understanding of women had never progressed beyond a horny adolescent's, despite the great sexual prowess they claimed. Their drug abuse and their crimes to support their habits had gotten most of them incarcerated. But women – more specifically their all-encompassing inability to understand, care about or otherwise have any meaningful contact above the waist with a woman – were second on their lists of insurmountable challenges. Convicts' grasp of female anatomy was sketchy at best; the female psyche might as well have been written in Mandarin as far as they were concerned. The word "woman" wasn't in their vocabulary. Not even "my old lady" or "chick," which had themselves become unacceptable terms since my old hippie days.

Instead there was the all-purpose "bitch," used to refer to any female human, and the slightly more ambiguous "my baby mama," whose name they didn't want to mention. Some had several baby mamas. Their idea of fatherhood began and ended with the act of impregnation. The more the better, casting their seed as enduring proof of their manhood.

Jose was the worst. Still in his early twenties, he had at least one baby mama, one daughter, one girlfriend who shared the step-mothering duties with Jose's mother, and another girlfriend on the side.

Those were the ones I knew of; there were probably more.

Jose, who didn't have a tablet of his own, was constantly commandeering someone else's in the cell to make phone calls to his harem.

"Denise," he would begin, "I love you, I miss you, I want to fuck you ..." They'd share notes about his daughter, for a moment or two he would sound like an attentive dad. But it wasn't long before his tone would change. "Do you love me? Are you waiting for me? If you don't, I swear to God I'll kill you..."

He sounded like he meant it. As soon as that call ended he'd call his other girlfriend.

"Do you miss me? I can't stop thinking about you, babe. I just want be with you, make a baby with you, fuck you forever ..."

In the cell Jose's main form of recreation was tormenting Georgie, the skinny blond would-be Chicano. Jose got more support when another inmate, a 21-year-old whiteboy named Lyle, arrived.

Georgie's sexuality was their preoccupation. They insisted he was gay, obsessing over the accusation. They repeated the innuendos and taunts over and over, until 19-year-old Georgie had nowhere to retreat to but his bunk where he would pretend to sleep for the rest of the afternoon.

"I just feel like punching you," Jose told him one day. "Giving you a hot one ..."

Belying his pretty face, Georgie was thick-skinned, resilient to the abuse. Jose kept it up until Georgie finally acceded. Jose hit him in the jaw, surprised when Georgie didn't flinch.

Watching the bullying was part of my cellblock education. It would have been suicidal to intervene, but Georgie wasn't expecting that. His reactions were complicated, some part of him even enjoying the attention.

His middle name was Dante. Lyle taunted him with the nickname

Tay-tay. One night Georgie convinced someone to ink three dots forming a triangle tattoo next to his right eye.

"Tay-tay got a tat!" Lyle and Jose repeated in sing-song cadence. "What a dipshit."

"It's on your face, where the C.O.'s can see it," added Mano, the voice of authority. "You didn't have it when you came in. It's not on your ID photo and you can't hide it. Not too smart ..."

"Tay-Tay got a tat ... Tay-Tay got a tat ...!"

I spoke to Georgie for the first time a day or two after I arrived in the cell. By way of introduction he told me he wasn't going to live to see twenty-one. He said it matter-of-factly, stoic resolve in the delicate features of his face.

"I don't care," he added. "I've already OD'd twice, they had to bring me back with paddles. I've been suicidal since I was seven. My mom died the day they took me into custody. My ex-fiance left me. There's nothing for me to live for."

Was this what my lawyer was preparing me for? They need you in there, Rick ... Was Georgie my mission? It didn't take long to realize first impressions were dead wrong when it came to the kid with the dyed hair. Whether or not he had stayed in high school long enough to graduate, he was smarter than his cellmates, probably smarter than all of them put together. He had built an entrepreneurial empire running prescription drugs to and from Mexico, making big profits selling whichever ones were illegal on that side of the border. His knowledge of pharmacology and brain chemistry was encyclopedic. He was the one who explained the difference between manic-depression and bipolar to me as knowledgeably as a doctor.

"Bipolar is immediate," he said. "It's a mood swing that can turn on a dime. Manic depression takes weeks to crawl out of."

From him I learned street terms like *zannies, roofies, black, green, ketamine* referring to opioids, uppers and downers with much longer official pharmacological names. When he had been free, Georgie consumed them in bulk, mixing and matching, speeding headlong on the highway to oblivion.

Incarcerated, he was always on the lookout for any contraband that had been smuggled into the cellblock. His drug habits were gleefully suicidal. He didn't drink coffee, he snorted lines of it.

At nineteen he was worldly yet naïve. He had learned to live on the street, carless, penniless, after being thrown out of both parents' homes. He had found a brief interlude of solace with the girlfriend he now called his ex-fiancee. She had invited him to her parents' upscale home in California and for a while he had glimpsed what a viable, if not altogether functional, family looked like.

Her parents were both law-enforcement officers; she had siblings who were into partying and guns.

The love of his life had tattoos on her arms of all the animals she had hunted. She would kill rabbits, then put their "lucky rabbit's feet" on Craigslist.

Georgie was brilliant enough to survive on his own, a savvy enough chameleon to dumb down to any situation he found himself in. He borrowed a chess set from Troy and started playing with me. It had been decades since the last time I played, he was just a beginner, but it wasn't long before he actually won a game without any help, other than carelessness, on my part.

Living on the street he was just playing his cards the best he could, not realizing what a terrible hand he had been dealt. White privilege is something unknown to most inmates in Pima County Jail. It wasn't their birthright, it can't be learned and they're not eligible anyway. Suicide might present itself as an option for them, but not self-pity. They've never had anything to compare their struggles to – they were too busy struggling with them. Georgie had already experienced things I still hadn't seen at three times his age. But, like Joni Mitchell, he didn't know life at all.

"You don't know anything," I told him. "Have you ever been any-where besides that trip to California? Did you even see the ocean? Do you have a driver's license? Have you ever been in a plane? A boat? You're two years short of being able to walk into a bar. Have you ever been in a college class, where you might discover how smart you are? You've never been to New York or Paris or ten-thousand other places. You've never driven cross country, you've never flown to Hawaii. You're just a kid. Why are you so damn determined to end your life before it even begins …?"

I couldn't save him. I couldn't even protect him from the bullying in the cell. But just maybe I could plant the seed for him to consider saving himself.

18

Mr. Inbetween

Cell 5's favorite TV series was the Australian-made "Mr. Inbetween." Adapted by a shaved-head, middle-aged actor-writer-director named Scott Ryan, the series was about a harried, divorced dad named Ray trying to co-parent his daughter with his successful ex-wife while making his living as a thug for hire. The writing was brilliant and sardonic, delivered with those Aussie accents that are hilarious all by themselves. Ray and his partner might spend a whole scene ranking all the film actors who had played James Bond. Sean Connery was the best, of course. Ray would philosophically quote the Dalai Lama, then beat the hell out of some lowlife in the next scene. When a neighbor called child protective services about Ray's parenting practices, he responded to the case worker's interrogation through his front screen door by repeating, "I don't answer questions."

He pronounced it *kweestions*. It became a cell slogan.

"I don't answer kweestions."

It was a weekly ritual, Mr. Inbetween night. We'd pull all the plastic chairs in front of the TV, like a little theater. I'd watch from my bunk above.

The show's title was apt for our group. Most of us were Mr. Inbetweens. Time in county jail, rather than state prison, is standard for sentences of a year or less. But many inmates' jail stays were transitional phases as we awaited prison sentencing. I had been taken into custody when I accepted my plea. I would have to go back to court – be part of the shackled parade of guys in orange – to hear the judge decide the length of my sentence within the options of my plea.

The prisoners rights attorney I consulted had been surprised that state prison was specified in my plea. A year was, by state prison standards, a short time. But when I asked my main attorney Susan if it wouldn't be better to stay in Pima County Jail for the duration, she insisted that was a bad idea. Jail time is flat time – you have to serve every day of the sentence. Prison time isn't; you do eighty-five percent, and there are other reductions that make it even shorter. State prison had other benefits, too, Susan said, although I couldn't for the life of me imagine what they might be.

Everyone would get called out of the cell from time to time for visits with our attorneys. They took place in a suite of soundproof offices a few corridors away. We were never sure when our attorney visits would happen. When they did, we'd be buzzed into the sally port to wait for a guard who would escort us. I'd be stuck in the sally port, just me and the security camera, for as much as a half-hour before a guard would arrive. It felt like the jail staff was taking their time on purpose, a little show of disrespect to my lawyer and myself, just because they could.

Susan would visit every few weeks to brief me for my court appearance. She was always well dressed, lawyerly attractive; her visits were also checks on my welfare, and state of mind. And how suicidal are we feeling today … ? I would share cell stories with her, careful to censor details that might be too alarming, or that could endanger me with the authorities or my fellow inmates. You never get used to knowing that you can't turn to the guards for protection. I would put a happy face on the week's developments, try to make jokes out of them, but the laughs we shared were brittle at best.

"Have you noticed face shapes yet?" she asked. Medical studies have shown that maternal drug use before birth can result in distinctive traits in their offspring later on. Wide foreheads; a vacant, confused, slightly crazed look in the eye; a belligerent set of the jaw …

Hmmm, now that she mentioned it …

Susan was hopefully anticipating that I would get the lightest sentence on my plea – a year of incarceration, followed by four years of probation. But we couldn't be sure until it happened.

For inmates, our court cases are the subject of endless discussion.

They're talking points almost as popular as fighting and sex. Everyone becomes his own self-taught advocate, although the number of convicts who go on to become actual attorneys – the ones they make movies about – are one in a million. Less, actually.

The rest of us know far less than we think we do, about almost anything ... just like most Americans who aren't in jail. We can probably thank Steve Jobs for that.

Sometimes the talk veered in more philosophical directions. Interpreting Bible passages is big among cons. No one in our cell was of that mindset, thank God, although I eavesdropped on one conversation where a few of my cellies were deliberating their chances if, in fact, the meek really shall inherit the earth. Mostly the topics were more mundane, like their plans to buy the newest model iPhone when they got out. Despite their sketchy abilities to make money lawfully, they were avid consumers, into nice cars, designer clothes, expensive colognes. A bunch of real dandies.

Occasionally efforts to combat the boredom had ingenious results. One day I looked out at a cell across the dayroom to see the inmates playing ping-pong. They had pushed their two plastic tables together, put a cardboard "net" in the seam between them and batted the plastic roller from a deodorant can back and forth over the net with paddles made from bowl lids. Most of the time the games were more dangerous. Fistfights in other cells were viewed like spectator sports through the windows.

For many young inmates, being incarcerated triggers the part of the brain that loves courting danger. They can't help it. Someone in Cell 5 would always have a smidge of tobacco smuggled in from outside that they would roll into a skinny cigarette. They would wait for lights out, then pull the TV cord out of the wall socket and hot wire it to produce a spark. This in turn would ignite a wad of toilet paper in an eyebrow-singeing flare-up. They would light the tobacco and head for the bathroom to share it. It was risky business. For openers, it could easily trigger the cell's smoke detector. They would seal the air vents to the outside as best they could, then wave wet towels around to try to clear the air. If the C.O. happened to notice, everyone in the cell would be rolled out whether we were involved or not, and sent to the hole. The discipline could add to our sentence and would definitely send us to far worse accommodations, of which there were plenty in Pima County Jail. All of this for a puff or two from a pin-thin excuse for a cigarette.

The smoking was mindlessly self-destructive, like so much else in there. Being in trouble was the only form of self expression lots of those guys knew. The volume of the TV was always cranked up to 100, blasting into the night, forcing them to scream over it. Then they would drink coffee at 10 p.m. to raise the energy level a couple more notches.

"Homey, swear to God, dawg, that fool was fuckin' crazy, nigga ..."

They repeated phrases over and over, a chorus of giggles like hopped-up hyenas until two or three in the morning. While they deferred to "Pops" to my face, I didn't make an issue of our generational differences. It was an uneasy truce. Best to just ride with it, I figured, take my chances that they didn't get caught and take me down with them.

It was riskier whenever we would get a new C.O. Female officers were rarely assigned to oversee the whole cellblock, but one night we got one. She was eager to prove she was tough enough for the job. Early in the evening she read Cell 5 the riot act when she discovered we were not in our assigned bunks. I was probably the worst offender, territorial about my beloved upper with its cherished view. Had she checked further she would have found that I had an extra mattress pad – jail's answer to a Sealy Posturepedic – provided by my young cellmates out of concern for my aching joints.

She was also responsible for overseeing the cellblock across the hall. She went over to check it and arrived back at 2-Romeo at the same moment I was being escorted back from my visit to the clinic that evening. I assumed the position – arms outstretched crucifix-style – for her to pat me down, just to be sure I hadn't picked up any weapons on my brief trip away. But suddenly she stopped.

"I smell smoke," she said, freezing into a stance like a pointer who's just gotten a whiff of quail. "Do you smell smoke?" she snapped at me.

"Uh, no," I said. My version of "I don't answer kweestions."

The smell had to be coming from Cell 1, the one closest to us through the vent in its door. But her voice was loud enough to be heard throughout the cellblock, quickly followed by the whoosh of flushing toilets in every pod. Cell 5 was no different, except for Georgie, who chose not to flush but instead to chug down the large cup of hooch he had been fermenting from oranges, bread, water and packets of sugar, ketchup and Kool-Aid. He spent the rest of the night regretting it.

The Cell 5 roster was constantly changing. Anthony Rodriguez had left; his final words, delivered to us by the C.O., were, "Tell every asshole in there to go fuck yourself."

His replacement, red-haired Alex Black, slept away his first three days on his bunk, then got into an altercation with a C.O. on the way to the clinic and was gone.

Bryce was next to go. His ex-boss posted bail for him at his next court appearance. Despite the prosecutor's admonition that Bryce was a dangerous drug dealer, the judge ordered him released. He would be out on bail through the holidays before returning to start a five-year prison sentence. Thomas went to court and got a two-and-a-half-year sentence. He returned to the cell where he spent each day getting more depressed until his departure to Alhambra the next week.

Two new guys took their places. They were both big boys, 250 pounds each, which didn't save them from all newcomers' fate, a spot in the upper bunks. Philip Worster arrived first, a red-headed forty-two-year-old from Massachusetts, with missing teeth and missing brain cells from decades of too much heroin. In jail he was getting methadone daily, which slowed him down even more. Shortly after arriving, he discovered the cell's meager collection of coloring book pages and the plastic jar full of well used colored pencils. He would spend hours at a plastic table, his bulk hunched over a partially completed page, endlessly arranging the pencil stubs by color and size. After three days, the page was no closer to being finished.

The other new guy was an Indian – a *chief* in prison parlance – named Clarence. He was huge. He arrived one night after I was already trying to sleep, face to the wall, blanket pulled over my ears. I didn't bother to get up to introduce myself, but heard him talking nonstop, announcing his presence in no uncertain terms, launching a game of Spades in which his smart-ass chatter never ceased.

The obnoxious bravado didn't make a good first impression, but over the coming days that changed.

Maybe it was because he instinctively deferred to me, or maybe it was because I liked having a Big Chief next to me, covering my back for my version of Jack Nicholson in Cuckoo's Nest. But Clarence had many talents. He was a barber. On the outside he worked as a short-order cook and was a master of combining soups, chili, and whatever meat pouches you had in your Keefe pack into a "spread," jail's version of fine dining. Unlike others in the cell, his attention span could handle a movie all the way through. He was fascinated when I made brief mention of my career in the entertainment biz.

One night we watched the series "House" playing in reruns. Noticing that it co-starred Olivia Wilde early in her career, I mentioned to Clarence that I had once interviewed her. Big mistake, I instantly realized. I had promised myself that I was going in to keep my previous life on Maui as secret as I could in jail, for my own protection. I didn't want anyone in there thinking I was famous, much less rich ... which, by their skid row standards, I most certainly was.

"You interviewed her? She's fucking unbelievably fucking fuckable. She's the most beautiful thing I've ever seen. You interviewed her ...?

Luckily the other guys weren't as impressed. They barely noticed. But something funny was happening to me with the TV. Every time I stopped to watch it, I saw someone I knew. Not knew in the conventional sense, but in the Close Encounters of the Celebrity Kind sense of my profession.

"They are not your friends." That line from the film "Almost Famous" said it all. It had been delivered by Philip Seymour Hoffman playing a cynical journalist advising an aspiring teenage Rolling Stone reporter about covering rock stars. They might drink with you, party with you, even smoke a joint with you, but they weren't like you.

That teenager would grow up to become the film's writer-director, Cameron Crowe. The line had stuck with me through decades of my career as an entertainment journalist and editor. Talking to thousands of those larger-than-life beings meant nothing to them; doing publicity was part of their job. To them I was anonymous, an interchangeable inconvenience. But I remembered every one of them vividly, like my own little sprinklings of pixie dust.

And now here they came on the cell's TV screen. Dennis Quaid doing spot commercials for insurance. Laura Dern at war with dinosaurs in "Jurassic Park." Brie Larson trying to help a giant ape in "Kong." Helen Hunt as the wife at home in "Castaway."

Joan Allen as the icy security agency boss in all the "Bournes" and "Death Race." Bryan Cranston as a dad undone by the nutcase his daughter is marrying in "Why Him?" Henry Winkler on NPR, once I got a tablet that worked and could listen to the radio app. Owen Wilson in "The Internship." Pierce Brosnan in "Dante's Peak." Kevin Costner in "The Untouchables." Robin Williams in "Mrs. Doubtfire" …

The list went on and on. I had talked to them all, not as friends but as something else, employees in the profession of being larger than life. My job was finding out what made them tick. Many of my interviews were on camera and are accessible on YouTube. They're a matter of public record. But then there were the stories behind the stories, the tiny glimpses of the "real" them. I had made a profession of pressing my nose up against the window of celebrity; I had spent decades getting paid to go to the movies and then write about it. Hundreds of the most gifted and gorgeous beings on the planet had graciously co-starred in my fifteen minutes of fame. And now here I was, dressed in orange not by choice, locked in a Tucson jail cell not by choice, as far away as you could get from the ethereal worlds they inhabited.

Talk about both sides now. Watching their parade on the TV screen was like seeing my life – my old life – unspooling before my eyes. It was also like the "Six Degrees" trivia game based on the concept that everyone in the movie business is connected to everyone else. Except instead of Kevin Bacon as the hub at the center of all the spokes, it was me.

19

Countdown

The days were counting down to my court date, and my exit from Pima County. Beyond Phoenix's ominous sounding Alhambra, the human corral where all Arizona inmates go for processing, no one knows where in the state they will wind up under the care of the Department of Corrections. You hope for a minimum security "two yard," which is easier than a three, which is safer than a four. Prisons, including the private for-profit ones, are big business in the Grand Canyon state. Forty-two-thousand inmates when I joined their ranks, third per capita in the nation, eighth in the world. That's not including the kids in cages and asylum-seeking families from the south who also wind up crammed into Arizona correctional facilities.

Out in the world where seasons change, it was fall. Plans for Halloween costumes were part of the news I got on the jail's pay phones and in my weekly video visits with Karen, Lisa, and on one occasion my ten-year-old granddaughter Lilie. Although my orange wardrobe was still disconcerting for us all, it was reassuring for them to see me on the screen. I still had all my teeth, and no tattoos – positive markers in my new reality. I looked fine, actually. Face untouched, upper body showing evidence of all the burpies, push-ups and body-by-Mano workouts we did several times a day in the cell.

"He's like the Rock," my roommates observed, "the Rick ..."

Lilie was somewhere between intrigued and scared silly about grandpa's new life. She was worried about whether I was allowed to do things like brush my teeth.

I tried to put her mind at ease. "I live in a room with eight other big, very immature men," I told her.

In fact, hygiene has protocols when you're incarcerated. The C.O. would hand out razors a few times a week, writing your name on the handle in Sharpie. You'd make what lather you could with a bar of soap; the razor had to be returned within fifteen minutes for disposal.

The cellblock had eight showers, half with no hot water, the others regularly in need of repair. You'd time your showers at the end of rec periods. If you timed it wrong or were locked down all day, you were out of luck. You washed underwear and socks – whatever you had worn to court, bought from the store or been bequeathed from other inmates on their departures – by hand in the bathroom sink. You could grind bar soap into flakes with a plastic palm brush if you couldn't afford liquid soap from Keefe. Georgie and Arnie had their own laundry businesses, washing other inmates' boxers for soups or shots of coffee. We'd get new oranges once a week, a couple of shirts, a couple of pairs of pants, all emblazoned with Pima County stenciling. You'd get a new sheet and towel, too, dumping your old ones in a rolling laundry bin.

I had more surrogate sons by now, twenty-one-year-old Lyle Lathrop being the latest. He was white, a champion swimmer in high school who had taken wrong turns ever since, all under the influence. He was facing charges including assault and possession of a sawed-off shotgun.

"Why couldn't I have had a dad like you?" he asked. "I wouldn't be in here if I had."

I had even found a way of neutralizing Jose – I made him my exercise partner, matching him push-up for push-up. From their cell across the dayroom, Troy and his guys could watch us working out in Cell 5. I was something of a physical phenomenon – hardly the strongest guy in the cellblock, or the toughest, God forbid. But I had the best work ethic, hands down. Considering that I was two or three times anyone else's age, no one messed with me, whether out of respect or pity. Plus, I had a posse.

My homework was trying to find the courage to back up the image. It was an acting exercise. It seemed to be working.

"I hate white people," Jose opined to Mano and Arnie one day, fully aware that I was in earshot in the cell. "They're soft, they're weak, they're dumb as shit, they think they're privileged …"

He paused.

"… Except for Rick. He's not like that. He's a Chicano, homey …"

A more accurate label would have been Hawaiian. Not by birth of course, but hanai, adopted. Living for a quarter century in multi-ethnic Maui, I was accustomed to being part of a cultural mix where each group got a piece of the pie. The culture was the part of Hawaii I loved most; it wasn't racial harmony per se, but mutual awareness and respect. Island diversity was something local comedians could joke about in stand-up routines, beginning with the way each ethnic group fractured the English language. Hawaii's not a melting pot but a mixed plate, a huge buffet where locals know how to pile their paper plates high with nourishing tastes from diverse roots and colorful traditions all over the planet. Knowing that you are a member of one race among many sharing a tiny dot in the sea produces humility and gratitude, rather than delusions of superiority over anybody.

Arizona jails and prisons are multiracial, too. There's just no aloha.

Jail is a four-letter word. When you're incarcerated and freedomless, a burger ad on TV borders on pornography. Daily life is not unlike the hurry up and wait of a movie set. Hours of debilitating boredom broken by moments of adrenalized panic. As opposed to my life quest to turn everything into a learning experience, in jail most of the time, the less you know the better. That's unless you want to make a career out of it. Lyle quickly mastered cell-to-cell sign language, forming letters with his fingers to spell out messages to inmates in other pods. He was in the loop. He was second in command of the cellblock's whiteboys. It was a dubious distinction in my eyes, but undeniably a position of power.

I in contrast was a one-man United Nations. I was sitting alone at the rec yard picnic table one day when suddenly all the other benches filled with Chicanos. It was a hastily called emergency council to address the manufactured grievance du jour. Nobody minded my presence, or asked me to leave.

Mano was head of the Chicanos, not only in our pod but in the whole cellblock. Ignoring our racial backgrounds, he gave me the respect he would his own grandfather, asking me from time to time just what I made of "this generation." Occasionally he would even share unguarded memories of times in his childhood spent with his uncles who were cowboys and taught him to ride and break horses ...

A semi-professional boxer, Mano had anger-management issues. His temper had resulted in an assault charge – I never got the details – that would send him to prison for a decade, until he turned forty. He exercised hours a day just to keep his temper under control. His mood was always touch and go, powder-key volatile, but that helped make him some sort of god to the rest of the cell. Jose and Arnie vied for his favor like preschool boys on a playground; behind their backs he was always evaluating their latest moves. He put me in a different category. Noting the way I interacted with the nurses, he observed, "You're there for the ones with daddy issues ..."

Other times he referred to me as "the don."

It created an illusion of security, even though I had already learned that in jail there's no such thing.

For every good C.O. like Montero and Crystal, the profession also attracted some real sadists. The kind who would make you grovel for a razor, or would stop you from getting hot water for coffee from the big electric urn in the dayroom. They were the ones who delighted in any opportunity to lock us in our cells, sometimes for days on end. There were all sorts of excuses for lockdowns. Fights in adjacent cellblocks. Once we heard an inmate "was missing" from the complex and a search was underway. Another time the rumor was of a suicide in the Towers. Then there was the night someone in the Towers set a fire in his cell.

You can never trust the information you get in jail; gossip and rumors spread at the speed of sound. Keeping us uninformed was one more way of keeping us powerless, especially in a population that wasn't too strong on critical thinking in the first place.

A GED was the only job requirement to become a C.O., which could be a foot in the door to becoming an actual sheriff. A fondness for bodybuilding and flexing didn't hurt your chances at advancement. Some officers were as covered with tattoos as the prisoners they guarded.

Were it not for the different color outfits they wore, it would be hard to tell which were which. Rumor had it that one of the older C.O.s had been an inmate earlier in his life. He wore high-necked black T-shirts to cover his prison tattoos that included, we heard, a swastika.

Although there were always radios and call buttons close at hand for the guards, I was struck from the outset that a single individual had the job of controlling more than seventy men considered by society to be extremely dangerous. 'Splain that one to me, Lucy … One night the cellblock got a visit from two very large sergeants who buzzed everyone out of our cells double-time down to a muster in the dayroom. Now, what is stopping this mob from overpowering the pair of them, I wondered idly. It was a moot point. The sergeants exuded an attitude that said, Seventy-two of you, two of us, bring it …!

They had heard about the irregularities in bunk assignments and a certain laxity in the cellblock's day-to-day operation. They threatened to roll out every man in there, reminding us that 2-Romeo was like Pima County Jail's Ritz-Carlton. Anywhere else in the complex was dirtbag in comparison.

They were intimidating enough to convince me to find my assigned bunk that night. But not enough to keep me from returning to my cherished upper a few days later.

The worst C.O. was on night duty, guarding both our cellblock and the one across the hall. His name was Kluggfurt. He looked to be in his twenties, his uniform shirt stretched across his chest, shoulders and arms. His face was pudgy with piggy little eyes under his short-cropped red hair.

I became aware of him one night at pill call when we were buzzed out, one cell at a time, to get our prescriptions from the visiting nurse with her rolling pharmacy. As I passed the cell next door, someone slid a letter through the door jam calling out, "Hey, homey, will you take this down to the mailbox …?

Instinctively I reached out for it, only to hear the C.O. bellow, "Touch that envelope and you'll be written up!"

The envelope could have been red hot, the way I backed away.

Kluggfurt wasn't above barging into our cell, grabbing washed T-shirts and boxers drying in front of air vents and tossing them out the door and over the rail to the dayroom floor. Forget smoking or actual misdeeds; he was on the lookout for the tiniest infraction. Mano's weight bar, cobbled together from a broomstick and a prison shirt holding a double thick garbage bag filled with water, would definitely qualify for serious discipline if Kluggfurt found it.

Inmates can file grievances if they think they're being mistreated; there are pre-printed form letters for that purpose. But, like the rape prevention fliers and hotline, they're all for show and a hedge against litigation – not for prisoner protection. In jail there's no such thing as prisoner protection. File a complaint and you'll be the one who winds up in the hole.

As much as Kluggfurt singled out Cell 5 for his wrath, he treated me differently. What was behind the way he took his time patting me down for trips to medical? I couldn't say. One time he escorted me himself, something unheard of. On the way down the corridor he even tried to strike up a conversation, telling me how he had spent his weekend as though he were talking to a friend. It was impossible to sort out whether he was a fundamentalist churchgoer; a zealous wannabe sheriff; a latent Nazi loving his power; someone genuinely concerned with saving me from the lowlifes I had fallen in with ... or if he was gay. Or all the above. Or some part of all the above. My guess was he couldn't sort it out, either.

But then finally, my court date came. They get the inmates up at three a.m., to get ready. You get a razor, you get a shower, hopefully you've got a clean orange shirt to wear. Kluggfurt tiptoed into the cell, woke me and Lyle who had the same date, and then just for good measure, went into the bathroom where Mano had forgotten to hide his weight bar. Kluggfurt brought it into the cell, dropping it in on the concrete floor to burst the plastic bag and discharge several gallons of water in a flood. Guys half asleep scrambled from their bunks trying to rescue their cardboard bankers' boxes containing their stash of food from Keefe from the suddenly drenched floor.

"Good morning, gentlemen," said Kluggfurt with a nasty grin. By the time I got downstairs he acted as though nothing had happened.

There were maybe a dozen of us from all over the jail appearing in court that morning. I still wasn't used to the routine, being chained together in groups of five, then being driven in a van with painted-out windows to the courthouse. We were herded into big shared cells, first at the jail, then at the courthouse at the other end of the ride. In that clockless space, the waits seemed endless. Most of us sat quietly, trying to get comfortable in the wrist and ankle shackles. But the extroverts in the group were delighted with the captive audience as they expounded on their inane conspiracy theories and biblical prophecies that just added to the torture for everyone else.

Being out of jail for the first time in more than a month, everything felt different, surreal. Underlying my disorientation, once we arrived in the courthouse, was a sensation it took me a while to recognize:

Women.

There were women in this world – not just one or two rare creatures in uniforms, but half the population. There were women C.O.'s wrangling chained-together lines of convicts with efficiency and wisecracks. When we got into the courtroom, most of the lawyers were women, well-dressed, well-spoken, like Susan. The judge was a woman, the gallery was full of women. Women were part of normal life, something I had almost forgotten in the testosterone-fueled freak show that had been my home for a month. Scarier still, I was already used to it.

No matter the length of the sentence or the seriousness of the offense, the cruelest, most unusual punishment of incarceration is the gender segregation. But truth be told, for most prisoners despite their claims of heterosexual superpowers, that part isn't punishment at all. It's a relief.

My wife, daughter and son-in-law were sitting in the front row of the gallery when we filed in, me at the head of the orange parade of humiliated inmates that had appeared so grotesque the first time I had observed one from the gallery. That was just a few short months ago, but it seemed like a lifetime now. The prosecutor in my case didn't bother to show up. Mercifully, neither did the victim.

The prisoners had been instructed not to make contact with their supporters in the gallery. Eye contact was the best we could do, striving for stoic tight smiles pretending everything was going to be all right.

When my case was called, Susan took her place next to me, briefly summarizing my case to the judge. She shared a letter of introduction and remorse I had written, along with the character references that had poured in from relatives and colleagues that read like eulogies for a saint. It was clear that the judge had finally looked at my file, something I had hoped would have happened months earlier.

"I've never encountered a defendant more contrite for his actions," she said. She acknowledged my wonderful career, my service to my community, my spotless record, my advanced age and recent health issues. Despite knowing better, some part of my mind still believed in Frank Capra moments. This would be the scene in the Jimmy Stewart movie where the judge emotionally broke from the expected outcome and actually did the right thing.

"Mr. Chatenever, it's clear that you made a mistake, but you are not a bad man and you do not belong in this hell …"

Yeah, right.

"… But there are the circumstances of the accident," she was saying as the reality switch flipped back on, "… the injuries inflicted on an innocent victim as a result of the accused's irresponsible recklessness …"

And there was the plea I had signed, sealing my fate, tying her hands to try to change it.

Did I want to say anything?

"Yes, your honor. On November 15, 2018, I made a horrible mistake…," I began, reciting the script I had mouthed over and over as I lay sleepless in my cell the night before. It wouldn't do any good, I knew, but I couldn't stay silent either.

"… In one second I changed several people's lives forever. I caused great pain and suffering to an innocent victim. I can only be thankful that his injuries weren't worse, and he didn't die. There hasn't been a day since when I haven't wished I could change places with him. But I can't …"

Out of the corner of my eye I saw Karen, Lisa and Angelo struggling to keep their emotions in check.

"… Lastly, I want to thank my wife, my family, the people who have stood by me. They forgave me, and are helping me find the way back, to forgive myself …"

I meant everything I said. But it wasn't enough. When you're a writer, words come easily. Sometimes too easily. That's what prison sentences are for, to make up the difference.

I got a year.

After I was transported back to jail where I'd spend the next week awaiting transfer to Alhambra, a counselor I had never seen before showed up in the cellblock to interview me. How did I feel about my sentence? he asked. Was it what I had expected? Did I think it was fair? Was I feeling suicidal?

He couldn't care less. I had been in jail long enough to know that. It wasn't about me. He was just doing his job, protecting the county from litigation in case I did something – something else – stupid.

I returned to my cell and turned on my tablet. There was a lot of online time left that I had already paid for and needed to be used up before I left. I flicked to the radio app. It was playing the Clash singing, "I fought the law and the law won."

20

Adios amigos

My sentence had been expected but still left me feeling agitated. For all the terrors of jail, everyone in there knows it's the minor leagues for the big show – state prison.

"Prison's better, you'll see," Bryce had told me over and over before he left. "It's for real, not like this shit show. I hate this place. But in prison, the inmates, the guards, everyone's a grown-up there. No posing, no screwing around, they take care of business."

Not a reassuring message since the only business I had observed in a while was fighting. And Bryce wasn't exactly a reliable source. He had been the cell's one guy to actually get into fistfight and not take it to the bathroom. With Georgie no less.

He lost.

Whatever set him off that morning, Bryce snapped, yelling, "You faggot!" before taking the first swing. But despite being outweighed by fifty pounds, pretty boy Georgie prevailed. He held his left arm out-stretched, his hand on Bryce's forehead, causing the bigger man to flail like a windmill. Picking his spot, it only took one punch to Bryce's jaw to bring things to an end. Bryce spent the rest of the morning nursing his chin and apologizing.

"I don't know what got into me," he said to Georgie, gingerly shifting his jaw from one side to the other. "That should never have happened ..."

Adding to me, "You should never have seen that. I really blew it, I'm ashamed ..." Bryce was ashamed a lot; it could pass for his mantra.

Fighting being the measure of the man when you're locked up, each new day, each new moment can bring the next throwdown. But if jail was amateur hour for prison, I didn't share Bryce's sanguine assurance that I'd do just fine the next step up. Each morning I woke up with all my teeth in place was a good day, I reasoned – but a moment of reckoning seemed inevitable. I was hoping for a two-yard at least, to bring a modicum of safety to the next chapter of this nightmare. I tried to ignore Mano's adage that real men don't do two-yards.

Sometimes I wondered if there might be a form of martial arts beyond what anyone knows yet, where I could blind someone just by looking in his eyes, or stun and paralyze him with my gaze alone. No luck so far. The closest I had come was reading The Teachings of Buddha with the takeaway that if you can overcome the fear of death – granted, easier said than done – immortality was yours in every second. And if you could overcome your fear of harm, no one could hurt you. You would be invincible. I was still working on that one, too.

In the meantime I bided my time. Clarence, the big chief, had been released, leaving cruel speculation and innuendo in his wake. Did he make comments about your appearance, too? Mano asked. Did it feel weird when he cut your hair? Did you ever catch him checking you out when he didn't think you were looking … ?

I hadn't minded Clarence's attention as long as it kept me off his enemies list. For some reason, no one had tried to intimidate me yet, on any pretext, even though it was obvious their rules weren't my rules.

Right behind misogyny, Homophobia is true north on inmates' moral compasses. At least that's what they claim. This of course is a transparent facade in a males-only domain, but perhaps the only firewall against wholesale rape and subjugation. Jail was the gayest place I had ever been, but pointing this out, even thinking it, was a recipe for disaster.

There were no glass mirrors on the premises, just palm-size plastic reflectors you could buy from Keefe, or the smudged dull metal plates over the bathroom sinks that yielded funhouse-worthy distortions. The screen of a turned-off tablet could also serve as a mirror, a dim one, for preening narcissists. Guys would flex their straightened arms then gaze down over them approvingly, rotating their shoulders to fully behold bicep then triceps, caressing every engorged vein with their eyes. Considering prisoners' loudly proclaimed disgust for all things homosexual, there sure was a lot of attention paid to the male body in there.

In Clarence's place came William Smith, a wiry little guy with a cast on one arm and assorted missing teeth attesting to decades of fighting behind bars. Imprisonment ran in his family. Was it his father or his brother who was in for life for murder? The other one was doing ten to twenty for a crime only slightly less serious. William's facial features were sharp and pointed, his eyes rodent-like, always on the lookout.

His fellow Chicanos recognized him as a natural born torpedo, prison slang for an enforcer tasked with delivering beatings whenever given the order. There was a candidate for his services in the next cell, a young guy with long hair to his shoulders, dyed primary red. Whether or not he was gay as some claimed, it was decided that he was definitely in need of a haircut. William hadn't been around very long before he got the job of delivering the message.

Cell life wasn't always that dramatic or dangerous, although attempts at kindness were generally regarded as a form of weakness. Big Philip Worster had taken over from Georgie as the main target of harassment from his cellmates. No one would bother waking him from his drugged slumber for meals unless I tapped his foot. They would joke about him as he slept; rolling their eyes in derision. But Philip had thick skin, a good heart and was even showing occasional signs of life through the haze.

"… When I was a kid in Wood's Hole, my parents took me to see 'The Nutcracker' ballet in Boston," he mused one day, his eyes staring into space, seeing the memory.

"… There was a Christmas tree that grew huge, right out of the stage …"

Another time he came back from medical with a strange look on his face. He rushed into the cell closed mouthed, scrambling to find a cup. Once one was produced, he opened his mouth and discharged its contents, the liquid methadone he hadn't swallowed for fifteen minutes. It was an act of generosity, in case anyone else wanted it. The sight of him disgorging into the cup made Jose puke.

Baby-faced Georgie was still the target of endless homophobic taunts, although my guess was he was, if not straight as an arrow, at least bisexual. He had become a regular part of the cell's exercise routine and was looking a lot healthier ever since he had stopped trading all his food for coffee to snort, and started putting on weight. He had also begun tutoring Jose for an upcoming test, GED prep, which was offered in prison. Long division was the challenge. Georgie would walk him through the steps like a patient teacher with the slowest kid in the class. When it came to smarts, Georgie was the one with the power. He had also gotten a haircut, removing the dyed blond layer on top, and was letting his facial hair grow into a goatee, looking more Chicano by the day.

On William The New Guy's second day in the cell, his mom sent him the biggest secure pack on the Keefe list. He hefted the huge bag up the stairs and then played Santa, handing out candy bars to each one of us. I got the Snickers, which I placed in my banker's box like a bar of gold. That afternoon on the rec yard, William approached me, wanting to talk.

"Hey, OG," he began. He knew I was awaiting transport to prison and he tried to allay any fears.

Mumbling, the way inmates without education or confidence do, prison was one thing he was an authority on. The only thing.

"You'll get a two-yard, no question, maybe a one ..."

I didn't know there were such things as one-yards.

"You're OG. Everyone will give you respect. When you get there, talk to the warden ..."

I didn't know you could talk to the warden.

"Tell him about yourself, let him know who you are, what you need ..."

"A laptop would be great."

"Tell him. He can get you one, no problem."

"Really?"

William nodded, a little smile on his battered face. I felt better than I had all week. It wasn't until a few days later when he asked me to help him fill out his Keefe order sheet that I realized he couldn't read. And that I probably shouldn't believe anything he said.

I was a short-timer now. The youngest guys in the cell were already moping around about my departure. Arnie had called dibs on my black

Champion briefs when I left. You could only wear DOC- issued white boxers in the joint. Lyle was miffed that I had agreed to Arnie's request.

"He's not even your race, OG."

Note to self: Don't do that again.

Discharges to Alhambra usually happened early in the week. It was already Wednesday, so I knew I had several days more before leaving. But then something strange happened. Going into my banker's box for coffee one morning, my Snickers was missing. I didn't know why I still had it – why I hadn't consumed it on the spot when William first gave it to me. Probably out of my goaty Capricorn habits of restraint and self-discipline, in contrast to most convicts' helplessness in the face of instant gratification.

I scoured the banker's box again, and again, rummaging through the plastic bags of noodles, coffee, cereal and a pouch of tuna – with jalapenos! – I had been saving for a special occasion. Had I consumed the Snickers in a senior moment now forgotten? Not likely. Eating a Snickers in jail would be a glorious occasion, right up there with Christmas, every bite an orgasm. Probably wouldn't have forgotten that.

But the alternative was unthinkable. Theft was utterly forbidden in the unwritten convict code, as serious as offenses get. Despite being made of flimsy cardboard with no possibility of a lock, our bankers boxes were sacrosanct. In Hawaii robbing one would fall under the heading of the most punishable crimes, called *kapu*.

I tried to put it out of my mind. But the next day there were fewer soups. I didn't keep a careful count, and ordered them as much for barter as eating. When guys in the cell would ask if I could advance them a soup until the next Keefe day I was usually good for it, only accepting the customary two-for-one interest if they offered. I hadn't placed a Keefe order that week. I was budgeting, calculating enough to last until I rolled out, when I would distribute whatever was left, shampoo and soap along with the food to my cellies.

The next day there was no soup, and the day after that no cereal. I couldn't ignore it any longer, sickened as I realized everything I had thought – the effect I could have, the changes I could make in their lives – had been self-serving delusions. Stealing from my box wasn't a one-off – it was a daily occurrence now. And since the cell was rarely vacated entirely, how could someone do it without everyone else knowing? The whole Pops thing, the whole OG thing – they been playing me all along. They all had to be in on it.

I mulled it over as I showered – I had gotten the stall with hot water for once – the morning before I'd probably be leaving. It hurt. Not the loss, although the thief had even taken my coffee now, but the betrayal. Then again, calling them on it wasn't wise. It would be the end of my safety. I should just let it go, chalk it up, keep my head down … but I couldn't.

Coming out of the shower into the dayroom Lyle was the first person I saw. He greeted me with a smile.

"Hey, OG …"

"Say," I began reluctantly, "do you know anything about what happened to my stuff …?" His smile disappeared. Not into anger, but confusion.

"What happened to your stuff?"

"Yeah, that's what I'm asking you."

"What happened to your stuff?" he repeated. My question wasn't registering.

"It's missing. Almost everything in my box, gone."

His face changed again, into fury this time.

We headed up the stairs back to Cell 5 together. We ran into Jose outside the door.

"Someone took Rick's stuff," Lyle told him. Jose's face went through the same transformation.

If these guys were collaborators, they were mighty fine actors in this latest chapter of my education. "Somebody tell Mano," said Jose. He took the job himself.

Mano's reaction was devoid of emotion, utterly efficient.

"Everyone's boxes out on the floor," he directed the cell, where everyone had returned by this point.

"Now."

With the boxes out from under the bunks it didn't take long to rifle through them. Or to find the tear strip from a pouch of tuna – with jalapenos – in the one belonging to William. He looked utterly blank when it was discovered.

"What the fuck?" said Mano, in William's face. "What's wrong with you? If you had asked Rick for something, he would have given it to you. You know that. What the fuck's wrong with you?"

William's expression didn't change.

"We'll take care of this tonight at nine," Mano went on, "at the C.O. shift change. You can fight back if you want. Your choice."

William nodded. Mano's questions to him – why? – were beyond his powers of analysis to answer. He had just done the only thing he knew how to do, and would face the consequences the way he always did. Like a convict.

We didn't think about it for the rest of the day. There were more serious matters to attend to. The kid from next door with the long red hair got rolled out that afternoon, and right after he left we had a C.O. at our cell door asking questions. The kid had reported that he had been ordered to get his hair cut by the new guy in our cell, supposedly on the orders of Mano.

"Anyone in here know anything about that?" asked the C.O. He was greeted with shaking heads all around as we looked at each as dumbly as the Seven Dwarfs ... if the Seven Dwarfs all dressed in orange.

"Didn't think so," said the C.O.

The point was irrelevant anyway. Before the haircut could transpire, the kid had stumbled on the stairs carrying two scalding cups of water for coffee back to his cell. He got third-degree burns on both wrists. He had been sent to medical; he wouldn't be returning to 2-Romeo.

After burning himself he called his mom on the phone in tears. She was fit to be tied when she called the jail authorities. Her next call would be to the Five O'Clock News, she told them.

Not our problem, was the collective wisdom in Cell 5. We had our own business at hand. Around nine that night Arnie approached me where I sat watching TV.

"You ought to go up to your bunk now. Maybe read your book ..."

I climbed the ladder. William stood across the floor, the rest of the cellies in a cluster facing him. Mano stood apart. Neither he nor I would take part. He was the official, like the timer at a boxing match. The other guys couldn't wait for him to give them the go-ahead.

Arnie had told me to look away, but I didn't. I watched as they converged on William, everyone swinging, their target's arms going up to cover his head in meek defense. They kept punching, then kneeing once he crumpled onto the nearest bunk. And I watched. Once upon a time, before this chapter began, I wouldn't have accepted this outcome. Not that I had been a fighter then, but there were principles I followed. And even though I was the victim of the wrong that had been done, I would have objected to the sentence being imposed. I would have taken William's side, out of liberal guilt if nothing else; or brushed the whole thing off, no harm, no foul, no problem …

William was in the fetal position now, the others on top of him. Was it for me that they were doing this? No one's pulling this shit on Pops. Or was it for themselves, for the sheer pleasure of it?

Yes. Both.

I watched the beating impassively. It was soundless, endless even though it only took seconds. I felt no outrage, no satisfaction, no sense of justice being served. There was no anger, but no horror at witnessing it, either. I knew far more than I had a month ago – far more than I ever would have wanted to – about the lousy cards that had been dealt to William, and most of the guys who wind up in jail. But I knew nothing, really. You went from enforcer to accused in this world on a moment's notice, often for no good reason. I didn't know how to live in a world that made no sense. And my sentence hadn't even begun yet.

Then Mano gave the signal, and it was over.

The guys climbed off, helped William unsteadily to his feet. Blood was trickling from one ear as he shook each one of their hands. The handshake was probably a protocol in the convict code I had yet to learn. I went over and shook his hand, too, I don't know why. We shared a look that couldn't be put into words, not apology from him not blame from me, but closure at least.

Kluggfurt gave me the official word a little while later.

"You're gone," he said. It would be another of those three-in-the-morning deals, I needed to get ready. I went back to the cell and started shuffling through clothes and bedding listlessly. I handed out what remained of my hygiene items to the others. I knew I wouldn't sleep that night, I didn't even try. But to my surprise, neither did most of them. They found things to do, make places in their boxes for the items I gave them – a drab of shampoo, one of those Keefe hand mirrors. Georgie went over long division problems with Jose. After a while they struck up a game of Spades. I lay on my bunk, closed my eyes, but couldn't keep them closed. I watched TV till Kluggfurt switched it off at 11.

When it was finally time to leave, I climbed down from my bunk. Mano appeared to be sleeping, but the kids were up, standing, waiting for me.

"See you around, Pops," called Arnie from under his covers.

"Let's get together when we both get out," said Lyle, "go shoot some pool or something."

We hugged. I nodded, knowing that it wasn't going to happen. I don't shoot pool.

Jose took his turn next shaking my hand, looking into my eyes before averting his. He couldn't think of anything to say.

William, a wad of tissue in his ear, looked down at me from his bunk. We nodded at each other.

Then it was Georgie's turn. "Thanks, Rick," he said, "for giving me something to want to do besides kill myself."

I could tell he meant it, but for how long? Kluggfurt buzzed the cell door open and I walked out.

Adios amigos. Vaya con Dios.

Next stop Alhambra.

21

Steiner

Before becoming the intake center for the Arizona prison system, Alhambra had been a mental health facility. This helps explain its Cuckoo's Nest architecture: low oppressive ceilings, long echoey corridors past rusty doors and slit windows, ceiling lights in metal cages radiating an anemic shade of yellow. Outside, in contrast, as though intended to soothe the minds of visitors worried about their loved ones, was well trimmed lawn and even two healthy, neatly barbered rose bushes.

Because of the high walls topped by guardhouses for sharpshooters, from inside you had no sense of being in Phoenix. You had no sense of being anywhere. The only part of the outside world that you saw was sky, adding to a sense of having been erased and then remade in a facility that caused rather than cured depression.

We told time not by clocks, but by counts when a phalanx of officers would arrive outside the cell door, ordering everyone out of our bunks and into the corridor to line up haphazardly against the wall.

I had the drill down. The C.O. calls roll. When he gets to your name, you bark out the last three digits of your ADC number – mine was 339331 – then you file back into your dungeon. At the last count of the night you learn if you're going to be rolled out in the morning.

"Chatenever …!"

"Three three one …!"

"You're leaving."

The C.O. said the words nonchalantly, like an afterthought, as though they were no big deal. But in Alhambra they trigger something akin to a Miss America moment: You fight back tears, overcome with emotions – beginning with just being amazed that you're still alive – as those around you put on smiles of congratulations to mask their jealousy.

It was a deja vu of my last night in Pima County, the hours before leaving spent too excited to sleep. There are the acts of charity – trading your mattress if you've got a good one for someone else's Gandhi-thin mat that you'll turn in when you leave. Bestowing your bunk space on the ground floor to someone with worse accommodations. Divvying up your toiletries – state-issued clear toothpaste, deodorant, liquid soap – among those left behind. When departure time arrives at four a.m., there are fist bumps and occasional handshakes, but no hugs this time. These dangerous, desperate, barely literate strangers with dental disasters for smiles and faded tattoos littering their chests have become your brothers, knowing things about you that actual members of your family don't. You will never see these men again … if you're lucky.

The one called Africa – he of the Harry Belafonte looks, the Motown voice and the Asperger's symptoms putting him at constant risk – was also in the group leaving. He led our ragtag platoon out into the hallway to join the dischargees from other cells. Everyone was in a four a.m. stupor, too dull, too worn down to be excited.

Our release was like playing the tape of our arrival in reverse. Standing along the same lines on the floor, me next to Africa, naked, scrotum checked, humiliated one last time before being allowed to dress again. We received new clothing, trading our shapeless Alhambra jumpsuits with the footlong crotch openings for snazzy orange pants with elastic waistbands and pockets. We got new mesh bags and clean white boxers fit for a heavyweight contender, stenciled with orange letters – ADC, Arizona Department of Corrections. Then we got our travel jewelry, shackles for our ankles, chains around our waists to clip our handcuffs to. Our footwear was flimsy shower flip-flops, ill fitting over socks. The plastic shoes shuffled on the floor under the clanking chains as we were led out into the yard where a dull gray bus with mesh over the windows sat waiting for us.

The inky night sky was showing its first signs of purple around the edges as the bus pulled out of the gate, passing nameless neighborhoods and interchangeable strip malls, joining the parade of vehicles heading for work as Phoenix woke to a new morning.

Being on a bus and not knowing where it's going makes you a refugee to nowhere. But whatever our eventual destination was, I had come a long way toward being able to pass its citizenship test.

Foreign to anything I might have imagined just a few months earlier, the outlines and ground rules of this new world were familiar to me now. The sociology of this realm was more like an animal kingdom documentary than something involving humans. We moved in prides, packs and herds through savannas where unfiltered testosterone wrote the rules and no one worried about whether the toilet seat was up or down. It was a male domain, but not exclusively. There were women too, here by conscious choice, usually in roles of authority. There were more of them than you might expect, many in correctional officer uniforms, more in nurses' scrubs. While some people might consider them trailblazers, they certainly weren't feminists … at least not according to the liberal connotation of the word, which is pretty much the only connotation it has.

Many of them had colorful tattoos wrapping their arms under their khaki uniform shirts. They were the objects of countless daily masturbatory fantasies and unfunny jokes They smoked cigarettes like Marlboro men, some chewed tobacco, and they dropped as many F-bombs into their conversation as their male counterparts. They dumbed down in futile pursuit of membership in the boys' club, not seeming to realize they were better than that. Their estrogen did precious little to soften what would rather be a battleground of masculinity devoid of feminine instincts or wisdom.

For all the posturing and preening of the inmates, like bantam roosters in a coup, few contenders actually vied for the alpha male title in any particular cellblock. There were, however, plenty of job openings a notch or two down. There's always the resident authority or loudmouth, for example. We had one on the bus. He started talking before the vehicle was out the gate and he never shut up. His voice accompanied the endless, formless suburban landscape of Phoenix passing outside the screened bus windows.

We were going to Buckeye, he predicted confidently, referring to a sprawling complex of medium security yards west of Phoenix. There we would drop off the most dangerous passengers, the ones in a caged-off section at the rear of the bus, before the vehicle returned the rest of us to a minimum security yard back in the city. Despite the assurance in his words, this made no sense. Why – aside from sadistic malice – would the Department of Corrections want to take us for a ride in the country if our destination was only a few miles from our starting point?

I hadn't learned yet that in the Arizona prison world, the guys who knew it all invariably turned out to be the most clueless clowns in the whole circus.

Out the windows the sun-baked subdivisions had finally given way to scrubby, leathery vegetation and the humble tranquility of the high desert. Red rock mesas stood like gigantic pottery and the jagged teeth of little mountain ranges took bites out of the cobalt blue sky. The chaparral panorama was bisected by a black ribbon of highway through the windshield.

The highway sign announcing the state prison came into view before the complex itself, ringed by a high wall of chain link topped by rolled razor stretching for miles. Chain link and rolled razor wire would become the window curtains of my consciousness from this point on.

A heavily armed gate and checkpoint provided access through the fence. Each of the yards within the complex had its own fence, its own gate, its own security. In convict lore, each yard also had its own history, measured in inmate stabbings, race riots, attacks on guards. By most accounts Buckeye – its official name was the Lewis Corrections Department – was a dangerous place.

Good thing it wasn't our destination.

After several more gates the bus arrived at the prisoner intake facility. My fellow riders were chuckling over Buckeye horror stories, especially the one on the news in recent months where the entire Steiner yard had to be evacuated after the inmates filled all the key locks with epoxy. From my seat I watched the driver exit the vehicle and open the baggage compartment under my window. But rather than stopping with the bags of the three high-risk guys, he was throwing all our mesh bags on the asphalt. Then he was back inside telling us all to get ready to get off.

Wait a minute, weren't we supposed to ...?

Our chains clanked around our ankles as we shuffled down the aisle, exited the bus and entered the office. The décor was pure prison, decades-old metal desks, lumbar-killing office chairs, gray linoleum floor, unshaded fluorescent tubes on the ceiling. A woman who could have been auditioning for the Nurse Ratchet role in a community theater production went over my medical charts, paying particular attention to my post-heart-attack prescriptions. For all the assurance I had gotten from fellow inmates that I would wind up on a minimum-security two-yard, it sure felt like they were signing me into this one.

My heart sank as a big guard led us out of the heated office and into a holding cell as long and narrow as a dog run. The morning sun was up, there wasn't a cloud in the sky, but the chain link walls offered no protection from the morning chill. It felt like it had been a long odyssey since leaving Alhambra, but it was barely eight a.m. In our new ADC logowear shirts we tried not to shiver, seeking sections of chain link warmed by the sun to back up against.

The gray bus had left by now, taking my hopes with it. A smaller van arrived a short time later to transport us to the Steiner prison yard I had been hearing so much about. Apparently they had gotten the locks fixed, but the first impression was hardly welcoming. A group of inmates in day-glo orange trucker caps listlessly raked the gravel around the scraggly ground cover and scrub brush that passed for a garden just inside the gate. The sun that had already begun baking the day seemed to have baked the brains of the inmates, too. The expressions on their faces were as barren as the landscape.

Steiner was a 3-yard and our little group was instructed not to interact with the convicts there, for our own safety. By now there were rumors that this wasn't our final destination after all. We were just passing through; this was prison's version of a Motel 6. But no one knew for sure. We would have an hour on the rec yard later that afternoon, we were told, after the others were locked down.

Our cell at Steiner was a dormitory, long and narrow with rusty bunks on either side of an aisle running the length of the room. The ceiling was high. Patches of hot, cloudless sky were visible through high windows under the eaves. There were electrical receptacles by each bunk but the face plates were all broken or removed, revealing knots and clumps of wire that would be dangerous if the power hadn't been turned off. The bathroom fixtures – urinals, toilets, sinks, showers – were around the corner in the L-shaped floor plan. The bathroom was Bed Bath & Beyond's worst nightmare, sending the message that good hygiene was for wimps.

Rumor had it that the cell was not in compliance for housing prisoners, but the authorities got around that by calling it a holding area.

Another group of prisoners had arrived from Alhambra the day before. They sprawled in bunks on one side of the aisle as we tried to find our bunk assignments on the other side. One of them remembered seeing me in Alhambra. He was Italian from New York; his name was Angelo but he already had the nickname "Baseball." He and another inmate played catch in the aisle using a rolled-up pair of socks for a ball. His friend was also from the East Coast, Connecticut. He was covered with tattoos including a rendering of his grandmother's face on the side of his neck. He bore an uncanny resemblance to an animated character, Shrek. His name was Art Morosco. He took to me instantly, saying I reminded him of the greatest man he had ever known, his grandfather.

"I'm not gonna let anything happen to you, OG," he promised. "Anyone comes at you, they've gotta come through me." He punctuated the remark by making a fist, covered with tattoos like a glove. It seemed like he had some experience in this field.

The cell could have been the set for a horror movie, complete with roaches crawling out of the bedding and a ceiling exhaust fan that creaked and rattled every time it switched on. The men in orange around me seemed straight from central casting – the thug squad. A tall, skinny black guy in glasses prowled the cell like a creature in a zoo cage, stopping to pound on the walls and windows, playing them like bongos. He sang as he drummed, a vague Motown-sounding refrain, off-key, over and over. It was impossible to tell if he thought he was musical – he wasn't – or if he was merely insane. Drugs will do that.

Another voice wafted from elsewhere in the cell. I didn't get up from my bunk to track down its origin. It sang a lament in Spanish. Had there been a guitar, had there been castanets, it might have qualified as flamenco. But in this setting it was counterpoint to the mad drummer

– lonely, haunting, scary. Baseball and Art played catch in the aisle. I lay on a scratchy gray blanket, knowing I couldn't shut everything out or make it go away by closing my eyes, but trying anyway. Art kept reappearing by my side bringing more blankets.

"Whatever you need, OG, let me know."

They gave us sack lunches when we arrived, the unidentifiable lunch-meat, the obscene peanut butter, popcorn, cookies, slabs of bread, all wrapped in cellophane. It doesn't take long to become adept with the cellophane, squeezing out scatological beads of peanut butter or flattening a transparent sheet of it into a plate to eat off of. You can even twist it tightly into something that passes for twine. They would bring us another sack for dinner.

The guards unlocked the cell at four that afternoon after the permanent population had been put away. Even at that hour well into autumn, the Arizona sun was relentless, beating down on the walking track that circled the exercise yard. Heavy taped metal bars provided racks for chin-ups, sit-ups, push-ups and other contortions in between. Towers for guards armed with rifles marked the perimeter, unoccupied.

Across the yard my new guardian Art scoured the ground and trash barrels for cigarette butts – a frowned-upon practice known as "sniping" that can get you a hot one in the bathroom – as I walked solitary circles around the track. Each time I passed the chin-up bars I stopped. Reaching up, crucifixionlike, I grasped the taped crossbar. Then I pulled, my feet leaving the ground, my head rising into the sky. Over and over in a futile effort to break the bonds of gravity, escape for a few moments into a better reality.

I sensed the eyes of the others around the track taking notice. "Look'it Granpa! How old did that guy say he was?" Doing pull-ups – as close as I could come to swimming in the absence of water – would become my salvation and my signature, one of the few ways I could turn on the endorphin faucet. You don't have much to work with in prison, you've got to make the best hand out of the cards you're dealt. But maybe Art would realize OG didn't need quite as much protection as he thought.

After rec, back in the cell, we waited and wondered, for what we didn't know. Uncertainty is a given in prisoners' lives, the trump card in the guards' hands. The less information inmates have, the weaker they are, and the more they manufacture rumors and fantasies to hang their flimsy hopes on.

The man overseeing our cell seemed higher ranking than a C.O., more like a warden. He was stocky and black, with a salt-and-pepper goatee, dressed in civilian clothes with a badge on his belt. He had a casual bossman demeanor, and something else – a sense of humor. At least what passes for humor in these parts. He brushed off any questions we asked like he was swatting flies. He quipped away all concerns – say, about the roaches – as just so much whining. We were in for a long stay, he told us, but then he was back an hour later calling names from a checklist on a clipboard. My name was on the list.

"Chatenever …," he called. I perked up.

" You're never leaving," he said, before pretending to recheck the list. "Oops, my bad. Get your stuff together, you're outta here."

Art and Baseball were also in the group being discharged. Guards led us out of the cell, around the track which was dark now, to the fence gate. There a pair of beefy C.O.s in black jackets and stocking caps took over. We were ordered to remove most of our newly issued clothes from our mesh bags and toss them in a pile on the ground. We were going to Kingman, a prison not operated by the Department of Corrections but by a private corporation, they told us.

"You won't be wearing orange there. You'll be wearing blue," said the C.O. who would be transporting us.

"Whoa, I've never been in a blue prison uniform before," said Art, sounding as excited as he would by a trip to Old Navy.

It was a lie. More prison guard humor. Before locking us into handcuffs and leg irons around eleven p.m., the guards advised using the restroom.

"You won't be able to go again before we get to Kingman," they said. "We'll be getting there around the time they open the gate, five a.m. Guys have pissed themselves, shit themselves waiting in the van outside the gate. We've seen it all. Just so you know …"

22

Kingman

The town of Kingman in northern Arizona is one of the old Route 66 map dots you fly through at 80 mph on Interstate 40, heading to the nearby Grand Canyon. From Buckeye you drive north, passing Las Vegas just across the state line. Arizona's famed highways are a lot less cinematic in the middle of the night. At least we were in something other than a institutional bus this time. It was a relatively new GMC passenger van designed for tour groups, with upholstered seats instead of hard molded plastic benches, and glass windows you could look out of. One of its few adaptations for transporting prisoners was a heavy clear plastic barrier separating the drivers' seats from the rest of the cabin.

"Don't sit in the first row," the driver warned us. "I brake hard, you'll do a face plant into the wall." Our hands chained to our waists would be useless to break the impact.

We sat three to a row, aware of the cuffs, especially the ones digging into our ankles. With no seat belts our bodies swayed shoulder to shoulder as the van followed the undulations of the road, rocking and rolling for hours through the night.

Kingman is another of Arizona's huge incarceration factories, one of "the new private ones." It houses three-thousand prisoners in three yards. One of them is a "PC" – protective custody – facility for sex offenders and other hombres in need of extra protection. Their ranks include convicted cops, and convicts who run up debts for drugs or gambling while they're incarcerated and now have guys waiting to settle the score.

The sprawling complex is called Kingman-Cerbat, named for the nearby mountain range that the sun rises over each morning. It's privately owned and operated by the Florida-based Geo Group, a prisoner-for-profit business that landed the contract after making a sizable campaign contribution to the man who went on to become Arizona's governor.

I didn't know any of this of course as I swayed in unison with the prisoner next to me, too excited and scared to sleep. The radio was tuned to a classic rock station out of Vegas. The song list that night sounded hand-picked for motivation, heavy on Journey, the Eagles, Elton John, Aerosmith, the Stones. Each song had been an anthem the first time I heard it back in the '60s and '70s when I still had my life in front of me. I had gone on to hear each group in person, for free, during my journalistic career.

Tonight the lyrics felt incongruous, cruel even, messages of false hope in an arid landscape.

We arrived before the gate opened and had to sit outside the locked gate with the engine idling. At least my seventy-three-year-old kidneys were cooperating. I tried to get a sense of the place through the windows, but in the darkness it was little more than fence, razor wire, industrial ducts and warehouse walls.

When the gate finally rolled open we proceeded through more gates, more checkpoints, more guards. Eventually we came to a stop and awkwardly exited the van on travel-stiff legs made even clumsier by all the chains. Our bound wrists didn't help our shaky balance climbing out. The cops lined us up facing the nearest wall. We were instructed to lift one leg then the other so they could unlock the shackles before moving on to our wrists. Once freed, we gingerly rubbed the skin the cuffs had rubbed raw. The leg irons left rings around my ankles through my socks.

Our entrance to Kingman was through a large garage door. The space inside was multipurpose – an intake center, storeroom and chapel with Bible quotations and the Lord's Prayer painted on one wall above a white board. Redefining the concept of "behind bars," there were no bars in Kingman. The buildings were all open warehouses and could have worked equally well as Foster Farms plants, only with men in neat rows instead of chickens. The bland walls were backdrops for groupings of plastic chairs, folding tables, industrial desks and stacked new mattresses still in cardboard packaging.

Our eyes and brains, bleary from no sleep and the long drive, registered bits and pieces of the scene. The staff here, male and female, didn't wear the DOC khaki we had learned to obey. Instead they had a newer, even more paramilitary look – cargo pants with bulging pockets, Desert Storm-style jackets, heavy belts clanging with gear, and high-topped black jackboots. If they preferred a more casual image, it was the same from the waist down, but bright blue polo shirts on top, with the Geo logo instead of a little alligator. The backs of all their jackets and shirts were emblazoned with SECURITY, a word I was more familiar with on the backs of T-shirts at rock concerts.

The only requirement for working at Cerbat was a GED. There were always ads on the Kingman radio station announcing job openings.

The intake officer, goateed with a shaved head like Mr. Clean in a blue polo shirt, strip searched us on entry, complete with the prerequisite scrotum flip to be sure we hadn't acquired any weapons or contraband since our last scrotum flip before departing. Once we dressed again we were herded into chairs in the middle of the room, in front of the whiteboard that still bore proverbs from the last chapel service. The nurse screening us this time was an older woman, thoughtful in her questions and possessing a quality I hadn't seen a while: kindness.

A feisty woman who identified herself as Sargent Kraft led the orientation. Colorful floral tattoos adorned her arms, obscenities laced her speech. She was funny and irreverent and warned us to stay away from her when she was in a bad mood, which she said was most of the time. She guided us through our paperwork. The Department of Corrections was in the process of integrating facilities that had remained segregated well into the twenty-first century. You had to sign a form saying you were okay bunking with someone of another race, otherwise you lost privileges.

Then Kraft eyeballed us for clothing sizes. A heavy orange jacket manufactured by prisoners with brass buttons and a gray blanket lining was an essential part of the Kingman wardrobe, since the winters were cold and the winds could be fierce. She didn't have one in my size when she handed out the rest of the apparel. I thought better than to ask whether the clothes came in other colors.

Then she gave us a crash course in something called compliance, which is what they've got in prison instead of individual identity for inmates. Compliance called for clean-shaven faces, tucked-in T-shirts, IDs clearly visible on the lanyards around our necks at all times. Failure to be in compliance could result in "tickets," disciplinary action or more time tacked onto our sentences.

We could get a change of appearance form for permission to grow a beard, but not all beards were created equal. Goatees were not in compliance, the authorities claimed, because certain styles of barbered facial hair were symbols of gang membership.

With stubby pencils we filled out a form known as "your 20 list," specifying relatives and others we wanted to be in touch with by phone or visits. Every name on the list had to go through a background check for criminal history. We were told it could take a month or more for the names to be cleared. That estimate turned out to be wildly optimistic.

In the world outside, cell phones are taken for granted as natural appendages of our bodies and minds. In prison, restricted phone access is one of the most demeaning, sadistic parts of the punishment. The authorities claimed the heightened background checks were to prevent drug deals and other illegal activity going down on the phone, but two months later my ten-year-old granddaughter still hadn't passed security clearance for calls. Neither had anyone else on my list.

In Pima County when you made a call, there had been cumbersome codes to enter on the keypad and a recorded message reminding you that all communication was potentially being monitored by a cop. But still, you were able to make as many calls as you could afford on the blue antique phones on the wall. Phone calls had been my lifeline to sanity. In Kingman for months the phones were a form of torture, repeating the message, "That name has not been approved," every time I tried to place a call. The so-called clearance process, which could have been completed in an hour if the officer responsible cared to, put me in an isolation chamber. It forced me to communicate the Jane Austen way, by letter, so that any contact with the world outside was guaranteed to be several days after the fact.

Finally Kraft got around to telling us about "the store." That was her main job at Kingman-Cerbat: property officer. Prisoner economics is a world unto itself, ranging from the most minimal transactions up to orders for hundreds of dollars. Barter is as alive in prison as it was in biblical villages. Keefe was the purveyor again, but the price list was different in prison. There were more items to choose from, from a three-cent pencil through white New Balance running shoes to a $200 TV. Soups were cheaper in prison, and you could buy tobacco. Pouches of tobacco and four-ounce plastic bags of coffee, along with the ubiquitous ramen packages, *soups*, served as the currency of the realm. On "store day" inmates would begin lining up in front of the commissary door before daybreak. Store day was a weekly little Christmas, even if your secret Santa gift to yourself was just a tube of toothpaste or a bag of tortilla chips.

I would learn all these details and nuances in the weeks and months to come. At the moment my woozy head was in sensory overload as Kraft delivered the spiel she had given thousands of times to new arrivals before us. She was cheerful enough now, she said, but warned us not to fucking try her patience if she was having a bad day.

Then we all scrambled up from our seats to claim a mattress, not the new ones in boxes but the battered ones as thin as yoga mats in a pile on the floor. With our mattresses over one arm, our mesh bags stuffed with clothes, blankets and a few toiletries in the other hand, we filed out of the storeroom and into the prison yard.

A cold wind was swirling sand and dust into pinpricks stinging our faces as we headed outside, trying to figure out which of the identical industrial buildings surrounding the huge yard was our assigned destination, Dorm 9. We kept stepping out of our shower shoes in the shifting sands. The wind turned our bed mats into sails, pulling us in one direction then another as we fought our way across the vegetation-free expanse like nomads in a Saharan dust storm. Welcome to Kingman, dude. Your new life has just begun.

The dorm housed one-hundred men on one side – the Alpha side – of a central wall, and another hundred on Beta side. Your low-walled cubicle was called .your "house," its floor plan barely bigger than a king-size bed, A metal single bed frame sat on one side of a narrow aisle, a cabinet and some metal shelves on the other. Everything was painted gray. My address was 09A03 – Dorm 9, Alpha side, bunk three – close to the front of the building.

The low partitions between our cells felt even more squat under the high ceilings, as though we had been sentenced to do time in an aircraft hangar or a Costco. All the occupants dressed in orange, the faded shades showing how long they had been there, how often the clothes had been washed. They went about their daily routines robotically in patterns both purposeful and meaningless. It all reminded me of those Uncle Milton's Ant Farms that we had as kids where you could watch the ants through the plastic walls of their container. The ants never realized they were trapped as they carried out their assigned tasks. They didn't know it was all for naught, beyond providing entertainment for some kid.

They were the chain gangs on Uncle Milton's Ant Farm, endlessly toiling to go nowhere, accomplish nothing.

The dorm's interior would become as familiar to me as the back of my hand. Pondering its ceiling – a grid demarcated by heavy brown metal girders, exposed water pipes and electrical conduit, with skylights and fluorescent squares at regular intervals – would became a form of meditation.

On the front wall, centrally located to oversee both halves of the building, was "the bubble," the raised platform holding the control console from which one officer could oversee all the prisoners in the building. In Dorm 9 when I arrived, two of those officers happened to be young women, C.O.s, Cressley and Portman, smaller in stature than almost all the men under than their charge, yet unquestionably in control.

On the back wall were doorways to assorted bathrooms, washers and dryers, an office, a classroom and a supply closet. One bathroom had urinals, another had toilets; both had a row of sinks on the opposite wall.

Providing for the excretory needs of a hundred confined men obviously entailed planning, engineering and logistics. A stenciled message over the door warned that smoking in the toilet stalls was punishable by disciplinary action, but that didn't deter those with a serious habit, or an attitude. It was intermittently enforced, depending on the C.O.'s mood. Some smokers further flaunted their offense by leaving ashes in the grooves of the handicap bars by the commodes.

The boxing ring requirements for "taking it to the bathroom" were left unwritten. I was far enough away on the other side of the dorm to mostly be blissfully unaware of these acts of settling scores, saving face by smashing in someone else's. You can't let anyone disrespect you. That's the beginning and end of the convict creed. There was one more bathroom, this one for shower stalls, on facing walls behind floor-to-ceiling white plastic curtains.

Relatively new washers and dryers sat against the walls on both sides of the shower room doorway. They were free to use, first come first served. If someone discovered unclaimed laundry in a washer or dryer, he would bellow "washer!" or "dryer!" loud enough for the whole dorm to hear until the guilty party showed up to claim it, hopefully before anyone lost patience.

Next on the wall came the C.O. III office. C.O.IIIs were upper level correctional officers, sergeants, who served as the administrators for the men in the dorm. Your C.O.III was the one you saw, or who saw you, about your status. The processing and bureaucracy for convicts was unbelievably cumbersome. It had gotten even more confusing when the statewide system bought a new computer program that left most of the C.O.IIIs staring at their computer screens as mystified as the big white dog on old RCA Victor record labels.

The clunkiness in the system felt like it was by design, just to make the convict experience a tad bit more inconvenient and unpleasant than it already was. I had yet to learn how dangerous its technology could be in the wrong hands.

Our C.O.III was named Villa. He was young and smart, but not especially motivated to put out any extra effort on any of his inmates' behalf. The C.O.III for the Beta side, whom we could also see for help, was a flinty yet grandmotherly woman named Sewell, who would go the extra mile for you … but didn't always get things right. Her office hours were more regular, and longer, than Villa's. When she wasn't behind her desk, she was outside smoking like a chimney.

The last door went to a classroom It was empty most of the time but available for an occasional class in Cerbat's education and rehab program. Or for weekly Bible studies sessions. Or early-morning yoga practiced by a handful of men in orange.

Everything was new, and there was a lot to learn. Then again, I had nothing but time to work on getting it down.

23

Politics

In prison when inmates say things are *political*, it's code for *racist*. It's simple. And complicated.

The day after I arrived in Dorm 9, I got the visit I had been dreading from the representative of "my race," wanting to see my papers. His name was Kyle – "but everyone calls me Coyote." He looked like Kurt Russell, if Kurt Russell were a weathered biker with a huge tattoo covering his chest in the style of a Jack Daniel's label saying, "Established in 1972." Coyote looked like he could have spent most of the years since 1972 under the influence, but still hadn't used up all the craggy charisma in the bottle.

He wasn't the head of Dorm 9's whiteboys – that title went to an inmate whose nickname was Ringo. But Coyote was second in command, formerly the torpedo, now the mailman. All outgoing mail went via a folder by his bunk; you put your envelope in the folder and he dutifully delivered it once a day to the mailbox outside the chow hall.

My hands unsteadily went through the manila envelope of my legal paperwork, finally finding the one court document I had – the five-page plea bargain outlining my two felony counts and the DUI misdemeanor.

"It was ag assault," I told him. "I hit someone in a crosswalk ... by accident."

"Drinking?"

I nodded.

The reason your race runs a background check on you is to be sure you're not guilty of the offenses prisoners themselves consider indefensible – child abuse, domestic violence and being a snitch.

Aggravated assault, which in most cases is intentional, is no problem. It even seemed like a badge of honor to some of them – Don't get Rick pissed, he'll run over you in his car.

Coyote looked over my paperwork skeptically, wanting more.

"We need your court transcript," he said. "Get it from your public defender. And whatever else they've got. Tell 'em you're indigent so you don't get charged for the copies. I'll loan you an envelope."

He had addresses for public defenders' offices around the state. I mumbled something about having a private attorney and not being indigent, wondering if that added up to two strikes against me. I wrote to Karen that night, asking her to contact my attorney to send the records to my new Kingman address.

Until the new documents arrived I was what was called "on blocks." It was prison's version of a probation period, when members of your race decide whether or not they can trust you, and whether or not you're a dick.

I took my meals with the two guys I had come in with from Steiner – my self-appointed bodyguard, Art, and Angelo, the baseball player. I was getting acquainted with others in my dorm, Chicanos and "kinfolk" along with other Caucasians. Some of them seemed friendly enough – someone loaned me a cup to use, someone else came up with a shot of coffee.

Whenever I could, I would head outside to walk the fence line around the yard's perimeter. Two times around was a mile. The Cerbat mountain range to the north and Oatmans to the south were dramatic through the chain link diamonds. Their jagged, purply silhouettes were magnets for my eyes – part dragons' teeth, part Rorschach test, part Western movie backdrop. Decades ago I had been a happy road warrior speeding through these parts on Interstate 40. The craggy mesas and pastel skies had inspired the Pixar artists doing backgrounds for "Cars." The mountains were constants in the daily uncertainty, rugged sentinels, their ridges and voluptuous valleys ever-changing in the days' shifting light. In the months to come, the mountains along with the sky and the sand under my feet would become friends I could turn to for company.

One day out walking I met an inmate from another dorm. When

he found out I was a journalist and editor, he got real interested.

"I'm writing a book," he said with a disarming grin. "I'll take all the help I can get."

I nodded, happy to oblige. "What's your book about?"

"It's about how God talks to me – and all of us – in dreams."

Not a promising beginning … but he didn't sound like a fundamentalist yahoo. His words were compelling, his face open and full of curiosity. Talking to him could have been a conversation I'd have about Buddhism, or on Maui about some new age topic less tethered to firm ground. His name was Jeff. He was in his early 50s, and although he had spent a lot of years in prison you'd never know it if you met him in a different place wearing a different colored shirt. He was handsome, engaging and smart, the kind of guy you'd totally trust to buy a car from, which was one of the jobs he had had in the world outside. Actually, he had been the agency sales manager.

He had grown up rich and privileged, the son of a successful real estate developer and golf course builder. In high school Jeff had been a state champion golfer who went on to college and was good enough to fantasize about the PGA. He was a golden boy with everything going for him, if he could just stop getting in trouble – over and over, it turned out – with women and alcohol.

Jeff was happy to help guide me through those early days at Kingman. He was a venerated figure on the yard and his presence by my side, along with his advice about what to do and what to avoid provided safe passage. It was a two-way street, not only for the suggestions I was making about his writing, but for the gratitude we shared to just have someone with a brain to talk to.

Some of the talk was about politics.

"I've become a CNN junkie," he admitted. "I never cared much about politics before. I grew up a pretty standard country club Republican and never gave it a second thought. But this guy Trump, what a piece of work. He is really and truly an asshole."

I couldn't believe my good fortune hearing his words.

The source of Jeff's political conversion was a woman named Claudia. His descriptions of her were glowing. He showed me photos in the little plastic-sleeve album you could buy from Keefe for thirty-five cents. In the photos the camera caught the irony in her eyes in every smile. He went on and on. She was a high-level administrator for a big defense contractor with a countdown clock on her desk showing days left in the Trump administration. She had her own nonprofit foundation devoted to various charities and rehabilitation programs around Phoenix. She was the kind of woman who got things done, and when Jeff learned of the freeze on my 20 list, he didn't miss a beat.

"Give me your wife's phone number. I'll pass it on to Claudia next time I talk to her." He called her every day. "She'll call your wife."

And she did. In those first couple of weeks Claudia was our lifeline, relaying messages to Karen, mostly where I was, and that I was okay.

Claudia did that kind of stuff all the time. She was suburban Arizona's answer to Mother Teresa. "That's just who she is."

I don't know how long it took before I realized that Claudia wasn't his wife, or even his girlfriend. She was married to someone else, she was a soccer mom. She was the opposite of the kind of women who got Jeff in trouble. She was instead a best friend, an inspiration, a muse, a conscience.

Jeff was my life buoy. Because we weren't in the same dorm, we didn't see each other all the time, but sought each other out for dinner, or sometimes to share walks around the yard. He got enthusiastic easily, punctuating conversations with a finger tapping your chest. His writing energy motivated me to do it too, in what would turn into the words you're reading here. He would pick my brain for writing tips, and in return gave me a book Claudia had sent him about writing creative nonfiction, titled "You Can't Make This Stuff Up." Despite thinking I already knew more than the author, I picked up a few tips.

Being true to the title was the best one.

His own book project was, as they say, interesting.

"What'd you dream last night ...?" he'd begin.

I could never remember. I wasn't sleeping all that well. A dream would have been a bedtime luxury, almost as good as a pillow.

So he would tell me his.

Jeff was no fan of evangelical religiosity, practiced in the Sunday night video services in the prison chapel. It was beamed in from a Phoenix megachurch and drew hundreds of Cerbat inmates to sing along, waving their arms in the air, grasping at salvation for a few happy minutes of believing they really meant it this time. But he was an expert on scripture, having read the Bible over and over.

Likewise, his study of psychology had been self guided, yielding an extensive body of esoteric knowledge. He would bring all of this to analyzing dreams, focusing on what seemed like the most mundane detail, the color of someone's clothes, the exact words they used. He would filter the signs he discerned through a derivation of Hebrew words and Freudian symbols, coming up with what always turned into an encouraging message to do the right thing. When you did, simple miracles happened.

Every time.

"You're sure that's God talking …?" I'd ask, "and not Jiminy Cricket?"

He was unfazed.

"Absolutely," with unshakable confidence.

When I suggested that his worldview was pretty similar to mine, which was based more on a magnificent network of Zen coincidences, he just smiled.

"Nope, it's God talking."

"But how does He have the time? How many billion people are on the planet?"

The logistics were staggering. I was thinking Santa Claus can do it, but only on Christmas Eve, and he has the whole year to prepare.

"How can He get around to everyone's dreams every night? I don't get it."

"That's because you don't know God," said Jeff, his smile and certainty unwavering.

A lot of our discussions took place at chow time, either in the dining hall or in the orange line snaking out across the yard waiting to get in.

"Chow," stenciled over the dining hall doorway, was an unfortunate word choice to a former entertainment editor who had spent decades editing copy about fine dining. The chow hall had big blue and green patches painted on its white walls around precise rows of metal tables bolted to the floor.

As in Alhambra, round stools were welded to the tables on metal arms radiating from the steel stalk supporting the table top. Apart from scale, with its primary color paint scheme the room felt more like a kindergarten than a facility for grown men.

The chow hall was the last bastion of institutional racism in an Old West justice system trying to get up to speed in a new millennium. At least up to speed enough to not lose its federal funding. Your race determined where you sat in the hall. I was already accustomed to Arizona prison anthropology and its five racial divisions: whiteboys, Chicanos, kinfolk, chiefs and paisas. The paisas were a group to be reckoned with at Cerbat – there were a lot of them. As opposed to the Italian origin of the label, paisano, these came from south of the border, Mexico mostly but elsewhere in Latin America, too.

They were boisterous and brotherly with one another, punching shoulders, yelling across the dorm or chow hall like a Spanish language radio station turned up to ten. The language barrier worked in their favor; few of the C.O.s spoke Spanish, so the cops were oblivious to the drug deals going down all the time.

Sitting "with your race" wasn't optional, it was mandatory. I never bothered learning which section belonged to which group beyond the whiteboys who occupied the two and half rows closest to the kitchen window where the chow was dispensed. It came on molded red plastic trays with no sharp edges, their compartments holding mushy concoctions only vaguely approximating the lively names on the menu: jambalaya, yakisoba, salisbury steak. The calorie count swelled with sliced bread, fried potatoes, canned fruit and vegetables, and lots – and lots – of beans. There were pancakes many mornings a week, in puddles of syrup with heart-stopping blobs of supposed butter.

The chow hall opened at five a.m. weekdays, later on weekends when there were only two meals. It dispensed sack lunches at noon, and reopened at five for dinner. Prisoners waiting to get in stretched across the yard, two and three abreast in a ragtag line. They cursed and smoked, taking lights off each others' cigarettes, stepping out of line to spit in the dirt. Smoking and spitting, that's how they rolled.

Movement was stop and go, the men proceeding in synchronized lumbering, shoulders and heads swinging side to side, reminding me of the drunken elephants in "Dumbo."

Forming lines was a major form of recreation at Kingman. "If you see a line, get in it," could have been the motto of the place. Lines at the commissary and property window were weekly occurrences. Pill lines at the clinic happened every morning and evening for prescriptions that couldn't be handed out more than one at a time. But chow was the mother of all lines.

In the morning it started forming in the darkness, before they opened the doors. If you arrived a little later the sky would put on a show, a lavender edge appearing over the Cerbat ridges in that moment of pure possibility before the sun appeared. At dusk the light show was over the other end of the yard, the sky awash with salmon pink fish bellies and stripes of turquoise and gold, before fading through purple to black.

The sky was the good part of standing in the chow line. The only good part.

Before dinner, inmates would congregate inside our dorm in front of the still locked door, impatient to be let out. When the C.O. buzzed open the lock, the cons would squeeze out like sand through an hourglass, some headed for the nearby cigarette lighter box on the wall, but most making a beeline for the chow hall. It was a daily stampede, many of them unable to keep from breaking into a run. Some traveled in twos, bromance couples in this womanless world, punching shoulders and laughing uproariously at meaningless jokes in their homophobic charades.

The paisas traveled in packs, joking, throwing fakes and jabs. Everything they did they did loudly.

The chiefs in contrast, always displayed a collective dignity, honor bound in tradition. Alcohol was their undoing, the reason most of them were here. Like other Arizona prisons, Cerbat had a sweat lodge for them. Fenced off from the main yard, its dome was formed from lashed-together saplings over a fire-pit dug in the ground. The dome could be covered with tarps for their centuries-old ceremonies.

CDs of chants would play on a boom box as the shirtless participants took turns going into the smoky sacred space. With the silhouetted mountains like slumbering beasts in the distance, the scene could pass for a vision from long before the white men arrived, if it weren't taking place inside chain link and razor wire.

In the chow line when chiefs ran into one another, the greeting would entail elaborate fist bumps and hugs. The encounters felt like reunions after months apart, even if the men had actually seen each other a few hours earlier that afternoon.

Most of what went down in the chow line wasn't that high minded. Or I should say, the fuckin' chow line.

In Hawaii, in pidgin, there's a term "dakine." It means something like this kind, or that kind. It's an all-purpose word, like a Swiss Army Knife of language, that can be used for anything. Noun, verb, adjective, adverb … it 's your go-to option when you can't bother thinking of the word you really want. It can be used in a sentence like, "You know … dakine!" exasperated if the listener doesn't know exactly what you mean.

Prison has its own word like that: fuckin'. Not only can it be any part of speech and mean anything you want it to, but inmates think it gains impact when repeated. "It's fuckin' fucked-up, dude, it's fuckin' funny as fuck."

My inner English teacher recoiled the first time I overheard someone sharing that sentiment in the chow line. I didn't realize yet that it wasn't a one-off, but an endless chorus whose theme and variations would be repeated every time I stood in the line.

"Shit, homey, that shit is fuckin' fucked up …" Just in case you didn't get it the first time.

When blacks did it, they added extra syllables and a mellifluous Barry White tone of authority. "That mufuka was fuckin' fucked up, you know what I'm sayin', Nigga … ?"

That was another essential, all-purpose prison word. The ultimate no-no of political correctness, it was the single word everyone I knew in my past life would have tied their intestines in knots to eradicate from their speech, thoughts or hearing. Yet it was perfectly acceptable on the yard. At least when coming out of the right mouth. The word referred to a human being, of the male gender as best I could tell, and usually came with a fair amount of affection, not to mention, respect.

Accompanying their fuckin' vocabularies was the distinctive way convicts laughed. Sometimes it was cackles that sounded uncomfortably close to a mental ward. Other times it was uncontrollable giggles bouncing back and forth, reminiscent of little girls in nursery school or a boy's choir singing a round. The jokes didn't get funnier, no matter how many times they repeated the punchline.

In the chow line "fuckin'" ranged from politics – "You know how many fuckin' people that fuckin' Hillary Clinton fuckin' had murdered?" – through sports – "The fuckin' Ravens got totally fucked by the fuckin' Titans, Nigga," – to culture – "Fuck, dude, fuckin' 'Ancient Aliens' was fuckin' out there last night, homey."

For all I knew, the paisas were saying the same thing.

It wasn't just my inner English teacher that recoiled. Every time a prisoner uttered the word, he was braying his ignorant cynicism and sealing his dead-end fate. I had five months, twenty-six days to go.

I hoped the condition wasn't contagious … or that I hadn't fuckin' already caught it.

24

Walking in circles

You need good shoes to walk the yard. Inmates have a choice of sturdy sneakers, all of them white leather, including New Balance if you can afford them. But the really big ticket item on the Keefe price list is your TV.

It's an off brand, Skyworth, institutional model. The case is made of clear plastic to prevent hiding contraband behind the screen. The screen is thirteen inches with no speakers but a jack for earphones. The newest model is flat-screen HD; it costs $200 plus tax and a coax cable.

It's way overpriced. Outside, on eBay or in pawnshops you can find one for less than $50. But for inmates without $200 there's another option – a yard TV. Yard TVs are used,. They become available when a prisoner leaves and puts his up for sale. They come in various vintages including old-school "bubbles" with bright, old-fashioned picture tubes. Yard TVs are less than half the price of new ones, but aren't always available. And there's a catch.

You can never be sure of the quality or history when you buy a yard TV. They're notorious for going on the blink as soon as they change hands. And yard TVs are, technically speaking, illegal. When you buy a new TV you get a receipt and your DOC number etched on the case proving it's yours. When quarterly or spot inspections take place in your dorm to check for drugs, hooch, porn or weapons, if you've got a yard TV it can be confiscated if the inspecting officers are so inclined.

There was lots of time to mull over the choice. It took a few weeks before you could order anything at all on the Keefe list. You had to have money on your books, which had to come in from "your people outside" and had to clear. All of that took a while. TV orders were known for getting delayed, sometimes for weeks. During the period of adjusting to your new life at Kingman, the new-or-used-TV? dilemma wasn't the most pressing thing on your mind.

But it's what Angelo wanted to talk to me about one afternoon. By now I had learned "Baseball"wasn't really his nickname – he just loved the game and couldn't wait to try out for the dorm team. He was a likable guy, as wry as Rodney Dangerfield. Like almost everyone else he was in prison for being an addict rather than a criminal … although that distinction quickly blurs. Before discovering drugs he had been a good kid growing up in a tight-knit Italian Catholic family. His relatives had put four-hundred dollars on his books for the big initial Keefe purchase. The money would cover shoes, extra clothes, lots of food, coffee … and a TV.

" … So I should buy a new one, right?"

We were out on the yard, sitting at one of the heavy brown metal picnic tables chained to the ground. The nearby mountain ridges looked sharp as knives in the bright afternoon sunshine.

"That's why they sent me $400. I priced out everything for them."

I nodded. He had already cast me as his surrogate father, even though we didn't even know each other's last names.

"Except …"

I knew where he was going.

In my prior life I had little knowledge of opioid addiction, beyond the ways I had seen it portrayed in squalid movies and TV cop shows about junkies, narcs and Mexican cartels. For all the decades thinking smoking marijuana qualified me as an outlaw, I was clueless when it came to hard drugs. The kids locked up around me were the worldly ones; I was the babe in the woods. But I had been in three facilities in two months now, and had gotten a crash course on the subject. For an overwhelming majority of prisoners, opioid addiction was the absolute source of light – and darkness – in their lives. It was the origin, the beginning and the end, as fundamental as breath itself.

I knew where Angelo was going.

"… If I get a yard TV, I'll have enough left to get high. Just one more time."

Yes, Virginia, heroin was available at Kingman-Cerbat. I didn't know how, or where exactly, and wasn't intending to ever find out. But everyone knew it was here. Kingman had a reputation for drugs throughout the entire Arizona prison system. Over the next months, I would begin connecting the dots, realizing why guys were sitting in the dorm, three to a bunk at three a.m., their eyes vacant and glassy reflecting the light from the TV screen. Or figuring out that inmates who came out of the commissary with gigantic plastic bags over their shoulders stuffed with the whole Keefe inventory weren't even hungry. The foodstuff purchase would pay for their drugs that week. Those with the most relentless habits built prisons within prison, their eyes furtive and haunted, their paranoia always just under the surface. The ones whose debt kept spiraling upward could look forward to getting beaten within an inch of their lives unless they could get to a C.O. first, requesting transfer to a protective custody yard. It was an ignoble escape known as "PC-ing out."

Jeff soon loaned me "Chasing the Scream," Johann Hari's journalistic chronicle of substance abuse and different approaches to treatment around the world. The author gives lots of attention to America's so-called war on drugs. It's an alliance of government enforcement and organized crime that essentially created the multibillion-dollar illegal drug industry, and gave mobs monopolies to run it. Among its lucrative byproducts are Arizona's corporate-owned prisons.

The man who conceived the war on drugs was the first commissioner of the Federal Bureau of Narcotics, Harry Jacob Anslinger. He was a creature of deeply held prejudices, a sadistic, natural misuser of power whose avid anti-drug crusade provided cover for his own morphine addiction. In his career, Anslinger added marijuana to the list of Class 1 narcotics, singlehandedly criminalizing the drug. Racial minorities were the real targets in his "war." In a single stroke he painted targets on an entire group of Americans, just for being black. Bebop jazz musicians were his obsession. Adding twisted lust to his pursuit, Billie Holiday was his bull's eye. Anslinger had launched his career as a protege of Joe McCarthy. He in turn found his own eager disciple in a young narcotics agent named Joe Arpaio. Joe Arpaio went on to become the sheriff of Maricopa County, state of Arizona, where the prison-for-profit industry is making a killing.

I never witnessed drug use in Kingman. I didn't know the details, I didn't want to. My journalistic impulses were on hold on that subject, trumped by my newly learned inmate's instinct to survive that took its cues from the three little monkeys with hands over their eyes, ears and mouths. But I knew enough.

Angelo and I were up walking the perimeter now, a rolled razor wire canopy above us. "... I should buy the new one. That's what I told my family I'd do. They trust me ..."

I didn't say much. He was pretty well covering the subject. I was just there to listen. Despite my new identity as a felon, just another man in orange with a number for a name, the needle on my moral compass hadn't gotten bent in the move. It still marked true north. Everyone – prisoners, guards, medical staff, the occasional warden – realized that about me as soon as they met me. I didn't belong here, but was available in case anyone got lost and asked for directions.

It wasn't really a conscious choice; it was just what I did. Surprisingly, it didn't appear to be generating resentment. Actually, the guys around me seemed to be honoring it.

What had my attorney said? "They need you in there, Rick ..."

On my resume I was a teacher as well as a writer, having taught for a decade at Maui Community College, which had recently dropped Community from its name. Making my living as a man of words had also taught me when to be quiet.

"... But getting high, just this once, they'd never know ... Those TVs are overpriced, I hate to pay that much ..."

Angelo and I kept walking. At some point, I spoke.

"You know what's right," I said. "You know how you feel. You know what you want to do. The part you may not know – but I do – is that you're strong enough to do it, for your family ... and yourself."

He nodded. It was clear he was in an agitated state, as the lawyers for the opposing sides kept arguing their cases in the courtroom of his mind. Over and over.

The next day was the deadline for filling out our bubble sheets. Angelo and I both ordered new TVs.

Encounters like that didn't happen every day. Sometimes a week would go by without one. But they happened enough.

Art, my ally from Steiner who looked like Shrek and had skeleton bones tattooed on the backs of his fingers, had once almost killed another inmate for saying the tattoo of Art's grandmother on his neck looked like Ronald McDonald. He had me pegged as his guardian angel.

"I can see your aura, OG. The light bends around your head and shoulders, glowing like a fucking halo …"

"It was yellowish green," he said.

"Evil bounces off you," he went on. "You were sent here to keep me safe …"

And here I thought it was just the reverse.

Art had a million stories. I never knew what to believe. There was the one about his family, the grandfather I reminded him of, a successful property developer who amassed a fortune creating marinas in Connecticut. Or his father, the Navy Seal, who had a garage almost as good as Jay Leno's, full of exotic cars. Now he had dementia.

Art had had his own cool cars and fancy speedboats growing up, before squandering it all when he got strung out on drugs. He had fought his way through one prison after another for decades. He had buried one son from a drug overdose, and saved a second one, but not his brain, when he resuscitated him. His idea of a good time "on the outs," was hopping a freight train in Phoenix, and heading north. He didn't do it the way Woodie Guthrie or the hobos in the '30s did.

"You hop a car carrier, one transporting Lexuses or Mercedeses. They're unlocked, they've got gas in the tanks. You turn on the heat and the sound system, and ride to Kingman."

He always brought his bike along, the latest BMX model.

"You hop off, check out the town, maybe go somewhere for pizza. Then you catch another train and head somewhere else."

I didn't want to believe him. The most outlandish origin stories I heard in Kingman tended to be products of monumentally deranged minds. The most sweeping one came from a guy claiming to be a paid

CIA mercenary, a former Mr. Arizona bodybuilding champ (twice), and the brains behind the biggest illegal steroid lab in Phoenix. The last time I saw him he was being accompanied out of Dorm 9 in handcuffs by a dozen C.O.s after being beaten up in the bathroom by an inmate half his size. But Art's tales were full of details, and vivid recollections, and remorse. And they always sounded true.

For all his family fortunes, including the seven-figure trust fund supposedly awaiting him when he was released in a matter of months, Art was indigent. He sniped cigarettes that he smoked constantly. He was always bumming things, a shot of coffee, a soup. He was adamant about receiving the free hygiene supplies they handed out to indigents – toothpaste, deodorant, a bar of soap, a small bottle of shampoo, a new toothbrush (two inches long so it couldn't be made into a weapon) – at store each week.

When we first arrived in Kingman together he tried to reach his mother, asking for twenty bucks to replace the holey old Riddell sneakers someone had given him. She never responded, which sent him straight off the despondent end of his mood-swing scale. I weighed the matter for several days, my better angel wrestling with my selfish inner dick as I considered the possible mooch-for-life consequences I might unleash with my action. Then I placed an order for a new pair of Ridells for him on my Keefe sheet.

"Don't get the wrong idea," I told him. "This is one time, the only time. Because you've got holes in your shoes, and it's beginning to rain."

The look he gave me was somewhere between astonished disbelief at the kindness of strangers, and the shatterproof devotion of a Golden Lab. I never regretted my decision.

Coyote was another ray of hope. Rather than trying to impose any sort of dumb whiteboy agenda in my mind, he was looking out for me, too. He went out of his way to get me hygiene products before I could order from Keefe, and to guide my steps through the unfamiliar minefield of prison life.

"Anyone comes at you is gonna have to get through me first, then the rest of the dorm. You're not just OG, you're triple OG," he said. Maybe it was the Kurt Russell resemblance, or the compassion I could see in his eyes still intact after he had broken every other part of himself he could get his hands on. Maybe it was his vulnerability struggling to pass his GED requirements at age fifty-two, but whatever it was got him to the top of my Good Guys list in a hurry.

Being incarcerated was messing with my biological clock, but that was proving to be a good thing. I wasn't feeling my age physically, maybe because of the constant shots of adrenaline keeping me alert as I tried to stay a step ahead of men less than a third my age. But there were other benefits, too. In prison – as opposed to the bleached teeth, beautiful people youth-obsessed consumer culture on the outs – older still gets credit for being wiser. To be OG was to be an elder, venerated here as much as in any tribal society. Doing my pull-up routine – ten sets of five, broken up by laps around the eighth-mile walking track in a practice I called "Communing with the Sky" – got unsolicited attention and respect from other guys working out. Strangers would come up and shake my hand. Staying strong was a way of staying sane; I didn't realize it would make me a made man on the yard.

Soon guys from the dorm were stopping by my bunk, just to talk. There was Walter, sentenced for joyriding on someone's Harley, without asking permission first.

"It was parked outside the bar," he said. "I left my Jaguar as collateral. I brought it back … three days later …"

This was Walter's first stint in state prison after decades of winding up in county jails, drunk and disorderly. He had been a pressman for a printing company, which gave us lots to talk about. He had worked his way through four marriages. But in the forced sobriety of prison, something had happened. Someone else had moved in, like a stranger answering a "For Rent" sign for his life. This new person was a good man, modestly reflecting on all the missteps that had left debris of wrecked relationships in its wake.

"My parents, my kids, no one wants to have anything to do with me. They don't trust me. I don't blame them."

"Well, let's see if we can do something about that," I said.

Chase had been nineteen, a former Eagle Scout, when he discovered heroin. He arrived in Dorm 9 with a row of stitches over one eyebrow, fresh from being sucker punched by someone in the van on the ride to Kingman. He was still just a kid who had been already been through a lifetime's worth of health threats including serious kidney disease. His health had been challenging enough for his single mom, before he started stealing her credit card to pay for his drugs. It wasn't the crime as much as his departure from her deep Mormon faith that had distressed her to the point of totally cutting him off.

"I can't communicate with her," he told me. "After all I've done, that's what I deserve." He would bring her letters to me to read. In them she pled for him to return to the faith. "See what I mean?"

"Those are the only words she knows to tell you she loves you," I answered. "Take that as your starting point …"

My new pals weren't limited to whiteboys. A Chicano named Bobby occupied the bunk next to mine. He hauled his TV up on the partition between our bunks before mine arrived. He let me borrow his Keefe price list to order from. He taught me what "lace up your shoes" meant – code for announcing an impending race riot on the yard. Ironically enough, if it materialized, we'd be on opposite sides. Bobby had a friend named Jesus (Hey-soos) who would shake my hand firmly whenever he came to visit Bobby. Jesus treated me like he would a priest.

Occupying the bunk on the other side of Bobby was an inmate named Trent. He was black but light-skinned, looking like a Caribbean matinee idol. Trent had been a body builder on the outs and was still in great shape; his job on the yard was running the rec office, checking out horseshoes (made of hard rubber for safety's sake) and other equipment and keeping the workout bars taped. Trent amazed me; he could do a five-hundred-piece jigsaw puzzle in an hour, then do another before lunch. We got into some serious film reviewing conversations whenever the cable movie channel would do a Clint Eastwood showcase.

These encounters didn't happen all the time. I was still working on remembering to keep my head down, and maintain a constant state of watching out. But rays of sunshine would sneak in. On my seventy-fourth birthday three months after arriving at Kingman, I was surprised by a birthday card full of little messages of hope and gratitude, and love. It was addressed to Alpha Wolf. Art had put a lot of energy into being sure everyone in the dorm signed it. All the whiteboys, at least.

"They need you in there, Rick ..."

Prison was proving to be every bit as dangerous and sordid as I had feared. What I hadn't anticipated was having the wherewithal to take it in stride. It didn't hurt to discover the Jesus card in my hand occasionally, even if its powers remained as mysterious to me as they were miraculous to others.

But when you get dealt the Jesus card, you damn well better play it.

25

Six degrees

Before being incarcerated, part of me still believed in happy endings. After walking the earth sidestepping serious trouble for more than seven decades, I was blissfully naive about bad things happening to good people. And, I assumed, one mistake, even a big one, didn't make you a criminal.

Well, so much for that.

Now I was stuck in a place where the joke about bending over in the shower to pick up the soap wasn't a joke, and I woke up each morning running my tongue along the backs of my teeth to be sure they were still there. "Living in fear" didn't begin to address the magnitude of the situation. No matter how many guys told me they had my back, I wasn't resting easy.

So I looked to Buddha for a little help. It was my version of Buddha, of course, who could have been Jesus' twin brother, or maybe a Photoshopped composite mug shot of the two of them. Buddha responded to my understandable concerns the way he often did, with a riddle:

What would happen if you stopped fearing fear? He left out the "Well, grasshopper …" part, and the martial arts lessons.

After all, until you really are in the jaws of the shark, bleeding – hemorrhaging is more like it – fear is just a fantasy, one of those unfunny jokes our minds get a kick out of playing on us. Whatever threat I could conjure – the Aryan Nation skinhead, the Chicano gang leader, the larcenist who got access to my bank account – did not exist. The jackhammer punches to my kidneys, the sound of my teeth clattering across the floor, the blood pouring from my nose broken in two places, the burning pain in my soul and elsewhere ... were just more of those mind games. None of it was real. Not yet.

So my first line of defense involved taming my brain. The second was writing a speech, like dialogue from a movie script, and silently rehearsing it as I walked around the yard. That way I'd have it in my mind if the occasion ever arose and I didn't totally freak out and panic. It went like this:

ME

OK, pal, I'm seventy-four. I've had a heart attack, I'm on blood thinners, my bones are brittle. And you want to fight me? You've got one shot, if you're lucky, before you get the shit kicked out of you by every whiteboy in Dorm 9. Then the rest of the yard gets in on it. My exercise pals will be lining up. What's left of you will get put on a body board and rolled out of here by a dozen C.O.s who hate fools like you for making their prison look bad. Once they sew you back together and put some staples in, you'll get more years added to your sentence on some four-yard where you'll be lucky if someone doesn't carve you a new asshole. And for what? So you can brag that you beat up an old man to prove what an ignorant, pathetic coward you are? Really? Well then, go ahead, pal, knock yourself out.

After feeling like I had it down, I started worrying when a little part of me wanted an excuse to try it out. In the meantime, I was getting more tutoring on my Buddha hotline. It came in the form of a slim paperback titled "The Zen Teachings of Homeless Kodo." Karen had picked up a copy in one of those neighborhood lending libraries in a cabinet nailed to someone's fence. You can't bring books in with you when you're sentenced, so I asked her to send me a copy.

This, like so many things about prison, isn't nearly as easy as it could be. Books sent to prisoners have to be brand new and can only be ordered from certain booksellers. Amazon's not one of them since it also sells used books. Once they arrive at prison, book orders have to be thoroughly inspected, not only for contraband, weapons or porn, but also for content.

"The Zen Teachings" made it through – no small miracle, since I doubted there was another copy in print in America. It's very Japanese. There's a cryptic black-and-white photo on the cover that may be some monks in black robes and coolie hats, or maybe they're umbrellas, walking in an alley in the rain.

Or it may be a picture of something else entirely, I'm not sure.

The book's authors are Kosho Uchiyama and Shohaku Okumura. They're both bald, bony Zen monks, the second the disciple of the first. They take turns commenting on the teachings of yet another Soto Zen master, Kodo Sawaki Roshi, who inspired them both. The chapters are short, adapted and translated from a series of weekly columns on the religion page of a Japanese newspaper in the '60s.

Although they became monastery abbots and renowned authors, the three teachers came from a tradition of being intentionally poor and homeless to remind them of their place in, you know, everything. So the book is a discussion between three generations of Zen masters, although the concept of a "master" in a religion that preaches selfless humility sounded like another riddle to me. Two of them are dead now, but Zen has always provided a happy home for ghosts.

The day the book arrived I started reading it on my bunk. On the first page of the first chapter was this story by Kosho Uchiyama:

"As a disciple of a 'homeless' teacher, I myself was homeless. I had to get daily food and provisions through takuhatsu, religious begging. Dogs often threatened me. Once a spitz jumped up and barked viciously. The chain tied to the dog's collar wasn't tight enough, and suddenly it came undone. The dog immediately cowed, whined, and retreated. It seems a dog barks overbearingly when chained, but loses nerve as soon as it's free."

I looked up from the book to see the men around me in the dorm, going about their daily routines and menacing postures like that dog on its chain.

Hmmm, I thought.

Could it be that the fear I was afraid of wasn't mine alone? Could it be colored orange, everywhere I looked? Could it be setting the agenda, could it be the secret that no one realizes everyone else is feeling?

The fear factor, it turns out, is the foundation of the prison system. It's in the DNA of everyone in orange, and everyone in khaki guarding them. Fear, and the broken spirit that goes with it, is what allows a single officer – a slight woman in her twenties – to hold total control over two-hundred dangerous men. Everything else – the tattooed, overdeveloped physiques; the "taking it to the bathroom" fistfights that broke out with depressing frequency, leaving blood on the floor followed by "knuckle checks" of everyone in the dorm to find the culprits – were bluffs. Macho posturing and preening were apparently the only options available for self-expression to confined men with limited imaginations. Cockfighting in Hawaii came to mind.

And so began my new routine, reading two chapters of "The Zen Teachings" each morning the way some guys read their Bibles. If I woke up early enough when most of the dorm was still asleep, I would put the teachings into action, or inaction, sitting there with legs crossed, meditating, my eyes on the white wall at the foot of my bunk until the numbers stenciled there – 09A03 – disappeared from view.

The Zen Teachings transcended time and space. Their thousand-year-old Japanese sentiments were life preservers tossed to twenty-first-century Americans drowning in consumer culture. The long-dead abbot could have been sending a personal letter to me when he wrote, "Each of us is born naked. For a short while between birth and death we put on various complicated clothes. Some wear luxurious garments, some rags, some prison uniforms."

The homeless, possessionless part of the teachings resonated too, somewhere inside me deeper than my head. Walking the yard by myself, sometimes I almost got knocked over by a sense of gratitude unlike anything I had felt before, for everything I could never possess.

The chain link fence framed everything outside the fence – the mesquite, the mountains – in endless tiny diamonds. It was prison's version of ancient Buddhism's Diamond Sutra that cuts through illusion to find the true wisdom of emptiness.

Jeff was long gone by now. He had mailed a request to the Department of Corrections, and was transferred to another yard where there were jobs for prisoners that paid more than twenty-five cents an hour working at a nearby chicken processing plant. So there was no one to compare notes with about what was going on on TV, which at that moment in time happened to be the first impeachment of President Donald J. Trump.

Just as well. Politics was not a place I wanted to go with anyone else on the yard. Actually, it had been a relief to be without a TV for those early months and to have been spared the piggy face, petulant temper tantrums and dolphin flipper arms. Besides there were far more interesting things happening on my television set. The strange sensation that began in Pima County of seeing someone I knew every time I pushed the power button was in overdrive at Kingman.

Here was Tom Selleck hawking reverse mortgages for seniors. Or Brie Larson eating a beetle in the Amazon rain forest on a National Geographic Channel adventure. Or Laura Dern growing up sexy in "Wild at Heart."

Blond Kelly Rohrbach co-starred with her red swimsuit in the remake of "Baywatch." She transfixed my cellies.

"You interviewed *her*? No way, OG."

Yep, and her "Baywatch" co-star Zac Efron, too. And Karen Gillan, whose naval was the highlight of "Jumanji." And Elizabeth Banks, crossing the line to direct as well as star in "Pitch Perfect." And older, more venerated figures like Colin Farrell and Pierce Brosnan and William Hurt and Clint Eastwood. I had talked to them all in that strange act of not quite journalism known as the celebrity interview.

I had started interviewing stars long before we moved to Maui. At my previous newspaper in Santa Cruz, I used to go on movie junkets to preview new releases and talk to the stars. Really big stars like Sidney Poitier, Michelle Pfeiffer, Richard Pryor, Mary Tyler Moore, Robin Williams and so many more. It was a strange sensation being that close to them for a few minutes, feeling the magnitude of their energy fields, until my paper finally reminded me what a conflict-of-interest movie junkets really are, and pulled the plug on any more free first-class airline tickets.

Now I couldn't watch a movie without one of them showing up. Every sighting flashed me back to the few minutes I had spent with them, the details and momentary infatuation recalled as vividly as most people remember their first kiss.

Making people fall in love with them was part of their job description. I was easy prey, too easy considering what a veteran, award-winning journalist I supposedly was. They in turn, provided tantalizing glimpses of what it was like to be them.

TV stars, too, Connie Britton, Emma Roberts, Evan Rachel Wood, Amber Heard doing L'Oreal Paris ads. When Ken Burns' PBS series "Country Music" treated Kris Kristofferson like the deity in blue jeans he actually is, it transported me to the Kristofferson living room in Hana, where his wife Lisa was taking a selfie of the three of us. She took another shot with her phone backstage at a concert, of Kris and his buddy Willie, with me in the middle. We looked like three happily confused old coots who had wandered away from the home.

I had been six years old when my mother died. Growing up in the Dust Bowl college town of Norman, Oklahoma, in the 1950s, I spent a lot of Sunday afternoons by myself, going to matinees for a quarter at rinky-dink picture-show palladiums called the Sooner and the Boomer. That's where I developed the irksome habit of falling in love too easily. In a stroke of cosmic good fortune, I had been able to parlay the affliction into a successful career reviewing movies. I put elaborate camouflage around the reality that it was probably still that six-year-old boy writing the reviews. I called what I did "cinemythology."

Westerns were my favorites when I was a kid in Oklahoma and were again as I watched them from a prison dorm in Arizona, just down the road from the town of Kingman that celebrated Andy Devine Days each year. Watching "For a Few Dollars More" one bright afternoon, Ennio Morricone's jangly music score echoed right out the dorm door and into the turquoise skies and pink mesas where Sergio Leone and Clint Eastwood could have been lurking like a couple of desperados.

Kevin Costner's "Wyatt Earp" ricocheted even closer. The actor once told me I had been the first journalist to do a cover story about him, many lifetimes ago. Now I had been to the actual places where some of Wyatt Earp's greatest gunfights occurred, from the aptly named town of Tombstone to the Tucson train station where Wyatt's statue still guards the platform. I had walked in his boot steps. But there was more.

Bolstered by his good aim, Wyatt Earp's sense of justice still prevailed in the craggy desert landscapes a century later. He wasn't much of an intellectual, but had his reasons for doing what he did. The bad guys killed his brother, for one thing. But his notions of justice being whatever he said it was, carried out with steely eyed vengeance, may well have put some ideas in Joe Arpaio's head, and set the tone for a lot of Western wannabes still enforcing the law, Arizona-style.

And now, in some giant sweep of karmic correction, after writing about other people's movies for so long, here I was making my own before I died. It used the same gorgeous Western movie sets, but was more modern, post-"Two Lane Blacktop," taking place in a seedier new West. And I was like Gary Cooper in "High Noon," cast not by choice in the starring role where playing the hero was my only shot at survival.

Playing the hero, as real heroes know, requires subduing the coward who lives inside every one of us.

It was the "Six Degrees of Kevin Bacon" game again, proving that everyone in the film industry has some connection to the "Footloose" star. It's a variation on what's known as the Butterfly Effect, in which everything we know in the world is connected to everything else.

I interviewed Kevin Bacon on a movie junket in 1988. Now I had inherited his marker in the game. Everything on my TV screen was within six degrees of me. From the guys with no teeth around me to some of the most gorgeous people to ever walk the earth ... everyone was a co-star in my crazy movie. We were all connected. We were all the same.

Interviewing movie stars I had learned that talent couldn't overcome insecurity. In fact it worked just the reverse. Being that beautiful didn't solve anything – it often made matters worse. This thing called the "self" was the biggest riddle of them all.

Years before I got to prison, when I was still leading a carefree live in a place many call paradise, I read this quote from someone named Cyril Connolly on my Zen Thought for the Day calendar: "We are all serving a life sentence in the dungeon of the self."

Now I was being reminded that the self in the dungeon wasn't the face in the mirror those stars on TV hawked products to beautify. It wasn't the biceps and triceps and pecs the guys on the yard worked out to make bigger. It wasn't the man who woke at three in the morning in a start, feeling so alone.

Instead it was the one homeless Kodo Sawaki described:

"It is brilliantly transparent like the deep blue sky, and there is no gap between it and all living beings. We cannot maintain ourselves by ourselves. Rather, when we give up I, we become simply the self that is connected to the universe."

26

Class act

The yard was abuzz. The VIPs were coming. A delegation of officials was on its way to inspect Kingman-Cerbat and we had been madly cleaning our houses ever since we got the news. The CEO – or was he the owner? – of GEO was traveling from Florida. Rumor had it that Governor Doug Ducey would be among the Arizona politicians and Department of Corrections heads accompanying him.

Dorm 9 was on their itinerary. Don't make us look bad were our orders.

When the entourage arrived, they formed a splendid parade crossing the yard. Men and women in black business suits were guarded by security officers looking fresh off the military transport from Afghanistan. The guards with all their special ops gear made the Kingman correctional officers look even more like rent-a-cops. There were dogs on leashes – huge, beige wolfy dogs twice the size of German Shepherds. They were magnificent beasts, undoubtedly trained to go straight for the throat.

The GEO boss must have been the man in the lead. He was dressed less formally than the suits, in a high school letterman's jacket with leather sleeves. He had an expensive haircut and a perfect Republican golf course tan. He was short, the kind of guy who owns NFL teams, savoring the power to buy and sell bigger, stronger men.

"Calm down," directed a C.O. when the procession arrived in Dorm 9. The inmates were as antsy as preschoolers. "This isn't a shakedown."

The procession of humans and animals reminded me of the triumphant parade at the end of "Peter and the Wolf," after they've killed the wolf. But it was surreal and upside down. The wolves were the law enforcement officers this time; we were the animals in pens. There was a tall black woman in the group, dressed all in black, as exotic as the Queen of Sheba. She turned out to be a high-level administrator at Kingman-Cerbat. In the coming weeks I would find endless excuses to ask her questions whenever she showed up doing rounds in our dorm.

They fed the VIPs a gourmet menu prepared by inmates in Kingman's culinary arts class. They didn't eat in the chow hall with us, but in the class's demonstration kitchen. The food was prepared in pots and served on plates that had never been used before, and were repackaged as soon as the officials left.

The GEO corporation was under investigation in Arizona at the time for its treatment of undocumented immigrants, including those well-publicized kids in cages in facilities closer to the border. It was just one of many lawsuits against GEO from all over the country. Among the charges were antislavery violations, forced labor conditions and failure to meet minimum wage requirements.

Officially speaking, the visit was to showcase how well prison reform was going in the state. The Arizona Department of Corrections had a new director and was in the process of adding the words "Rehabilitation and Reentry" to its name. But the guy in leather sleeves couldn't have cared less about prisoners; he was just a little rich man checking the balance sheet on one more investment.

Any break in the 24/7 monotony was a godsend. One Saturday, heading out of the dorm to the pull-up bars I heard an electric guitar. The twang seemed to ricochet off the nearest mountain range, its purple ridges looking like they had been cut by a kindergartner with dull scissors. Following the sound to its source, I got to the chain link-fenced corridor between our yard and Cerbat North next door.

Squeezed between the fences, a band of inmates was playing. Guitar, bass, drums – not great, but not bad, either. The sound was dreamy, not agitated, one of those Grateful Dead woozy raptures that went on and on. The sky was paintbox blue, the autumn air crisp; the scene as mellow as things ever got at Kingman.

A group of inmates had gathered along the fence, listening and swaying if not quite dancing. A similar group lined the fence on the north yard side. After a break, a second band of musicians took over, singing in Spanish this time and getting even larger audiences along the fences.

It was a free afternoon concert like hundreds, thousands, I had been to, beginning in college and continuing through the slack key guitar and ukulele festivals on Maui every summer. It was so pleasant, the orange men smiling and rocking to the beat, it took a while to realize something was not quite right. What was wrong with this picture ...?

And then, finally, the answer came:

No women.

It was so obvious, the beautiful presence of women being such a taken-for-granted part of normal life. But that was the old normal. When I mentioned my realization to guys who had spent years, not months, incarcerated, they hadn't even noticed.

Culinary arts was the best, but not the only class at Kingman. The prison was officially a "program yard"; education and training were part of its mission. There was GED prep, including practice sessions leading up to the actual exam. If passed it would reduce an inmate's sentence by a few months. Other classes ranged from vocational skills like carpentry to seminars in cultural diversity and re-entry. A class called Parenting Skills got a lot of interest after the attractive young mother who was teaching it showed up in the dorm recruiting.

High school equivalency was the goal for the general population. I figured I was going to skate by that dimension of the prison experience until I got a chrono – that's prison talk for a memo – telling me to show up for the re-entry class beginning next week. Art got one too.

It started at eight-thirty a.m. Monday, but at eight-fifteen our dorm got a call that it had been canceled that day. Ditto for the next class, and the next. Scheduling conflicts kept conveniently occurring. But then, finally, it happened.

The instructor was a C.O.III from a dorm across the yard; his name was Whitworth. He had a brown goatee and glasses, and an Okie-from-Southern-California accent. The curriculum came from the same cookie-cutter that stamped out most Kingman classes – twenty guys sitting around tables in a dorm classroom, doing workbook exercises on Xeroxed pages. Some of the chapters were pragmatic: preparing a resume; applying for Social Security or a driver's license; getting a job; balancing a checkbook; handling taxes and insurance. But others were on more abstract topics – self-awareness, perception, attitudes, life skills and relationships.

Whitworth was a likable guy. He had spent decades working in prisons, but wasn't comfortable in the role of teacher. He'd rather talk, with an easy-going drawl and encyclopedic memory for details, about the boxing match on TV last weekend, or the NFL season, which was going into high gear. His strategy was to have members of the class lead the discussions.

"Substance abuse and rehab are the only things I'm qualified to teach," he said. In a career where asserting your authority matters, he was tough enough, but self-effacing, too. He had married his wife... twice. He was hardly an authority on women, he confessed. He had raised a bunch of kids, including at least one of the neighbors'. He was all for prisoners learning to take responsibility for themselves, but wasn't on any high horse about dispensing advice. His own life was about as much as he could handle.

In the first class we had to go around the table telling a little bit about ourselves.

When we got to me I said I was twice, maybe three times the age of anyone else in there. It was a slight exaggeration – Whitworth, Art and at least one other guy, Terry, were in their fifties. But it was close enough. It was my first time in prison, I continued, the first time I had ever been in trouble with the law. Before that, I had been a journalist, editor and teacher for decades.

"And then I made a helluva mistake to get here."

After class I approached Whitworth.

"You know, I've taught college English for a long time," I began. "So, if there's anything I can do to help ..."

He cut me off right there.

"You can do the whole thing," he said.

Which is how the fall 2019 Re-entry course at Kingman-Cerbat State Prison became Mr. Chatenever's class.

"I don't know much about prison," I began when Whitworth brought me to the front of the room at the next session. "And I only know one way to teach. It begins with treating everyone with respect. And letting you know what I've learned in my life. And actually being interested in what's on your mind. And providing a safe place for you to share it."

I brought Art to the whiteboard with me, as the class secretary. And to literally watch my back. He may have been covered with a carnival sideshow's worth of tattoos, but he had beautiful handwriting. He had taken art lessons as a kid. It was another legacy from that beloved grandmother whose face he wore so proudly inked on his neck.

"You may not think that you have anything to say ... but you do," I told the guys around the table, eyeing me skeptically. "I'll help you discover what it is."

Big surprise. They went for it.

Especially the early chapters, where perception, social attitudes and personal awareness were the workbook topics. The lesson plan, such as it was, was almost identical to the way I taught English at Maui College, where the challenge had been to reach local kids from homes where English wasn't necessarily the language their parents spoke. And what was coming back to me – enhanced by considerable knowledge of substance abuse and extra-legal activities across the map of America – was the same, too.

The guys opened up. They responded to the new sensation of being listened to with respect, maybe for the first time in their lives, the way a parched rose bush reacts to a garden hose. Their brows furrowed with efforts to answer my open-ended questions. Their words came with a healthy dose of self-reflection for the lives they had lived and the mistakes they had made up to that point.

"You've still got time to change," I told them. "You're young enough. You've still got a whole life in front of you. My journalism career began after I turned thirty.

"But it's up to you."

There was an edge that hadn't been there when I taught at the college. A new dimension earned by self-flagellation; a new stance stemming from being in orange, just like they were. I was one of them. I had fucked up, as badly as they had. Worse, actually. My mistake almost killed someone.

I had journeyed to a new world since the last time I taught a class, but these guys were quick studies.

We all knew we had things to learn from each other.

Whitworth loved it. Here I was teaching his class for him, deferring to him whenever the discussion veered in the direction of the law, prison regulations, substance abuse, getting clean, and the odds on next weekend's NFL schedule.

"You're the best teacher on the yard, Chatenoover," he'd say, and mean it. Regulations specified that an inmate couldn't officially teach a DOC class, but hey, no harm no foul.

"I'm only sorry I can't pay you," he added.

"No worries," I answered. The pay scale, twenty-five-cents-an-hour, was one more Department of Corrections kick in the groin as far as I was concerned. And what I was getting from the class was more than worth it. Way more.

Among the posers, bodybuilders, well-intentioned but clueless women, and playground bullies who found gainful employment as C.O.III's in the Arizona prison system, Whitworth was a rarity. He was a mensch. Once, before my phone privileges kicked in, I got a letter from Karen about a health emergency she was experiencing. Even though it was days later, Whitworth let me call her on his phone as soon as he found out. The C.O.III's in my dorm wouldn't have done that.

I started making regular visits to his office, ostensibly to touch base about how the class was going, but more just to share a few minutes with a normal human being. He always dropped whatever he was doing when I showed up, even if he steered the conversation to football as soon as he could. He displayed prodigious knowledge of every game that had been played the previous weekend, along with stats on everyone who had played every position on every team every year … college as well as pro.

"You're one of the good guys in here," I told him.

"Yeah, well, if you're gonna put me in your book I want some money for it," he answered.

My "students" would lapse into personal stories, sometimes painful, before a lightbulb would switch on over their heads signifying epiphanies large and small. One of them, an Indian, would go into long rambles, about his kids, about his elders, about his tribal traditions that were still vital and brimming with soul despite the forces of America trying to beat them down, as they had forever.

I taught the way I conducted interviews. It's a process I still don't understand, all these years later. I would skim the workbook chapter, collect my thoughts, then wing it. It was akin to channeling, opening my mouth and seeing what came out. Prison Rick was a lot like Maui College's Mr. Rick ... just a little harder edged, a little more tough love, a little less liberal correctness.

"What's honesty?" I asked one day, in the workbook chapter on personal values. Blank stares around the table. No wonder – it was a trick question, impossible to answer.

"Yeah," I acknowledged, "that's a hard word to define ... but it's basically the face looking back at you in the mirror ..."

Whoa now, where had that come from?

Behind me, Art was covering the whiteboard with his elegant printing, turning what I said into well organized outlines and lists. It was brilliant. And when he spoke, his comments were smart, too, belying the fact that they came from a mouth that had had twelve rotten teeth removed by the prison clinic's free dental service. He was alert and well-spoken, making me think all those tall tales about family fortunes in Connecticut may have actually been true, before he discovered drugs.

"They need you in there, Rick ..."

Now I had another nickname beside OG to greet me when I worked out on the yard: "Hey, Teach...," before they'd shake my hand.

The teaching stretched through the holidays, Thanksgiving, Christmas, the Super Bowl.

Whitworth said he'd excuse anyone who picked the Super Bowl winner from attending the next class. In our dorm we had an office-pool-style betting grid, ten by ten squares. It cost a soup per square to enter, and paid off with about twenty soups, or bags of chips, or tubes of sunscreen or whatever else wound up in the pot, each quarter. It was extra super that year because my team, the 49ers, were in it for the first time in a long time, playing Kansas City. I bought extra squares on the grid, not because I cared about winning – I was trying to wean myself off soups, actually – but to help fill up the sheet. The number squares were chosen at random; I got some good ones.

Watching football in a prison dorm will never be mistaken for your favorite sports bar. For openers, it's almost silent. Everyone is tuned into his own TV, the announcers' voices and roar of the crowd relegated to earphones. But even without a TV of your own, you can follow the game by the cheering, or spontaneous applause of your fellow inmates. It's clear which convict is for which team, immediately. Considering the heightened emotions of a championship game, and the issues some prisoners have with anger management, it seemed slightly dangerous to be in such close quarters. But then again, what's not dangerous around here? It's prison – remember?

One of my squares in the pool was zero-zero. Great numbers betting-wise, covering lots of frequent football scores… like the 10 to 10 halftime tie, and the 49ers' 20-10 lead at the end of the third quarter. Each time a quarter ended, the pool organizers showed up dumping piles of ramen on my bunk. It was soup Christmas at my house.

The funny thing was, rather than resenting me or even being jealous, the guys in Dorm 9 were genuinely excited every time I won. It was something uncommon, a warm, fuzzy feeling that almost made up for the game's miracle finish and final outcome.

"Should have picked Kansas City, Chatenoover," Whitworth waxed philosophically at the next class.

But the best part of Super Bowl 2020 was the halftime show, hands down. Shakira and Jennifer Lopez, bare-legged, oozing sensuality, leading a stageful of dancers in synchronized twerking, choreographed porn, Busby Berkeley eroticism shot from crotch-cam POV, a national observance of Latina-powered, nearly X-rated frenzy.

Now, try to imagine the effect of all that on hundreds of sex-starved prison inmates whose understanding and interest in women went no deeper than the parts of their anatomies featured in the gyrating spectacle. The performance got spontaneous hoots, cheers and applause from all the orange boys in the hood. After its breathtaking climax a single voice rang out in the dorm:

"The shower room is closed. Don't even think of going there."

27

Big mistake

The Super Bowl win should have been the end of this book. Life in Dorm 9 had become predictable, at least. There was still the occasional fight that brought squads of guards scrambling through the doors to overpower an out-of-control inmate or two before escorting them out in handcuffs. But mostly it was Groundhog Day, the same old same old, on a tape loop. Twice a week there was class to relieve the boredom. Teaching had given me a role, a purpose in the orange wasteland. I had a job, planting new ways of looking at things and tiny rays of hope in brains where they had never been before.

It was early February, there were less than three months to go before my release date, April 26. And that wasn't counting the senate bill.

Almost from the moment I arrived at Kingman I had been hearing about the senate bill. It was a piece of legislation supposedly set to kick in at the beginning of the new year that would reduce almost everyone's sentence from the current eighty-five percent to sixty-five percent of time served. If you had a year, that translated to about eight months of incarceration; if you had passed the mandate test, that took another couple of months off. Jeff had had a copy of the bill, but it was written in legislative language neither of us quite understood.

In prison, counting your days is everyone's preoccupation, repeated like a mantra from your first waking moments to your last thought before falling asleep. The senate bill was the wild card, changing the calculation. The senate bill was what I would discuss with the Queen of Sheba warden lady whenever she showed up. That, and whether I would ever be able to drive again. She was like my own personal blast of sunshine. Art would come find me whenever she made rounds to our dorm. She always seemed happy to talk to me, another miracle considering our, uh, difference in status.

Obsessing over the senate bill was like catnip – prisoners couldn't let it go. But it could also drive a man crazy. An intense inmate named Bowie could talk about nothing else until the fateful day he wound up running back and forth on the low wall separating two rows of bunks. He had the look of a feral animal, trapped with no way out as squads of C.O.'s in the surrounding aisles, each armed with handcuffs, tried to corner him the way small kids might with a kitten. He had just learned he hadn't qualified.

His was an extreme overreaction; in truth almost no one qualified.

Art and I would go over and over our senate bill status with the C.O.III in our dorm, Villa; and then we'd go visit Whitworth in his office. They'd call up our files on their computers. Art was looking good. There was some problem with me.

"It looks like you qualify, Chatenoover, but they're not giving it to you," Whitworth told me.

"Why not?"

"Beats me."

When Villa, who was better with technology tried it, he came up with an answer.

"It's because of your prior," he said.

"But I don't have a prior," I reminded him. "When it comes to crime, I'm a one-off."

He nodded. "It's just the way the computer reads your charge."

"But that doesn't make sense," I pointed out, sounding uncomfortably Spocklike.

"How do we know that someone didn't punch my info into the system wrong? Hitting one wrong key can have huge consequences."

"No, it's just the way the system reads the code," he answered. "The result's the same." End of story.

The senate bill was turning out to be just one more rumor on the yard, one more convict fantasy that you'd desperately grasp at, winding up with nothing but air slipping through your fingers.

Art's release date was a few weeks ahead of mine, earlier in April. But he kept getting notified that he was the rare case where the senate bill actually applied. He could be released any week now.

"Whoa, now, you lucky bastard," I said, struggling to keep a lid on my envy.

He wasn't so sure. Instead of elation, the news set off another of his not infrequent bouts of depression.

"Believe me, OG, I'd trade places with you if I could," he said, looking more mournfully Shreklike than ever.

The speeded-up release date didn't thrill him. He was even talking about forgoing the mandate, serving out every day of his full sentence. In prison this is known as doing "flat time."

What was going on? I didn't get it.

And then I did.

He didn't want out.

A lot of guys in prison don't want out. For many it's the only life they've ever known. They'd talk about yards they had been on the way my friends compared notes on past European vacations. Their rap sheets were what they had instead of resumes. For all Bernie Sanders' talk about American socialism – a hot item during primary season on TV each night – anyone really wanting to know what American socialism looks like should spend some time with the Arizona Department of Corrections. What you learned in school are humans' "basic needs" – food, clothing, shelter – are all taken care of in prison. Your only responsibility, as Whitworth regularly pointed out, was making your bed each morning. No one even checked for hospital corners.

Kingman resembled a facility for wayward youth at least as much as a penal institution. It was known derisively among its residents as Camp Snoopy. They hated what it implied about them to be on such a wussy yard, but then again, few of them were well suited for real life on the outside. The only thing they had any real skill at was making bad choices. And they were lazy.

The smart ones realized but wouldn't admit, prison had another plus: It was a place that kept you sober a whole lot easier than you could do it on your own.

I was still a newbie, but now I got it. No wonder Art, and so many other guys in there, felt the way they did. They knew prison was as close as they would ever get to a safe, secure place called home.

So I was ready to ride out those last few months. My phone privileges had kicked in, two fifteen-minute calls a day mostly to Karen. Like "The Music Man," by now I knew the territory. No longer did I spend every moment looking over my shoulder or checking for walls to back up against. News on TV was talking about some viral epidemic that had hit China; a case had just been diagnosed in the state of Washington. There was something womblike about having my bunk to crawl into each night. It didn't feel like safety exactly, but I was no longer a stranger to those big skies over the Western movie sets. This was my temporary home on the range.

That would all change a few mornings later when my name went up in big letters on the whiteboard in Villa's office. Art's bunk was right outside the office; he was the early warning system for bulletin board news. He bellowed it out across the dorm.

I bounded up from my bunk and headed over to knock on the door. I had the routine down, and got along well with Villa. He was young, his arms were big from working out, he had a little Clark Gable mustache. He was a protege of Whitworth, who was always talking about how smart the younger man was. Villa just didn't work as hard, wasn't as soulful. I never got much satisfaction from our meetings.

"What's up?" I asked him, pointing to my name on the board.

"Second Chance," he said.

"What's that?"

Second Chance was another Department of Corrections stab at rehabilitation. It was a program for inmates two months from the gate, geared toward re-entry and reducing recidivism. There were classes, counseling, job placement. I remembered Jeff telling me I should get to a re-entry yard if I could. It sounded like some sort of reward to me, like an honors program … until I remembered just where I was. I looked over the paperwork, which was basically just a single page to sign. It specified that on completing the program I would look for work.

"But I'm retired," I pointed out to Villa. He just shrugged.

They offered the program on two different yards in the state. Manzanita in the Pima County complex was one of them. That was huge. If I could get myself delivered back to Tucson, that would eliminate the headache of Karen having to drive across the state to pick me up.

"It's a two-yard, right?"

Villa nodded.

"Should I do it?"

He shrugged.

So I headed over to ask Whitworth.

"They can tell how old I am from my computer profile, right? Why would they want me in their program? I'm retired. I'm not going to be looking for a job when I get out."

"They probably want you to teach there," Whitworth ventured. "They'll put you to work teaching as soon as you get there."

Made sense, assuming that whoever was administering the program had done his homework, figured out who I was and what I could do for them. It was kind of brilliant. Totally wrong, but kind of brilliant.

I signed the form. It was up to the program whether or not to accept me.

In the next few days I tried to learn more. I asked other prisoners – granted, never the most reliable sources – but the more I learned, the more I realized I had made a big mistake. The Second Chance program, I heard, was sponsored by the Arizona Association of Realtors to train guys to become licensed apprentices for contractors flipping houses. The classes were all vocational, in the trades. I'd be useless as a teacher. There was nothing I could do in the program, except train to be a plumber's assistant. The one good thing was that you got a voucher for hundreds of dollars' worth of free tools, clothes and boots even, so you'd be ready to go to work.

Worse, if you got there and didn't want to stay, you could be cited for refusal to accept housing and moved to a far worse yard somewhere else.

My heart was sinking.

Maybe, hopefully, they'd turn me down. It was the weekend now. On Monday I decided, I would go into Villa's office and cancel my request. I tried to put it all out of my mind. The Oscar ceremony was on

TV on Sunday night. Laura Dern, the love of my life for the thirteen minutes we shared on the Maui Film Festival stage, was up for best supporting actress. Dorm 9 didn't have a betting pool on this one, but I could keep score of how many close encounters I had had with these beautiful beings from other galaxies.

The show had just begun, the glamorous red carpet strolls, the on-ly-in-Hollywood brand of excitement when a sergeant I had never seen on the yard before showed up in our dorm. He looked like a movie star himself, with an easygoing, non-Kingman smile. He talked to the guard in the bubble, and the guys around me noticed they were looking my way. I didn't notice myself. I was engrossed in the show, where they were getting ready to announce best supporting actress when I got called up to the bubble.

"Chatenever," said the charismatic sergeant, real friendly like, "pack your stuff. You're rolling out first thing in the morning."

Just like that. I was numb, in shock. I felt like Art – I didn't want to go.

I was unable to focus on any more of the ceremony. Art was the first in the farewell delegation, swooping over vulturelike to my bunk to claim my mattress and pillow, plus assorted hygiene products, T-shirts, boxers and socks that he traded for his own holy ones that I would turn in when I left. I packed two banker's boxes with my meager belongings that passed for treasures now: my books, my TV, my Koss earphones, my battery powered beard trimmer. I could take the clothing I had ac-tually bought – the sweatshirt and thermals, the orange stocking caps we called beanies, the too-small workout shorts. There was my photo album in its soft plastic sleeves, with pictures of the kids and Karen and Lisa along with the family shots my sister had sent. The glossy freeze-frame smiles from happier times had helped me make it through countless nights. There were files and manilla envelopes of legal documents and classwork; packets of every letter I had received. And there were my notes and notebooks, my lifelines for the past five months, the items I most feared losing or being confiscated.

Young Chase came and sat on my bunk for his last father-son ses-sion. Walter spent a long time hovering over my bunk, shooting the breeze to avoid anything heavier. Other guys swung by, in pairs or one at a time, everyone working to avoid getting emotional. Somehow, in prison where nothing counts for much, my leaving felt like a big deal.

After they turned out the lights and everyone went to bed, I lay on Art's wafer thin mat too keyed up to sleep. After playing Kingman to a draw, I was off the next morning into a total unknown. A place to have to prove myself, all over again, one more time. It felt more ill advised by the moment, but there was nothing I could do about it now.

Just like everything else in the last year of my life.

28

Segue

When I retired after twenty years as the entertainment and features editor of The Maui News, I continued writing a weekly column for the paper. It was called Maui Connections because I worried that many people wouldn't recognize the title I preferred: Segue. It's pronounced "seg-way," it can be a verb or a noun. Segues are known to music composers, filmmakers and radio DJs. The word describes a seamless transition from one movement, or scene, or mood, or state of being to another. Could it be one prison yard to another?

A good segue is invisible. But then again, life itself might be called The Big Segue.

A full moon washed the chilly winter-black sky as I took my final walk across the Kingman yard. I carried everything I owned in two cardboard boxes; my feet crunched in the sandy gravel. The buildings around the gigantic sandbox of the yard were dark silhouettes, slumbering and peaceful at this hour.

I knew the drill by now, the ankle shackles, the chain around my waist to attach my handcuffs to. Being transported with other prisoners was a new experience each time, but always awful. I was the first passenger, directed to the furthest back seat in the last row of the van, effectively trapping me in the corner farthest away from the doors. At the next stop we picked up guys who had been in the hole, young yahoos who took the bench in front of me, proceeding to giggle, play grab-ass and for all I could tell, masturbate, all the way to the next stop. Each new convict was a grim threat, an ignorant, foul-mouthed dangerous stranger, even more paranoid and pumped up than normal to be so vulnerable in such close quarters.

The trip followed the steps of my incarceration in reverse. The van made infrequent stops where the guards distributed sack lunches with the inevitable peanut butter packed in cellophane like a poodle walker's poop bag for us to eat. We stopped at Buckeye, its dog-run cages and dingy office familiar territory to me now. Hours later we stopped at the Florence yard south of Phoenix, where we sat in another big cage and ate more sandwiches. I had forgotten to take my meds before we left that morning, and barely had any water all day. Dehydration seemed preferable to having to urinate for those long chained hours on the highway.

The day was clear, the sky Arizona menthol blue. The view out the windows of scrubby desert, the endless sprawl of washed-out Phoenix suburbs, the autopilot flow of traffic through the windshield all came as a mild shock. The sunbaked panoramas were plain if not ugly, their patterns predictable and unremarkable enough to be invisible. But to my weary inmate eyes it could have been a brand-new world beheld by the first Spanish explorer of the region. My traveling companions now included a black man with a walker carrying his meds in a plastic bag; and a big blond white guy who seemed to know everything about every prison yard in Arizona from personal experience. He was a little concerned about moving someplace new, because among his tattoos was a swastika from his earlier Aryan Brotherhood days. Now the symbol was like a bull's eye for trouble if he didn't wind up surrounded by whiteboys wherever he was going.

Our Florence stop was to pick up more prisoners. We were out of the van and into a big cage, trying to squeeze more peanut butter onto bread. It's a challenging task when your wrists are chained to your waist. The black dude, whose name was Montgomery, was also headed for the Second Chance program at Manzanita. Aryan man said he knew the yard well.

"It's small," he said. "The fuckin' dorms are small, the yard's no bigger than this fuckin' parking lot."

You could probably fit five of this fuckin' parking lots onto the yard at Kingman, and still have room for the softball diamond. My buyer's remorse since signing the Second Chance paperwork just kept getting deeper.

"Everything's close together. It's weird, kinda fucked up," Aryan man continued.

"But it's a two-yard, right?"

"No fuckin' way. Who told you that?"

Deeper and deeper …

The familiar cityscape of Tucson came into view. Then it flashed by the van windows, so near yet so far away, before the vehicle left the freeway and pulled into the Pima County state prison complex late that afternoon.

Surrounded by miles of chain link, its guard towers ominously like a medieval fortress, Manzanita was one of several yards in the sprawling facility housing almost five-thousand inmates. It was an equal opportunity incarcerator; security levels ranged from two to five.

We were herded off the van and into a big receiving room full of large cages. No one bothered to unlock our chains. The boxes of our belongings were unloaded but we couldn't get to them to retrieve things like my meds or a sweatshirt to buffer the chilly wind that kept blowing the room's doors open. We staked out sections of benches in the cage, no one making eye contact. They gave us more sack lunches, more peanut butter. There was a big Igloo water container and paper cups in the cell, but just working the spout or getting the cup to my lips was tricky with hands still chained to my waist.

The staff didn't seem in any hurry to speed our processing, which included an interview with a nurse. My blood pressure was through the roof, my upper body shivering in the orange T-shirt and pants that were all we had been allowed to wear for transport in the van. They offered flimsy protection from the February chill.

I had crisscrossed this parched state only to get back where I started, trying to outrun the verdict that had been handed down at the scene of the crime by the hipster I almost hit, then made official months later in a courthouse just a few miles from where I now sat: I was an old man.

The guards wouldn't get my sweatshirt for me, but one finally brought me a prison-issue, brass-button, blanket-lined, inmate-manufactured orange jacket. This one was close to my size at least, and didn't feel like it was tearing my rotator cuffs every time I put it on.

We waited. And we waited some more. Our ranks kept shrinking as new detainees were parceled out to different yards. We were the last. The black guy, Montgomery, was in the cell with me, on a paranoid rant, sure that someone was stealing his belongings from his banker's boxes which were somewhere out of our view. Finally a van showed up to take us to our new home. The afternoon light was fading down to a lavender horizon as we drove the last stretch, passing one industrial-looking, chain link-fenced yard after another en route to Manzanita. The driver was chipper, trying to be helpful.

"You're too late for dinner; they'll get you sacks when you arrive," he ventured. "They'll have to go through your property boxes, you'll get your stuff in the morning."

At least what the property officer – who would make Sergeant Kraft back at Kingman look like a saint in comparison – decided not to confiscate. My earphones would be a casualty. The officer would claim my repair of a broken earpiece was a "modification – not in compliance." Montgomery would fare far worse. A lot of his stuff didn't make the cut, for the most nitpicky of reasons, just to remind us who was the property officer here.

We were passing a huge warehouse-looking dorm building now, like the ones at Kingman. "That's Catalina," said the driver. "It's a two-yard."

"Well, what's Manzanita, then?" someone asked him.

"It's a three. But special. The Second Chance program is there. It's a medical yard, there's a hospice dorm, and a mental health unit. It's sorta like a two-yard, but not exactly."

I could tell Montgomery and I were sharing the same anguish, mentally rehashing the choice to come here, realizing what a dire mistake it had been. And that was before we even set foot in Dorm 1-A.

Swastika man had been right. Everything at Manzanita was tight and compact, especially after the expansiveness of Kingman. The dorms were divided into Able and Baker sides, each with bunk beds for forty-eight prisoners. The ceilings were low, most of the bunk beds at right angles like "L's." You shared your tight floor space with the guy in the other bunk. Even without bars between the cells, the room felt claustrophobic and dim. What light there was came from a few dungeon-style slit windows, and urine-colored illumination over the aisle that bisected the room. The lights never turned off.

My cellie in the top bunk was also a fresh arrival, a handsome young Mexican kid named Alberto. He was big and strong, a former boxer and mixed martial arts guy. It would take a while for us to sort out whether he would be a bullying tormenter or a loyal protector, one of my sons. All of the new arrivals were exhausted from the long day's drive, but had a hard time falling asleep realizing, each in our own way, what we had left behind, and what a poor choice we had made.

It didn't look any better the next morning. The other inmates in Dorm 1-A seemed older, seedier than the general Camp Snoopy population ... and they were supposedly the hope of the prison system, the ones selected for Second Chance who had at least a shot at making it on the outside.

Things got worse when we were let out for chow and I saw the inmates pouring from the other dorms. They were even older, harder edged, a scary bunch living in a mental vacuum that hope had exited long ago. Their tattoos and the scars on their shaved heads were sinister. Their jutting jaws missing teeth looked like shoddy Bondo jobs after a car wreck. Every word I overheard coming out of their mouths was "fuck." They weren't zombies, technically – just men who had burned up their futures and were now in suspended animation, the basically-waiting-to-die state of being that passes for life in prison. The cons in wheelchairs were the worst. There were lots of wheelchairs per capita at Manzanita, sometimes creating hand-propelled gridlock. Cons on wheels were, I would come to learn, were the surliest of anyone there.

The chow hall was smaller than Kingman's, and said "Dining" over the door. It was a reminder that Manzanita had initially been a women's facility. That explained other quirks, too, like the absence of urinals in the bathroom. The line waiting to get in the chow hall was, at least, short. The metal tables inside were long, family style. You could sit anywhere with anyone, regardless of race, as you tried to keep down the stuff they fed you.

For the new arrivals, all of us somewhere on the grief scale for hav-

ing put ourselves here, there was lots of acclimating to do. The Second
Chance program building was across the yard from the Second Chance
dorm. My first intake interview was with the program's C.O.III, a big
fella named Bigelow. He wore his badge on his belt. He had a distinctive
accent that sounded to me like New Orleans (it wasn't), an LA Rams
lanyard for his ID around his neck, and a jovial spirit that I would come
to learn was unflagging.

Looking over the records of my case, he shook his head.

"Shit, man, you shouldn't even be in here." He didn't mean Second
Chance – he meant prison in general.

"What happened to you … fuck, it could have happened to anyone."

"Tell me about it," I answered.

He shook his head again.

"But what am I supposed to do now?" I asked. "I was told I'd be
teaching in the program … probably not, huh?"

He considered the possibility, his face in its perpetual little smile.

"Getting back to Tucson was the biggest reason I did it. If I leave
this program, am I going to get punished, shipped out to a worse yard?
Someplace far away?"

He didn't know the answer to that one, either.

I was in invisible quicksand, homeless now, adrift, at the mercy of
the punitive, indifferent bureaucracy.

"So what should I do?"

"Why don't you stay?" Bigelow said, his smile like sunshine.

Two offices down the hall was Steve Montoya, one of the program's
two case workers. Short, stocky, he was an ex-cop with tattoos on his
muscular arms and a round moon face that could have passed for Hawaiian. In fact, his wife was Hawaiian, and they had a vacation trip
to the islands coming up. His screen saver was a shot of a free diver
underwater. I should have felt right at home, but didn't.

Looking up from my files, he tried to size me up.

"Now why would a seventy-four-year-old man want to be in a Second Chance program?" he began, sounding like Columbo unraveling
a scam. "What brought you here?"

"Bad information," I answered honestly. "The authorities at Kingman don't really know what this program is. They advised me to come. They thought I'd be a teacher here. I thought it was some kind of honor."

He shook his head. "There's not much this program can do for you. You don't need a job, or any training ..."

"Maybe there's something I can do to be of help ..."

He still looked suspicious.

"Well, you better figure it out," he said finally.

"Can they move me to the Catalina two-yard, so I can stay in Tucson, at least?"

"No guarantees," he said. "You wanna leave, they'll decide where to send you. DOC doesn't always do the right thing, the efficient thing, the thing that makes sense.

"Think it over," he concluded, his suspicions unabated.

As I had been reminded on a daily basis since this nightmare began, I was at the mercy of ... everything. When you go to prison you surrender your personal wants and needs at the door. Your well-being is one thing the authorities can agree they couldn't care less about. There's no customer complaint department. You put yourself here, it's your problem. Deal with it. Why do you think it's called prison?

I had new options to deal with. Not good options, but options. Welcome to Manzanita, dude.

29

Father Time

It would take a while to get in the groove at Manzanita. The skeptical case worker soon realized what the jolly C.O.III had known instantly: Gaming the system wasn't my plan – it was beyond my skill set, actually. So they sweetened the offer. If I stayed in Second Chance I wouldn't have to formally complete the program. I wouldn't have to write essays. I wouldn't have to do the mock job interview. I wouldn't have to look for work. I wouldn't have to do a resume, but could use the time to update my old one if I felt like it. I was welcome to go to classes. And they'd see if there were things I could do to help out, sort of like a grad student.

I felt like a bonus baby. Relatively speaking.

Walking back from the chow hall later that afternoon, someone called me over to where he stood by Dorm 1. He lived on the other side of the building, the B-side. He was black and wizened, with bad teeth and evidence of a hard life all over him. His nickname was Pac-Man, I don't know why.

"Where you from, OG?" he asked. "You ain't from around here."

How could he tell?

"It's the way you walk. You got swagger," he answered.

That, I knew, could be dangerous. Superior was one thing you didn't want anyone in orange thinking you thought you were. I didn't think I was. Apparently neither did Pac-Man. It sounded like a compliment.

"Yeah, it's the way you carry yourself, OG. You ain't from around here."

The classes, it turned out, weren't vocational after all. That was the other Second Chance program, the one in Phoenix. This one was geared toward rehab and counseling, character development and practical life skills, from balancing a checkbook to parenting. The goal was to curtail recidivism.

The first class I attended was led by a perky bank administrator who came to the yard once a month to teach fundamentals of finance. She was cute and funny, especially for an accountant, full of good information even if her ultimate motive was to sign up new clients as soon as the inmates were released. She was feisty, with no aversion to being politely appreciated by a roomful of horny men. She knew they were mostly there to stare at her sweater, but hey, that went with the territory.

Most of the classes were taught by inmates who had been certified as Recovery Support Specialists, RSSs.

Unlike the Second Chancers who were months or weeks from release, the RSSs were serving long sentences for serious offenses. They had been bad hombres, but had turned their lives around with the training. Among them were Seth, a member of Aryan Brotherhood in his youth who still had menacing tendril tattoos around his neck. Now he was studying theology. And Apple, a soulful black preacher man with a Barry White voice who spoke in metaphors. And Carlos, a short Chicano, as round as he was tall, who had been a pimp and a strong-arm man in his prior life.

The head RSS, the one coordinating the curriculum, was Polynesian. He was Kawika, the name the Hawaiian version of David. Being around Kawika made me feel like I was home in the islands. He was a Power Point whiz, so all the classes came with nifty visuals even if I had to restrain my inner English teacher from correcting the spelling and punctuation.

I went to all the classes. I looked forward to them each day. Lots of the guys in there were bullshitting and hustling; that was all they knew how to do in a classroom. They would raise their hands to answer every question, but couldn't string a sentence together without throwing in "You know what I'm sayin'?" at least three times. Others, though, were doing some serious soul searching. I didn't raise my hand much, but everyone listened when I did. The differences between me and them – case workers and RSSs included – were obvious, but no one held that against me. When I told them I had been a journalist and editor, some inmates – the bold ones – asked me to read their essays or help compose letters to their victims, one of the program requirements. Or they showed me their poetry. Apple, who had self-published a whole book of theology, brought me chapters to read.

"I saw you in a vision last night," he told me one day as we waited to go into class.

"You were the proofreader," he said. He made the word sound more biblical than grammatical. Another time, in a class where we had to do role-playing, someone dubbed me "Father Time."

The OG effect was kicking in again. Inmates started coming to me almost as soon as I arrived at Manzanita, for one thing or another. I would walk the fence line with them, listening like the father they needed but didn't have back when it would have made a difference. My cellie Alberto, who had become my wingman by now, would tell me all about growing up in his large Mexican family, bouncing back and forth across the border, sometimes all of them sleeping together in a van.

"We were poor, but I was always happy," he said. "I didn't know what I didn't have …"

His strength and martial arts prowess had made him a torpedo on his last yard. He cried after he beat people up, he confided to me, and had resolved never again to "lay hands on" anyone.

Alberto had created a whole entrepreneurial circuit shoplifting iWatches from stores, then selling them to provide for his girlfriend's lifestyle choices. He got popped when he got careless one day. He was smart, charismatic, had a strong work ethic and a supportive family. His sister was a doctor. He was in his early twenties, with plenty of time left to get it right the next time.

I told him all that. In case he needed to hear it.

The OG effect was beyond my control. At least I had enough sense not to get in its way.

Steering me through the world of Manzanita was an inmate named Phil Marshall, better known as Blackie. The nickname didn't come from his considerable prowess as a tattoo artist, but from childhood when his skin would get very dark in the summer sun. Phil was in his fifties, but in my mind we looked like brothers, both of us with close white beards and short cropped gray hair around the weatherbeaten crow's feet at the corners of our eyes. Or father and son. When he learned I was writing a book, he suggested Benicio Del Toro for his role in the movie.

He was like the mayor of the yard. He knew everyone, and they all deferred to him. Swagger – ?

Blackie had it to spare.

Now, tattooing is a violation of prison regulations that can result in serious discipline if caught. It required procuring the equipment, making the ink, then posting a lookout at the door for the hours Phil would do one eager inmate after another, their eyes filled with tears as they fought off the pain, on his bunk in the farthest corner of the dorm. His work could be intricate or expansive – sleeves like fine filigree on forearms, a striking three-dimensional cross covering an entire back. Being a master practitioner of this forbidden art didn't disqualify him from high status in Second Chance. He had completed the program months earlier, but days before his release he got a surprise from the Department of Corrections. They pushed his release date back several months, citing some technicality in his sentencing. Those little DOC surprises, it turned out, happened all the time. It was prison's version of Catch 22, more DOC humor

Rather than turn bitter, Phil stayed with the program. He wasn't an RSS because he hadn't done the training, but was like a noncommissioned officer, working in the office and serving as a liaison since he lived in the dorm with the rest of us. He was the one I initially asked for advice about whether to stay at Manzanita or not.

He had spent almost all his adult life incarcerated for a never-ending rap sheet of robberies, house break-ins and car thefts.

"I was a bad guy," he told me earnestly. "You wouldn't have wanted to know me then, or see me when I'm high. It's just bad."

It was all because of drugs, alcohol. And now that life was over, finally. He was sober; it was going to stick this time. There was certainty in his voice when he spoke about it. He wasn't fearing being released – he was looking forward to it for the first time. He was experiencing a new sensation – confidence that he could make it on the outs.

We couldn't have been more different. He was a Chicano who had wasted what education he had. He was a lawbreaker from day one. One morning, to lessen his sentence, he went around with a couple of cops identifying homes and businesses he had broken into. Before noon, he had solved most of the open cases on their books.

But, he told me, he had never been violent. He was a reader of scripture, a believer in biblical prophecy that he insisted explained everything wrong with America at the moment. It was all preordained, predicted in great detail thousands of years ago if you knew how to read the texts. He was a champion of the state of Israel, because of what the Bible said. His family members were Fox News watchers, Donald Trump lovers. Phil liked Trump, too, because he supported Israel.

"Now, which part of what he said about Mexicans did your family miss?" I asked him. He had no answer.

We couldn't have been more different. We got along great.

He would roll his eyes whenever he showed up and CNN was on my TV, making the sign of the cross for protection if he saw Nancy Pelosi's face. I in turn would needle him about Trump, going to great lengths to share everything I knew about malignant narcissism, money laundering, victimhood, tax fraud, entitlement and pathological lying.

"All politicians lie," he pointed out.

"True enough, but some of them are capable of doing more than one thing at once. They're not all certifiable sociopaths who flap their hands like dolphin flippers and whine like spoiled brats whenever they open their piggy little mouths. They're not all shills for Russia …"

What was happening to me? Hadn't I promised myself not to go there? In the interest of self-preservation? And yet inexplicably, here I was in a place beyond fear where my biggest concern was that it might be me who started the altercation on the yard, facing off with a couple of strutters who revealed tattooed swastikas on their flabby bellies when we all took our shirts off to work out.

Besides having forgotten that I was seventy-four with health issues, it had utterly slipped my mind that I didn't know the first thing about beating someone up … while beating someone up was the only thing these guys knew the first thing about.

Whether Phil initially saw himself as my guide or guard, or me as his teacher, everything soon equaled out. The respect was mutual. We had things to learn from each other. We would have long conversations about everything, including taboo topics like religion and politics, on one of our bunks or the other. We never missed eating meals together. He clued me in on how the system worked. He was an avid listener to my adventures in movieland, and a sponge for the lessons I had taught in my classes. He was as smart as I was. Our opinions of our fellow inmates were pretty identical.

"OK, if Benicio Del Toro is going to play you in the movie, who do you think should play me?" I asked him one day. "Sean Connery's too old … Maybe Richard Gere, because he's a Buddhist …"

"There's someone…," he began, searching memory before hitting on the answer:

"Larry David," he said. "He'd be perfect."

I had never been in counseling before. It hadn't seemed necessary. But in the classes about character, each session built around a word like Responsibility, Vulnerability, Honesty or Courage, I felt doors opening into myself. Having wrestled my shame to a draw by now, going down these new corridors dressed in orange felt somehow more beneficial than if I had been doing it with my buddies on Maui in a men's support group for aging artists and silver-haired beach boys.

It took five trips around the chain link perimeter to make a mile at Manzanita. The dorms and other buildings were squat and close, the spaces between them layered with razor wire barriers before your eyes finally reached the low lavender mountain silhouettes under tequila sunsets on the horizon. The Kingman vistas had been beautiful and liberating; these were just the opposite. Oppressive. The yard was on the flight path for Tucson's mammoth Davis-Monthan Air Force base. Sleek, flat-gray jet fighters flew in close formations like geese with their tails on fire, low to the ground, engines roaring above our heads.

It felt like I had blown out my shoulders with all those pull-ups at Kingman. Plus, the chin-up bars on the new yard were an inch or two higher. My feet didn't quite touch the ground when I hung from them, increasing the pull on my shoulders. Luckily, there were some elliptical machines on the yard, relatively new judging from the glossy green paint. They had rower arms, padded seats and fulcrums letting you pit your body weight against gravity five-hundred times per workout. Facing forward, backward, overhand, underhand, I'd do a lap around the fence between each set. My shoulders were spared, my endorphin craving sated – I was a happy camper.

Relatively speaking. At least until Covid-19 showed up.

Novel coronavirus was in the news, almost from the moment I had arrived at Manzanita. The first case in New York was announced at the beginning of March. New York Governor Andrew Cuomo's televised press conferences became part of my morning routine before going to class; his brother, CNN commentator Chris Cuomo's on-air struggles after contracting the disease were on my screen every night around chow time. I'd squeeze the peanut butter out of the cellophane and watch Chris struggle to breathe.

The reports, especially from the streets and hospitals of New York City felt apocalyptic ... but far away. Numbers in Arizona were in single digits, and most of those were in Phoenix, Maricopa County.

It was business as usual on the yard – go to class, work out, eat, sleep, count your days left, get up the next day and do it again.

Second Chance was a pilot program, a stab at the rehabilitation part of DOC's new mission. It was a work in progress, well-intentioned but running a gauntlet between knives out on all sides. There were the hard-ass prisoners, some even in the program, who weren't about to let their guards down long enough to sing Kumbaya. Second Chance acknowledged that the root of the inmate mentality was fear – a dangerous thing to admit, a vulnerable place most convicts couldn't let themselves go. Their armor, their body ink, was all they had, all they knew, all they were.

On the other side were the old-school Department of Corrections administrators, convinced that inmates were irredeemable, deserving nothing besides a never-ending price to pay. Hell, boy, if it ain't cruel and unusual, it ain't punishment. They couldn't wait to see Second Chance fail, to prove their point.

My regard for the Second Chance staff, in contrast, went up by the day. Whatever these tough guys lacked in sensitivity and psychological training, they made up for with commitment, and actually caring for the guys in their charge. They were in the trenches, shining beams of light into dangerous spaces the rest of society would prefer to keep dark and safely locked away. They were redeemers.

They kept pressuring Phil to teach a class, and he finally settled on selfishness as the topic. Kawika was helping him do research, and they kept running their findings by me hoping I would jump in and take the whole thing over. There were three kinds of selfishness, we discovered. The usual kind was the carcinogenic sin of envy, that could never get enough to be satisfied. Then there was the good kind, the selfless kind, like Mother Teresa's, where helping others helped yourself. And finally there was a third kind, the neutral kind, where you fulfilled yourself first, in order to be of greater service to others. The night before the class was supposed to happen, Phil developed a severe case of stage fright and told me he wasn't doing it. He looked like a little boy on the first day of kindergarten.

"Whaddya mean?" I asked him, incredulous and angry.

"I'm not doing it," he repeated, getting more emphatic the more scared he got.

Apparently, from what he told me later, the look on my face convinced him to change his mind. That was an example of the good kind of selfishness.

I volunteered to teach a class, too. It was on Communication Skills – personal, as well as professional. One of the lessons I taught my college classes felt even more pertinent here: Communicating, learning like six-year-olds to "use your words," was a valuable way to access your emotions, and meet yourself, and put your life in balance. I snuck in a part about what a drag it was to hear, "You know what I'm sayin'?" all the time. And how useless the word "fuckin'" was. Kawika worked with me on the Power Point; I threw in some photos off the internet of me on stage interviewing Maui Film Festival honorees, to illustrate one-on-one communication. Phil hung on every word of the presentation, quoting whole sections of it back to me weeks later. And Bigelow came up with a new nickname for me. Movie Star.

Life felt manageable, especially in prison where everyone does the cellblock shuffle – two steps forward, two steps back. If you hadn't been bipolar when you started, it didn't take long to catch it. Depression was the constant undertow; everyone would struggle like ocean swimmers trying to keep our heads above water. There might be hits of elation, maybe a letter on your bunk with new photos, or an endorphin high after exercising, or a chance to play OG and help someone get something sorted out. But everyone also knew they never turned the lights off in the dorm. It was a lesson you learned from seeing them on at 3 a.m. on far too many mornings.

Still, my months until release were turning into weeks. Being paranoid about getting one of those DOC surprises like Phil's that hit guys just days from the gate, I kept asking Bigelow to check my status, harping on whether there was anything I needed to be doing, any final paperwork.

"Don't worry," he assured me. "Everything's on track. You're looking good, Movie Star."

30

Surprise

The onset of coronavirus in Arizona was like waiting for a hurricane in Hawaii. You learn that it's coming from radar and the meteorologists long before it arrives. They plot it on their computer maps as a vivid swirl of primary colors, yellow, red and green, like huevos rancheros, surrounded by the blue of the ocean. Although hurricanes may pack winds stronger than a hundred miles per hour, they approach at a snail's pace. They lumber. The meteorologists plot the hurricane's path in the shape of a cone, widening with possibilities for veering or turning as it nears. The islands sit in its path on your TV screen, unmoving targets. Hurricanes are on the weather report days before landfall, moving with inexorable slowness, taking forever to arrive. You watch them advance, frozen like an animal in the crosshairs of a gun sight, stuck on your island unable to do anything but watch. And you wait. And you wait.

That's Covid-19 on a prison yard.

By the middle of March it had arrived in the Grand Canyon state. Not in the numbers that were still paralyzing New York, and much heavier in Maricopa County than anywhere else in Arizona, but still enough to freak everyone out. We'd get reports from the outside about panic buying in Tucson supermarkets, resulting in near-fistfights and whole aisles of empty shelves. People lined up for hours waiting to get into Costco. Businesses were ordered closed. Video on the evening news showed deserted streets, like a movie in the aftermath of zombie takeover. Local governmental and medical officials kept issuing mixed messages. No one had any idea what to do.

Tucson's penal institutions – from Pima County Jail to the state prison complex – seemed afterthoughts in the not-quite hysteria gripping everything else. They were just another problem without a solution as the disease shredded the normal patterns of society. Our case workers, who went home to their families every night, were reacting like macho men, playing it down, not convinced it was as dangerous as the doctors warned, not even convinced it was real.

Calling home didn't yield any better information. We'd make the calls from Manzanita's phone kiosk out on the yard where two rows of bright blue, push-button '70s-style pay phones sat on metal stands bolted to the ground. Each stand had a round metal stool attached to it. There was no such thing as privacy in the roofed, open-air space. Using the phone required punching in a code, then repeating the voiceprint you had recorded when you got to prison. Everyone recorded the same words, "United States of America." If a bunch of guys sat down to make calls at the same time, their voices spoken into their handsets in ragged unison sounded like a twisted Pledge of Allegiance from the dark side.

Authorities on the news were advising something called "social distancing," frequent hand washing, hand sanitizer, and wearing masks. As prisoners we could do the hand washing part, but good luck with the anything else. Living in close quarters with almost fifty men in bunk beds made social distancing – whatever that meant – impossible. Likewise for the chow line, and the bolted-down stools that put inmates shoulder to shoulder in the chow hall. Masks – ? Although a few of the guards started wearing them, risking being called pussies by their coworkers, there were no stinkin' masks for the prisoners. And as for hand sanitizer, it contained alcohol, so we didn't get any of that, either.

Two guys in the dorm had severe coughs that caused them to hack all night, keeping the rest of us awake and scaring the hell out of us. They both went to the clinic, but then were sent back with diagnoses that it wasn't Covid-19. Pneumonia, maybe. They couldn't breathe, for sure. But it wasn't Covid-19. The number of cases kept going up each night on the news. Occasionally a local or national report would focus on the special challenge presented by incarcerated prisoners in a pandemic. It wasn't as though the authorities weren't aware of it. They just didn't have a clue what to do. All family visits were canceled, all nonessential staff were ordered to stay off the yard. Eventually Second Chance's two case workers were ordered to work from home; we never saw them again. The guards, C.O.IIIs and other essential staff who had to report to work each day were now all required to wear masks. But still, the measures felt like bandaids. The prisoners were still maskless, still meeting in our classroom shoulder to shoulder, still on top of one another in the dorm and chow hall.

The official word was that there were no positive cases in the Pima County prison complex. If you believed that.

"It's gonna be like the green mist when it hits," I told Phil. "It'll creep under doors and into every dorm, no one will be spared ..."

My inner B-movie writer was embellishing a bit.

"... It'll hit everyone. Now, according to the experts, most folks have an eighty percent chance of beating it, of suffering nothing worse than the flu. If they even know they've got it. Unless you're seventy-four years old, with heart disease and who knows what else. In that case the green mist has your name on it. It's looking for you, dude. Once it hits the yard, you're a dead man walking. It's been nice knowing you ..."

Strangely, it wasn't fear talking. Homeless Kodo had recalibrated my fear response, making me fatalistic instead of afraid. The difference was lost on Phil. I was speaking metaphorically. He was taking my words literally.

He was in his fifties, which wasn't exactly a safe demographic, either. It was about this time that he started having anxiety attacks in the chow hall.

Being one of the oldest guys at Manzanita, at least outside the hospice dorm, I made an effort to alert the authorities to my special vulnerability.

"Yeah, that's bad," Bigelow agreed. "You better be careful, Movie Star."

I even sent an inmate letter to the prison officials, pointing out I was less than a month from release, nonviolent, and in the highest-risk category for the disease. I never heard back. An assistant warden showed up in our dorm a couple of times, checking things out. I pointed out to him that if I got sick, and died, it would be a bummer for both of us, public-relations-wise.

Wouldn't it be easier to just send me home a few weeks early?

That made sense, he agreed. But there was no way DOC would do it. And so we waited.

Sometimes they'd lock the whole yard down, a pickup driving from dorm to dorm bringing us our meals. Phil thought that was a good solution. It kept us safer, he thought. I wasn't so sure. I lacked his acquired immunity to claustrophobia. And besides, how could we be sure we weren't locking ourselves in with the virus? Then they tried sending nurses around to each dorm to take everyone's temperature. Then they stopped. Then they opened everything up again, hardly a reassuring move by now, sending us back to the chow hall that Phil could no longer enter without getting dizzy and hyperventilating.

Rumors kept flying that someone on the yard had it. The chaplain, someone I had never seen, reportedly tested positive, and was in quarantine. The official word from Department of Corrections was that the yard was clean. But who knew?

In the meantime my TV was still sending me messages, playing the Six Degrees game in my head with celebrities I had interviewed. I knew whole scenes of "Bay Watch" and "Jumanji" by heart; I thought of Bryan Cranston as an old friend every time I saw him in a movie or on "Breaking Bad" reruns. Then my acquaintances spread beyond the movies to TV newsrooms. One of CNN's pandemic authorities was epidemiologist Dr. Larry Brilliant. I had interviewed Dr. Brilliant, relaxed and comfortable enough to ask if that was really his name, a year earlier in the Haiku, Maui, living room of his dear friend, spiritual teacher Ram Dass. The two of them, along with Dr. Brilliant's wife, had first met in the '60s in India, as devotees of the same guru.

I thought of Ram Dass as my dear friend, too. We had spent countless occasions together on Maui, where he had lived for years after suffering a debilitating stroke. I was his go-to guy for stories in the newspaper. I was also sometimes part of the adoring group who joined him in his weekly ocean swims. I would find excuses to interview him every six months or so. It was always an honor. It was always bliss. Once when I thanked him after a phone interview – a challenging exercise ever since aphasia had impacted his speech – he answered, very slowly, "It takes two to tango."

Ram Dass died while I was locked up. We all die. That had been his message in his later years, getting more obvious the older he got. I was connected to Ram Dass, everyone was connected to everyone … or, was it just my TV playing a cruel joke on me, flashing scenes of my life before my eyes, which some say happens to drowning men in the moment before death?

Who knew? You couldn't be certain of anything anymore. And we waited. My months to go had become weeks, and now were days. Re-acting to the virus the Department of Corrections had stopped moving prisoners from yard to yard, so as Second Chancers were released, they weren't replaced. The dorm was emptying out. Almost all the upper bunks were vacant now, a semblance of social distancing in effect. Each morning we'd wake up, see if we could still breathe, then get on with the day. The case workers were long gone, but Kawika kept a semblance of the program going. Social distancing be damned, classes were still meeting. Guys were submitting resumes, and, surprisingly, getting job placement once they were released. Bigelow, now wearing a mask, would open the classroom and chaperone the sessions the way the case workers used to.

My time to release could be measured in hours now, just three days more, when Bigelow told me to stop by his office after class. He still called me Movie Star, but there was a look of worry I had never seen before in his eyes above his mask. Phil and Kawika seemed to know something, too, their eyes avoiding mine in the classroom.

After class I headed for Bigalow's office.

"Sit down," he advised, closing the door behind me.

I did.

"Do you have something in your past?" he began. "A sex charge …?"

I felt his words in my solar plexus, knocking the wind out of my lungs. I stared at him dumbly. I didn't know what he was talking about.

"They're not releasing you," he continued. "The processing office in Phoenix says your charge isn't eligible for the mandate. You've got to serve your full sentence, flat time … I won't tell you how many more months …"

I hadn't taken a breath since he began. Finally, I spoke.

"There was one incident," I began uncertainly. "I hit someone in my car. One time. My C.O.III at Kingman said there was a prior offense on my record, but there was no prior. It's a mistake in my file. There was one event. I could have killed someone, but didn't. It all happened in one second. One time. By accident. What sex charge …?"

Bigelow looked perplexed.

"The woman in the Phoenix office said something about a sex charge," he answered, reaching for his phone to call her back.

"She can explain it to you."

When he got the woman he put her on speaker phone. She had an English accent, like Mary Poppins. She called my file up on her computer and started to explain, but then thought better of it. Instead, she asked me my version of what happened that night.

So I told her, the scene unfolding one more agonizing time, the screaming voice calling out from the side of the van, my eyes momentarily seeking its source, returning in time to see the body hit my windshield in sickening slow motion.

"There's something not right here," said the woman. "Who was in your vehicle with you?"

"In my vehicle?" I answered. "There was no one with me. I was alone."

"There's something not right here," she repeated. "I need to investigate this further, and talk to my boss. He's gone home for the day."

She told Bigelow she'd follow up and get back to him. Then she hung up.

I was in a daze. So was Bigelow. When he had spoken to the woman earlier, she made it sound like the case was closed.

"Well, at least she left the door open this time," he said. "Try to get some rest tonight."

Yeah, right. Now I had gotten my own DOC surprise, just like Phil. I felt unsteady on my feet as I left the office. The sunshine hit like a blast furnace as I left the building. Phil and Kawika were outside waiting for me.

"Are you OK?" asked Kawika. I didn't know.

"We can make it work," Phil tried to assure me. "They can move you to Catalina for the last three months. We can make it work."

I didn't know. Everything inside me, my courage and resolve, had been timed to my release date, three days away. Now my insides felt like a balloon deflating. I didn't think I had anything left, much less three months of it. I was in shock. I didn't have a clue what just happened.

Phil and I walked back to the dorm in silence. When we got to my bunk I pulled out the tattered manilla envelope holding my legal records – the cops' accident report, the plea bargain, the transcript of my court case.

"You're better at reading this stuff than I am," I told him. "Maybe you can make sense of it."

He read each page slowly, nodding to himself. Finally he figured it out, but then had to be careful how he explained it to me. He borrowed my pen and wrote a word on the side of his hand: "child." He didn't want to say it aloud, for fear of being overheard.

I had gotten things wrong, it turned out. I was guilty of two felony counts in the plea my lawyer had cynically called "artful." For all these months of telling people I was in for Aggravated Assault with a Deadly Weapon, that technically was the charge I would be on probation for once I got out of prison.

What I was serving time for was the lesser charge, Endangerment, for having put the pedestrians in the crosswalk in peril.

Phil didn't want to say the word, because in prison, it was almost always linked with the one he had written on his flesh: "Child Endangerment." Those two words were one of those prison taboos; an unforgivable sin you were never safe from retribution against at the hands of your fellow inmates.

Any suspicion along those lines would have been a target on my back every day of my incarceration. Even though I wasn't guilty of it. Having a child in the car that you're impaired while driving is like a DUI on steroids. Phil had learned the lesson the hard way: if there's a child in a house you're breaking into, you're also guilty of child endangerment. Physical, emotional and sexual abuse fall under the heading, too. Someone in some office had been careless, either misreading my charge or hitting a wrong key when he put it into the computer.

"It was just a mistake," said Phil. "They'll fix it in the morning."

I wasn't sure I believed him.

"What if they don't?" I asked.

One grand jury, eight months, four prison facilities, more than a hundred employees of the Arizona Department of Corrections had planted the knowledge somewhere deep in my soul that I was powerless in this world. There were plenty of honest, smart, compassionate people working in the department.

And a few who were not. Those were the ones who didn't make mistakes. If you tried pointing out a mistake to them, they would just dig their heels in deeper. The power of their power was the power to misuse it. That's precisely what the president of the United States had pardoned – and praised – the sheriff of Maricopa County, Arizona, for doing. For all I knew, the boss of the woman with the Mary Poppins voice could be one of those guys, too.

Alberto and the other guys in the dorm could sense there was something wrong. They stayed away from me. Phil would pop over to my bunk to reassure me, but it didn't help. I don't know how much I slept that night, which parts of my swirling thoughts were awake, which parts dreams. I tried to imagine how I would survive the coming months, the temperature already hitting a hundred on the yard, the virus lurking, ready to strike at any moment. Phil would be gone, the program would be suspended, I would be alone in the dorm, with the swastika guys out there whenever I worked out on the yard. I was too numb to respond, too numb to feel fear.

What was the old adage again? Whatever doesn't make you stronger kills you.

This new scenario was playing like a tape loop in the mind of someone different from the man who had been handcuffed in a Tucson courtroom eight months earlier. I had changed. I was now accustomed to wearing the same orange clothes twenty-four hours a day, sleeping in them on a lumpy mat, eating peanut butter squeezed from a cellophane bag. It was hardly Jesus among the lepers and criminals, but I might have paid enough dues to be one of the wise men, by now. And to my astonishment, there were silver linings. For all the times I had realized how essential a laptop and a phone would have been to record this horrendous chapter of my life, I had instead been forced to break my addiction to them. I had retaught myself the art of handwriting, the mindset of pondering. My brain moved more slowly, more disciplined, like the ancient Hawaiians before written language arrived. I had been forced to seek answers you couldn't find on Google.

My orange T-shirts had become monk's robes, cementing a bond with those bony old Zen masters.

Everything taken away hadn't destroyed me. Just the opposite. It had liberated me. I was no longer a consumer, squandering the priceless moments of my life trying to decide between meaningless product choices. I was locked up, deprived of freedom, yet in direct touch to the universe. I had never been more alive.

The next morning I could barely eat my breakfast, impatient for them to unlock the yard so I could call Karen. I had to let her know of the developments in Phoenix, that I might not be released this coming Sunday after all. Trying to explain it would be hard enough, especially without knowing how it was going to turn out. We might need to call a lawyer. My feelings bounced between hopeful and crushed, my blood pressure probably off the chart. It was limbo to the max.

I was on the phone to her trying to convey it all, when Phil showed up by my side. "Bigelow wants to see you in his office," he said. He was smiling.

"I'll be over as soon as I get off the phone," I told him. Only having two calls a day, you couldn't afford to waste one of them.

I was still on the phone when Bigelow himself showed up. He hadn't been able to wait in his office. Over his mask, the twinkle was back in his eyes.

"They fixed it," he said. "You're good to go, Movie Star."

The woman in Phoenix had been good for her word. It wasn't even eight a.m. yet; she had brought it to her boss' attention first thing. Phil's explanation of what had happened was exactly right. They were able to fix the mistake as easily as it had been made in the first place, with a couple of keystrokes.

When I got to Bigelow's office, he called her again to thank her.

"I felt horrible about how that man must have spent the night," she said. She really was Mary Poppins after all.

So I was home free, but wasn't entirely buying it. That wouldn't happen until I actually exited the yard, passed through the gate under the razor wire arch, got picked up in the parking lot and drove away. You're discharged from prison in reverse order from how you came in. They put you in a cage with other guys being released, all of them talking about how high they're going to be and how many blow jobs they're going to receive by the time they get to Phoenix. They take your orange pants and shirt and replace them with blues, mom-style jeans and a sky blue T-shirt. They give you a month's worth of meds.

They all say, "Don't come back."

"Don't worry," you answer. "I won't."

In my last class on Friday, Phil called me to the front of the room. Last words were a custom, a tradition in the program. A lot of the guys could barely put a sentence together, because of shyness, their lacks of education or confidence, or the powerful emotions they were trying to put into words. I didn't have that problem.

I thanked Bigelow, the RSSs, "the artist formerly known as Blackie." I thanked the guys in the dorm, I thanked the program itself. And then I relayed the story of what my lawyer had told me in the dark days before I was taken into custody, "They need you in there, Rick ..."

"Wow," said Phil afterwards. "She really said that to you? So that's what you've been up to."

My last Saturday, the guys in the dorm played kickball. It's a game that involves kicking a soccer ball then running the bases like baseball. Its popularity is limited to kindergartners and prison inmates, and almost invariably results in grown men showing up at the clinic with muscle sprains or worse. I knew better than to trust my knees or my seventy-four-year-old equilibrium to try to play. I was always the scorekeeper, which was sometimes as dangerous as other places I had been since I started dressing in orange.

After the game there was another farewell ritual for me, most of us feeling as awkward as young boys trying to say good-bye.

That night in the dorm I parceled out my stuff, clothes going to guys who still had a while left, hygiene products to others who asked. Phil had bought my TV, paying in soup installments for weeks. He was acting as an agent for a buddy in the B-side of the dorm who still had years on his sentence and had a business renting TVs out to new arrivals.

Guys showed up at my bunk a few at a time. Alberto and B.K., who always called me Mr. Chatenever and hung on my words like gospel, whisked me away to the yard where we talked until the guards locked it down. Then we came into the dorm and talked some more. It didn't seem like there was anything to say, but they didn't want to let me go.

The next morning I got up, balled my bedding into a heap and threw it into a big laundry hamper. My books, my letters, the beard trimmer, the black-and-white marble-cover composition books that would become these words were all in one bulging cardboard banker's box. Phil and I said goodbye. We had each other's numbers. We knew this wouldn't be the end.

I walked out of the dorm to Manzanita's heavy gate where I waited for someone to buzz me out, unable to get Bob Dylan out of my head. The lyrics were changed just a bit, like I was.

> *Well the emptiness is endless, cold as the clay*
> *You can always come back, but you can't come back all the way*
> *Only one thing I did wrong*
> *Stayed in Arizona a day too long.*

Karen would be arriving in an hour, pulling up in her white minivan. She'd have a mask for me to put on. We'd stop by our daughter's house, see the grandkids, the youngest ones having been told that Gramps had been back in Hawaii all this time. She had rented an Airbnb for two weeks for me to quarantine in. Everyone thought that was a wise precaution, considering where I was coming from.

There was going to be a lot of adjusting to do, a lot to learn and relearn. The world had totally gone to hell while I was away.

www.ingramcontent.com/pod-product-compliance
Lightning Source LLC
Chambersburg PA
CBHW060918120626
46553CB00001B/374